When Your Past Is Hurting Your Present

Sue Augustine

HARVEST HOUSE PUBLISHERS

EUGENE, OREGON

Cover by Left Coast Design, Portland, Oregon

Cover image ©Mandy Pritty/Digital Vision/Getty Images

WHEN YOUR PAST IS HURTING YOUR PRESENT

Copyright © 2005 by Sue Augustine
Published by Harvest House Publishers
Eugene, Oregon 97402
www.harvesthousepublishers.com

Library of Congress Cataloging-in-Publication Data
Augustine, Sue.
    When your past is hurting your present / Sue Augustine.
        p. cm.
    ISBN-13: 978-0-7369-1537-3
    ISBN-10: 0-7369-1537-0 (pbk.)
    1. Christian women—Religious life.   2. Change (Psychology)—
Religious aspects—Christianity.   I. Title.
BV4527.A94   2005
248.8'6-dc22   2005001503

Printed in the United States of America

06   07   08   09   10   11   12   13   / VP-MS /   10   9   8   7   6   5

*For my beautiful daughters, Sheila Marie and Lori-Ellen,
precious gifts from God who have been a constant delight
and incredible source of inspiration, comfort, hope, and love—*

and

In memory of my mom

Acknowledgments

Even though my name is on the cover, I could only write this book because of the love and support of so many others. I'd like to say thank you...

...to God, who is always ready and more than able to transform a hurtful past into a bright and glorious future;

...to my husband, Cliff, my prayer partner for more than 25 years, who has pushed me to pursue the best God has for me, and who is adored more than he'll ever know;

...to my four beloved grandchildren—Kurt, AJ, Alexandra, and Cassie—whose infectious enthusiasm and sweet innocence have taught me much about living in the moment;

...to my fun-loving sisters—Lois, Carol, Ticha, and Ruthie—who offer me tremendous opportunities to "get away from it all" and be a kid once again;

...to my pastor, Rev. Peter Cuke, who speaks faith and truth through his consistent and uncompromising teaching of the Word;

...to all my dedicated friends, who prayerfully support me, and with whom I can feel free to process my innermost thoughts, views, and ideas;

...to the many women who graciously allowed me to interview them and share their stories in order to bring enlightenment to others, even though most of the names in this book have been changed to protect their identities;

...to all the wonderful people at Harvest House Publishers, for their faith in this project—in particular Barb Sherrill and Teresa Evenson, who believed that my personal story of overcoming a tragic past was one that needed to be told to encourage other women to move beyond the fears that cripple their dreams, and Shana Furjanic, for her expert work in editing the manuscript;

...and last but not least, to my cat, Daffy, who gives me enormous joy and comfort as she snuggles on my lap or warms herself under the desk lamp while I work into the wee hours at my computer.

Contents

A Glimmer of Hope

WHAT IF YOU KNEW THAT IN THE NEXT 21 DAYS you could finally leave your past behind? If you could start over with a brand-new beginning after only three weeks, what would you be willing to do to see it happen? Chances are, if you believed the damaging effects of your past could be altered so suddenly, you'd be receptive to making some significant changes and trying some new concepts.

That's exactly how I felt a number of years ago when someone suggested to me there was a way out of the despair, disappointment, and heartache I was experiencing, and I didn't have to spend the rest of my life in therapy searching for the answer. It gave me hope to think I could move from a past that was harming my present into a future filled with potential and possibilities. The best part was that it could happen naturally and quickly. After suffering a number of devastating and disturbing events that left me overwhelmed and feeling like a failure, I was baffled and confused, with nowhere to turn. What I want to share with you are the powerful truths that so dramatically transformed my life. I'm excited because I know they can do the same for you!

It's a well-known fact that in 21 days you can form a new habit pattern, develop fresh routines, or create different comfort zones for yourself. For example, it takes approximately three weeks to be at ease in a new job position or feel comfortable when you move into a new house. If you purchase a different car, it's about 21 days before you've adjusted to all the gadgets and remember which side of the gas pump to pull up to when you're purchasing fuel. It's the same when you've switched storage drawers but keep returning to the one where you used to keep the cutlery or your underwear (hopefully not in the same drawer!). I've often thought this is why a three-week vacation could be dangerous. In that short time, you might create an entirely new lifestyle for yourself—and it wouldn't be so easy to go back to the original one!

In this book, there are 21 chapters, seven in each of the three major sections. There's also something noteworthy about the number seven. It seems to be a significant number to God, because it is mentioned many times and for many purposes throughout the Bible. For example…

- When talking about healing our wounds—
  The moon will shine like the sun, and the sunlight will be seven times brighter, like the light of seven full days, when the Lord binds up the bruises of his people and heals the wounds he inflicted (Isaiah 30:26).

- When talking about trusting and obeying God—
  By faith the walls of Jericho fell, after the people had marched around them for seven days (Hebrews 11:30).

- When talking about hearing from God—
  At the end of seven days the word of the Lord came to me (Ezekiel 3:16).

- When talking about rest—
  For in six days the Lord made the heavens and the earth, the sea, and all that is in them, but he rested on the seventh day. Therefore the Lord blessed the Sabbath day and made it holy (Exodus 20:11).

These are just a few of many references. I want to encourage you to read seven chapters a week, one each day—you can complete this book in 21 days. The chapters are brief, but what you discover on these pages during the next three weeks could mark the turning point in your life. Twenty-one days is not a long time to invest in your future when you consider how long you may have been struggling to rise above the things of the past.

Starting to Move On

Contrary to what many popular books, programs, TV shows, and workshops will tell you about dealing with a damaging or disturbing past, it's not essential to continue examining, scrutinizing, and belaboring the details of what's over and done. You've probably already tried that, and it hasn't worked so far. I want you to know it's possible to start over—to move from an imperfect past to a future that is brighter and more promising than you've ever imagined—without investing in a lifetime of intense therapy or exhaustive self-analysis.

While it's good to look back long enough to understand why you feel the way you do, God tells us in His word,

> *Forget the former things; do not dwell on the past. See, I am doing a new thing!* (Isaiah 43:18-19).

For hundreds of years, well-meaning psychologists, therapists, and counselors of every stripe have sincerely attempted to help us "get past our past" by reliving it, retelling it, or dissecting all the dreadful particulars, much like we do frogs in a science lab. The Bible tells us we can let our past go because *"if any person is in Christ he is a new creation; the old has passed away. Behold, the fresh and new has come!"* (2 Corinthians 5:17 AMP).

I know God's promise is true because it's happened to me! My life has gone from tragic to triumphant, from devastating to victorious, without years of struggling and striving in heart-rending therapy sessions, probing into what happened in the past. On the other hand, I do believe that analyzing our inner self and examining the various ordeals of a hurtful past can be valuable learning tools when done constructively and in the right setting. You may see professional therapy as a beneficial tool in your personal renewal, but what I want to do in this book is introduce additional steps and optional fundamental principles that are compatible with appropriate counseling, whether or not you choose to use both. The concepts and biblical principles found here literally have the power to take you from defeat to victory once you apply them and adapt them to your own situation.

The first step is to believe it can happen. It has been my experience that miracles have a habit of happening to those who believe in them and anticipate them. Life has a strange way of giving us what we expect from it. For example, if you expected to get nothing from reading this book, guess what? That is exactly what you'd get. Expect God to act in your life and start looking for your miracle—now. It might be on the very next page.

As you begin to make adjustments and alter your attitudes, beliefs, habits, and behaviors, remember that the changes you make don't have to be astronomical to get astronomical results. Sometimes we think that in order to experience exceptional transformation, we need to do something extreme or radically outrageous. The truth is that it's often the smallest change in one direction that makes the biggest overall change. Even one idea, when implemented, can be life-changing. Like the colored-glass patterns in a kaleidoscope that are completely transformed with the slightest rotation, your entire life could be altered with one small adjustment. Any single change you make while reading this book could turn out to be the one missing link in the chain of events in your life.

I realize each one of the steps presented here could fill volumes, and you can certainly find other books out there covering many of the topics. However, my desire for you in writing this book is to pull all the steps together into one cohesive, interconnected approach that is simple, realistic, and achievable. If a particular area captures your attention (and I hope it does), that's great. Go on and read additional books about that topic. The messages of others—in the form of books, articles, sermons, and seminars—have greatly influenced and encouraged me. Over the years, I have read countless books, listened to numerous speakers and preachers, made a myriad of notes, and collected scores of articles. I am deeply grateful to all those who have gone before me, opening doors, breaking down barriers, and leading the way to help others.

As you move from a past that encumbers and impedes you into a glorious present and on toward a promising future, I am convinced you will find what I did. Others will notice changes in you and ask how you did it. You will have many opportunities to share with them what you have discovered. This brings to mind an impressive candle-lighting ceremony I attend each year at Christmastime with my family and friends in a historic nearby town. In early December, an evening stroll begins with hundreds of people gathering around the old clock tower. With everyone holding an unlit candle, we join in singing some Christmas carols. Then the first candle is lit, and in turn, the next one from that one, and the next two from those, and so on until everyone's candle is lit. What a beautiful sight to see a frosty winter night suddenly illuminated by all those candles glowing together. It always warms my heart no matter how many times I experience it.

In the same way, as this message changes your life and you begin to radiate inner peace, joy, and strength to handle daily challenges, you will be able to go out and add light to another's life. The words to a children's song from my Sunday-school days encourages us to "brighten the corner where you are." Once you begin to brighten your own corner, the more light you'll have to share with others, and the brighter our world will be.

With the principles I'm going to share with you, I was able to rise up from the pit of my dark, desolate past. By the light of these concepts, keys, and principles, I believe you can do the same. As you make the journey from a painful past into a fulfilling future, remember that living in freedom is not merely a luxury. It is a vital element in accomplishing your God-given life purpose. I pray that you discover all God has in store for you. I know you've never imagined anything quite like it, because the Bible tells us,

Eye hath not seen, nor ear heard, neither have entered into the heart of man, the things which God hath prepared for them that love him (1 Corinthians 2:9 KJV).

So get ready. You are about to conquer those obstacles that have been encumbering your dreams, and I am delighted to travel this path with you.

How to Get the Most From This Book

It's been said we read best when we read with a personal goal in mind. As you go through this book, I encourage you to take it personally. In other words, continually relate the material back to your current situation, relationships, and interests along with all their challenges and obstacles. Most of all, resist the urge to think, *Wow, so-and-so sure needs to read this book!* Why is it that when we come across powerful, life-changing material, right away we think of someone else who could benefit by it? Fight the temptation. Trust me—the message is for the one reading the book!

There are a number of other reasons we are not transformed by what we read. One is that we do not put new ideas and principles into practice. It's not what we know that makes the difference, but what we *do* with what we know. Knowledge is great, but it's only *potential* success until it's combined with action. For instance, how much knowledge do you have regarding the importance of fitness, exercise, diet, and nutrition? Chances are you do not need more knowledge, just action! As you finish each chapter, try writing out your own personal, strategic plan. List those steps you intend to implement as a result of reading that portion. Be very clear as to what you will do differently as a result of what you've read. Implement those new ideas as soon as you can. The more quickly you can put a concept into practice, the sooner it will become a habit.

Keep a journal or spiral-bound notepad with this book, along with a good pen. Write the title of the book on the front cover, and as you go through each chapter, make your own summary notes of things that are meaningful and pertinent to your life. This way you'll end up with a miniature version of the book—one that emphasizes those ideas that are especially significant to you. Feel comfortable writing in this book too, underlining significant passages, and using a special marker to highlight ideas that stand out. It makes them easy to spot when you go back later to review.

Spend time meditating on what you've read. Too often we put a book down and immediately get back to what we were doing before reading. To meditate simply means to reflect, ponder, contemplate, and mull over. Allow yourself some time each day to do this. When you read the quotes, try to reflect on their meaning. When there are Scripture verses, look them up, compare them with other versions, and memorize some of them.

Finally, the very best way to get the most from this book is to move from being the student to the teacher. Pass on what you have gleaned. Without trying to transform others or push information on them, you can simply impart what has inspired you to make changes. While you cannot change another, you can be a positive example and a good role model. Others will come to their own discovery at the right time for them. Though you can change only yourself, you can pass on what excites you to others. Happy reading—and enjoy the journey!

> If I can aid one in distress,
> If I can make a burden less,
> If I can spread more happiness,
> Lord, show me how.
>
> GRENVILLE KLEISER

Part One

Relinquish Your Past

The past is a bucket of ashes, so live not in your yesterday, nor just for tomorrow, but in the here and now. Keep moving and forget the post-mortems.

CARL SANDBURG

Forgetting what is behind and straining forward to what is ahead, I press on toward the goal to win the prize for which God has called me heavenward in Christ Jesus.

PHILIPPIANS 3:13-14

To relinquish...

Synonyms:

Let go, leave behind, depart from, let pass, abandon, give up, turn your back on, forsake

Antonyms:

Keep hold of, hang on to, preserve, maintain, continue, prolong, promote, cultivate, foster, further, advance

Chapter 1

Yesterday

It is not the experience of today that drives us mad; it is the remorse or bitterness for something which happened yesterday.
AUTHOR UNKNOWN

Forget the former things; do not dwell on the past.
See, I am doing a new thing!
ISAIAH 43:18-19

YESTERDAY IS HISTORY. WE KNOW THAT. No one has to tell us there's no going back. We cannot relive any part of it or change one thing about what has already happened, nor can we make it go away. Yet even though we don't intend to dwell on the past, most of us continue to carry at least some fragment of yesterday in our hearts. With all its unique sorrows and joys, whether it's helped us to grow or not, and if we've learned much or nothing, our suffering has shaped who we are. We have been changed by it. We would not be who we are today had we not fallen or been pushed down, and learned to pick ourselves up again and again.

Consciously or not, past events can play over in our minds much like a video on auto-rewind. On one hand, there are some "good ole days" of yesteryear we'd return to in a heartbeat. On the other hand, we are haunted by experiences from ages ago that have left us dealing with heartache, remorse, bitterness, or humiliation. If you are like so many of us women, you're attempting to go through life's journey carrying around some pretty heavy baggage from days gone by.

Whether your bags are packed with resentment, regrets, fear, anger, unforgiveness, or doubt, my guess is you know intuitively that hauling all of that paraphernalia around everywhere you go is dragging you down—mentally, emotionally, physically, and spiritually. Whether your pain is close to the surface or hidden deep within your heart, what happened yesterday holds you back from becoming all you were intended to be today—crippling your hopes and dreams for a victorious tomorrow.

At times, it may seem as though you and your past are one. Sometimes we can fail to differentiate between what has happened to us and who we are today. If you have a hard time getting beyond that damaging mind-set, let me encourage you right now. *You are not your past!* Although you are changed and shaped by past experiences, who you were yesterday does not control the person you have the potential to become tomorrow. In fact, who you were when you began reading this book is not who you can be once you've finished. Events of yesterday do not have to govern today. Your past does not dictate your future. The time has come to lay that baggage down and leave behind all the struggling and striving. You can be set free as you journey forward into a balanced, healthy, and rewarding future.

In an old story, a man trudged wearily along the road, straining under a heavy burden on his shoulders. A pickup truck overtook him, and the driver stopped to offer him a ride. The man was relieved and happily accepted the offer to sit in the back of the truck. But after he climbed in, he continued to carry his load on his shoulders. When the driver arrived at his destination, he pulled over, walked to the back of the truck, and asked his passenger why he had not laid his burden down. The man replied, "I felt it was enough that you would carry me. I could not expect you to carry my burden, too." What a wasted effort! There was no need for him to continue hanging on to this heavy load. You and I often continue bending beneath the weight of what happened yesterday—tormented and plodding wearily through the present and on into the future.

Lightening the Load

Let's start now to lighten your load as we travel together for the next three weeks through these chapters. For the best results, use the journal and pen I recommended you keep with the book to record your own personal "ahas" and insights as they occur to you. Find a comfortable spot, get cozy, snuggle up with a cup of your favorite tea or coffee, light a candle, and envision me there with you. On our voyage, we'll be discovering 21 powerful and practical ways to change habit patterns and let go of this heavy load we needlessly lug around. Freedom from the past is our destination. Our ultimate goal is liberation from anything that hinders our progress, keeps us from reaching our God-given potential, holds us back from realizing our dreams, and stops us from fulfilling God's purpose for us here on this earth.

So be prepared. From this moment on, your life may never be the same. You are on the threshold of a brand-new day, a bright tomorrow, and possibly an entirely transformed life. I believe there are no coincidences—it's no accident you have picked up this book. Chances are there is something in your heart right now, telling you it's time to leave your past behind because there's a magnificent future waiting up ahead.

A familiar adage declares, "When the student is ready, the teacher will appear." Be on the lookout for your teachers—you never know in what intriguing form they will appear. My prayer is, because you are ready to relinquish the harmful aspects of your past and move beyond all that has crippled your dreams thus far, the Holy Spirit will be your teacher, using the principles in this book to play an even larger role and fulfill a greater purpose in your life than either you or I can begin to imagine. The Bible describes a God, *"who by His mighty power at work within us, is able to do far more than we would ever dare to ask or even dream of—infinitely beyond our highest prayers, desires, thoughts, or hopes"* (Ephesians 3:20 TLB). This moment in time could be your turning point.

Do You "Have a Past"?

For starters, what if I were to ask you if you have a past? Sounds scandalous, doesn't it? Of course you have a past. We all do. Your past includes everything that has happened to you right up until yesterday. Minute by minute, the past is being created. It's always catching up to you. Just when you think you've got yesterday taken care of, another "past" creeps up, and you must decide how you will deal with it.

When your past is hurting your present, it's nearly always caused by one of two things:

1. remorse or regret over something done by you
2. bitterness or fear caused by something done to you

In other words, either you've been a victim of circumstances and external conditions beyond your control—your environment, your upbringing, the actions of others, religious or cultural customs, societal traditions, or natural causes—or you are experiencing the consequences of your own choices, decisions, behaviors, and actions. The past that's hindering you now could be something as recent and clear-cut as words spoken in anger to your child yesterday that you wish you could take back, or the hurt you are feeling because of the gruff way your husband treated you in front of company the other night.

That past may be further back, such as last week when you abruptly lost your temper at work, an embarrassing moment you endured at the dinner party a month ago, or dreadful memories of the times you were teased in school for being overweight, awkward, slow, or shy. A hurtful past for you may be as deep-rooted and complex as the demeaning and soul-destroying things you were told while growing up, the abuse you suffered as a child, an adulterous affair that ruined your marriage, the shame of having to declare bankruptcy, the dismay of losing your job, or a horrible accident that took the life of someone you loved. In any case, hurts from your past can linger, coming back out of the blue to interrupt your present life and rob you of joy without any warning.

From interviewing hundreds of women internationally, I am convinced each one of us has something from yesterday we wish we could erase or recreate because its lingering regrets and disappointments are having an adverse effect on us today. If you have ever fallen flat on your face, totally blown it, or felt your life has been botched up completely by external circumstances or other people, then you know the past can still be affecting your present. If you've ever put your foot in your mouth—or, like me, if you do it often enough that you need to get yourself some chocolate shoes (my friend reminds me that a closed mouth gathers no foot!)—or humiliated yourself in some embarrassing situation ages ago, you might still be mortified today whenever the memory of it comes flooding back to haunt you. Whether you've been the victim of another's inappropriate, immoral, or illegal actions, or you are living with the consequences of your own mistakes or flawed choices, the past may still be hurting you.

Moving Out of the Rut

Our past consists of the good, the bad, and the ugly, and the ideal thing to do is savor the best and forget the rest. It's probable you are yearning to do just that, but even though common sense says it's simple, it's not always easy. Maybe you're ready but don't quite know how to get started. It could be fear, doubt, or anxiety holding you back. I can tell you I know firsthand what that is like. The things I was afraid of kept me stuck in a rut for years. But by implementing the same principles in this book, I was able to get beyond those fears and see my life dramatically transformed.

When I think about my past life compared with today, the contrast seems incredible. My former existence was filled with apprehension, loneliness, and despair. Yesterday I was a victim. Today I am a survivor. Yesterday I was shy, insecure, and pessimistic, and made poor choices for myself. Today, I am confident and feel assured I can walk hand in hand with God through any trial or adversity life puts in my path. Yesterday, I endured domestic violence and lived each day with a dire sense of hopelessness. Now, I am healed and able to go out and encourage others to make positive choices that will transform their lives.

My dilemma began like that of so many other young girls. With extremely low self-esteem, I had virtually no confidence, doubted my abilities, had little faith in my potential, and questioned my personal worth. In school, if I achieved good grades I attributed them to luck. If my marks were poor, I took the blame and believed it was because I lacked intelligence. Although I made friends easily at first, I often sabotaged those friendships because I was convinced that once someone really got to know me, the relationship wouldn't last anyway. When things were going well for me, I believed I must have simply been at the right place at the right time. When they weren't going well, I assumed I had brought it on myself. It's not surprising I found it difficult to accept any compliments, acknowledgment, or words of appreciation, and longed for the approval of others.

The choices I made at that time reflected my poor self-image. While in my teens, I attracted a man with the same low self-esteem. In spite of his volatile temper and an extremely rocky dating relationship, I married him right after high school. I still remember standing at the back of the church, a teenage bride about to walk down the aisle, when my Dad leaned over to whisper, "Sue, it's not too late. You don't have to do this. You can change your mind." My parents knew what a terrible mistake I was making.

Within weeks, I knew it, too. We were both young and emotionally immature, and did not have the skills to handle the stress and pressure of a new marriage. Arguments escalated into abuse, and for the next several years I was a battered wife. Much of the time, I had to creatively cover my bruises, swollen lips, and black eyes with cosmetics. I was hospitalized with more serious injuries on numerous occasions. Some of what I endured included a ruptured kidney, fractured jaw, and broken nose. Because I did not give in easily but fought back, the episodes intensified. Eventually I realized I was turning into a person even I couldn't like, let alone love or respect. My life eventually became a blur of police sirens, doctors' reports, hospital visits, and family court appearances. Yet I continued to go back to the relationship time and time again, desperately wanting it to work and hoping against odds that our relationship would somehow improve.

Why I Hesitated to Leave the Past

You might wonder what drew me to that marriage in the first place and kept me returning to such an explosive and harmful situation. Often during interviews and at women's retreats where I share my story, I get asked why I stayed. If you have been in a similar situation, I am certain you will be able to relate. If you have not, it may be difficult to understand. Many of my audience members vow they would leave after the very first incident. One thing I have discovered through my own experience is we cannot make a judgment until we are actually in the situation. We really don't know how we would respond, only how we plan to or hope we would.

Besides, each situation is unique in so many ways. Some women I've talked with have had the good sense and courage to get help after the first incident. I stayed, attempting to handle it on my own, for a number of reasons. For one thing, my life wasn't bad all the time. As with most difficult relationships, there were good times mixed in, which sometimes gave false hope that the situation would improve. As well, I had learned from necessity to make a life for myself within the marriage, with simple pleasures and innocent delights—designing and sewing my own clothes, baking bread, doing crafts with the children, spending time with friends, oil painting, and reading good books. And like the weather forecast, "cloudy with sunny breaks," there were just enough intervals of sunshine—love, passion, laughter, and joy—in our home to keep the hope alive.

Also, I took my wedding vows seriously and was committed to making the marriage work in spite of what I mistakenly felt was merely a relationship problem. I saw the abuse as being the "worse" part of *for better or worse.* Further, in those days (the late 1960s), separation and divorce brought disgrace to families and were not openly discussed in society.

Aside from that, this man was my childhood sweetheart and the only man I'd really been close to. Although we'd had a troubled dating relationship since I was 13 years old, and even though I often witnessed the consequences of his fierce temper, especially when he became jealous, I somehow had a warped and distorted view of these outbursts of rage. I saw them as a form of extreme passion and intense love, resulting from his jealousy and the fear that he might lose me. (With my own low self-esteem and my longing to be needed, this made sense to me.)

I believed also that, once we had a family, all this would change. Because my husband had had a difficult childhood, I felt he simply needed to feel secure within a loving family and home of his own. Add to that the religious teachings I had received growing up and the deeply imbedded beliefs from childhood that couples marry *'til death do us part,* and it may become a little easier to see why I was willing to tolerate this behavior. I saw these outbursts as being a type of sickness. I was ready to fill the role of nurse. It didn't seem appropriate to leave someone who was not well. Of course, there were always his promises that the cruelty and violence would never happen again, and I desperately needed to believe that was true. Yet deep down inside, I knew intuitively this was not the case. Eventually, I had to resign myself to the fact that, should I choose to stay, my options were limited…and this was going to be my future.

Being abused by a loved one sets up two conflicting natural instincts: the impulse to hide out in what should be a safe and secure environment (the family home), and the gut feeling to want to flee a dangerous situation. Naturally, with the fear of the unknown, I was torn. Most of my days were spent learning new ways to cope with my former husband's fits of rage in order to survive the predictable bumps and bruises. Periodically I tolerated nearly unbearable episodes of abuse. Numerous times I was strangled—on several occasions, I was left for dead.

My physical constitution was being damaged by all the stress I was enduring, and eventually I became infected with a rare blood disease that nearly took my life. My own emotions became so out of control that I said and did things that were out of character for me, and that made me feel responsible for the resulting violence. Deep in my heart and soul, I accepted all blame for most of the incidents and went on a perpetual journey to improve myself.

After we had our two little girls, there were times when the only thing that got me through the night was having those chubby little arms wrapped around my neck, pudgy cheeks pressed up against mine, and precious toddler voices whispering, "It's all right, Mommy. Everything will be okay." But I knew that it wasn't going to be okay. I knew I had to make changes—if not for myself, then to protect my little girls.

The beautiful marriage and family life I dreamed of as a young girl had turned into a veritable nightmare. We were heading for divorce. It took several years before I finally found the courage and wisdom to make the break from the past that brought me to where I am now—a happily remarried mother of two and grandmother of four, traveling the world as an author and conference and retreat speaker. What a difference between yesterday and today!

Your Time for Renewal

Now I am free from the past and able to share with you the steps I took to recovery, with complete healing and total forgiveness. You may not be in a state of crisis as severe as mine. Or maybe your situation makes mine pale in comparison. In any case, each of us must deal with some heartache, grief, or other stumbling block from our past that hinders our future. There is a way to stand tall, take charge, and refuse to let the past cripple your dreams and hold you back from living a victorious life. Whatever challenges you are now facing, I want to offer you the hope that things can improve. I want to bring you comfort and encouragement during your time of renewal.

There are so many variables when it comes to identifying elements from yesterday that continue to haunt us today. Perhaps you can identify with some of these heartbreaking circumstances, traumatic events, and difficult situations others have shared with me. They have endured these over the years and, in some cases, continue to struggle with them today:

- rejection in childhood
- being teased or bullied in school
- feeling inadequate around your family
- having a domineering or alcoholic parent
- feeling like a failure or an outcast
- suffering abuse of any kind (emotional, mental, physical, verbal, or sexual)
- being an unwed mother
- giving up a child for adoption
- having an abortion
- living with a demanding or controlling spouse
- being deceived by a loved one
- undergoing separation or divorce
- suffering miscarriage or the death of a child
- enduring the loss of a loved one—a family member or friend
- suffering from lost dreams and crushed expectations
- attempting suicide
- having an unfaithful spouse
- being raped

- going through an adulterous affair
- living with drug or alcohol addiction
- performing criminal activity
- losing a job or home
- being falsely accused of something
- being stood up at the altar

- declaring bankruptcy
- feeling like a failure as a parent
- going through depression and hopelessness
- letting someone else down
- being abandoned
- suffering betrayal
- being robbed

These are just a few of the experiences that can bring heartache and cause us to get stuck in the past. Most of us have experienced some of these tough times. Nearly everyone I spoke with could identify with at least one, and in many cases, several of the above. In some strange way, it is comforting to know that we are not alone in our suffering. But now, the past is not yours anymore. You have today and tomorrow ahead of you.

How thankful I am for the miraculous way I have been so completely healed of the past! How glad I am that I have this awesome opportunity to share that with you! Although I can still remember what happened and how much it hurt at the time, the memories are merely scars. And as a dear friend once pointed out to me, scars don't hurt. They're what's left behind after the injury is healed. With each scar, I can recall exactly how, when, and where the wound happened, and even how much it hurt at the time, but the pain is gone. These scars don't hurt anymore. Come with me now out of a hurtful past and into a place of complete healing, restoration, and total renewal!

I appreciate what Ralph Waldo Emerson said when he very wisely encouraged,

Finish every day and be done with it. You have done what you could. Some blunders and some absurdities no doubt crept in; forget them as soon as you can. Tomorrow is a new day; begin it well and serenely with too high a spirit to be encumbered with your old nonsense. This day is all that is good and fair. It is too dear, with its hopes and invitations, to waste a moment on the yesterdays.

Hold on to the promise of hope for tomorrow. You can be free from the past—at last!

Chapter 2

The Promise
of Hope

*Hope is the feeling you have that
the feeling you have isn't permanent!*
JEAN KERR

*Weeping may endure for a night,
but rejoicing comes in the morning.*
PSALM 30:5 KJV

IF YOU HAVE EVER FELT HOPELESS, HANG ON! The night you're enduring may seem long, but there is joy coming in the morning. Incredible
changes are going to take place in your life as you begin to relinquish
your past and renew your present. God promises, *"I plan to give you hope
and a good future"* (Jeremiah 29:11 NCV).

Hope and Its Opposite

At one time, every young woman had a hope chest. It was a time-
honored tradition, a gift passed on from mothers to daughters designed
for putting aside linens, quilts, dinnerware, cutlery, and other items for

their household while anticipating eventual wedded bliss. My mother had one. It was a beautifully carved wooden chest we kids loved to rummage through. By then, it held her wedding gown, bridal veil, photo albums, scrapbooks, pressed flowers, and other keepsakes. Some were mementos from the days she and Dad were courting; others came from their wedding day and first few years together. There was also a selection of baby clothes and handmade knitted outfits my sisters and I had worn.

Simply recalling that exquisite chest brings its distinctive cedar aroma back to me. It's as real to my senses as if I were back in the family home, lifting the lid this very moment. Each time I would sift through all the keepsakes carefully stored away, I would imagine how Mom must have felt as she added yet one more item in anticipation of marrying her life partner—whoever he might be. I am sure there was an element of dreamlike mystery as she would envision the man, the relationship, and the life ahead of her.

Hope is like that. It is filled with optimism, grand expectations, and the joyful anticipation of good things to come. It brims with magnificent possibilities and lofty dreams. Emily Dickinson said, "Hope is the thing with feathers that perches in the soul." The *Oxford Dictionary* says hope is "expectation and desire combined, clinging to a mere possibility." Most of all, hope is something we absolutely cannot live without. It is vital to your heart and soul, and is as essential to your life as air and water. You need hope to cope—it's necessary for your very survival. Hope enables us to conquer tremendous odds and overcome exasperating obstacles that would otherwise hold us back.

The opposite of hope is despair and gloom. The psalmist wrote,

> *I would have despaired unless I had believed that I would see the goodness of the* LORD *in the land of the living* (Psalm 27:13).

Because of the abuse that had taken place in my past, I went through a devastating time of despair and hopelessness, even though I had been set free from that situation. There were times when loneliness would overwhelm me. I would not get dressed and would just stay on the couch. I didn't want to talk to anyone or leave the house.

The typical response to hopelessness is to hide under the covers, stay in the dark, or be engulfed in mindless television watching. But that isolation, along with filling our minds with toxic information from watching talk shows, soap operas, and the news all day, sends us spiraling further downward into a pit of despair. Eventually, my negative thoughts became a lifestyle. Rather than exposing myself to being hurt again and again, I simply refused to believe anything good would ever happen to me. The result was, I began to expect to be hurt—and I was. Disappointment is painful. This was one way I could try to protect myself.

Little did I know God was there with me the whole time. When I began to study the truths in His Word, I discovered my negative beliefs had naturally been bringing more negativity into my life. It became clear that my negativity had to go. I needed to let go of my past and move into the future with hope, faith, and trust in God.

Here's what I discovered: There is no room for your past in your future! When we have trials to endure and challenges to overcome, hope for a better tomorrow is surely the way out. *"Hope deferred makes the heart sick,"* according to Proverbs 13:12, *"but when the desire is fulfilled, it is a tree of life."* Even when we know and trust God, every one of us can still have periods of discouragement, depression, and even despair. But the more we place our hope in God, the quicker we'll be able to see His hand working to set us free. Biblical hope is closely related to faith. I'm not sure you can even have faith without hope because hope is the foundation on which faith is built. Genuine hope believes, regardless of the circumstances, everything is going to turn out all right. Faith is trusting in the One who can make it so.

The Power of Hope

In a fascinating experiment, two groups of adults in separate rooms were asked to hold their hands in buckets of ice water. The first group was told the test would last only three minutes; the second group was given no time frame. All watches and clocks were removed. When the time was up, the organizers found the participants in the first group were able to keep their hands in the icy water for the entire three minutes and believed they could have endured even longer if necessary. The members of the second group could not even last three minutes. What was the difference between the two? The group with no time frame had been left without the hope of a certain ending. Therefore, the ordeal had seemed even more agonizing.

Hope is very powerful. A hopeful outlook can improve the body's defense system against toxins and disease. Hope also gives us the stamina, determination, and fortitude we need to help us survive even the most devastating, disheartening, or demoralizing conditions. It can provide more courage and endurance than we ever imagined possible. It's amazing what we are able to tolerate when we have hope that there is an ending in sight and believe better days are coming. It's been said that hope sees the invisible, feels the intangible, and achieves the impossible. Faith in God and hope deep in our hearts is crucial no matter what our present circumstances are.

Aside from believing we will recover, we have to know deep down we have what it takes to survive. We can have this assurance because God has promised that "*he will neither fail you nor forsake you*" (Deuteronomy 31:6 TLB). Even though we can trust God that something better is coming, we don't need to know what it is. Things might not turn out the way you've planned. In my case, I can't tell you that my story of surviving devastating domestic violence ended with "and they lived happily ever after." However, as I went through the legal, emotional, and spiritual journey of dissolving an 11-year marriage and starting a new life, I did it with the assurance that God Almighty had a plan and a better way. "*'I know the plans I have for you,' says the Lord. 'They are plans for good and not for evil, to give you a future and a hope'*" (Jeremiah 29:11 TLB).

Somerset Maugham wrote, "It's a funny thing about life; if you refuse to accept anything but the best, you very often get it." When I first heard that quote, it brought new hope for a freedom I had never experienced or even imagined. I had always felt bound to the past and never even thought I deserved to have a happy life. But I was getting desperate, so refusing to accept anything but the best sounded very appealing to me.

I want to encourage you by letting you know there is hope for you and your situation, whatever you are dealing with. God is intimately involved with every detail of your future, and His desire is for you to be an overcomer. Isaiah reminds us in the Old Testament,

> *Those who hope in the Lord will renew their strength. They will soar on wings like eagles; they will run and not grow weary, they will walk and not be faint* (Isaiah 40:31).

Get ready to discover the way out. Start believing that the best can happen and don't accept anything less!

Leaving Behind the "Hope Thieves"

There is a way out. Your life is not written in stone, based on what happened yesterday. Regardless of what has been done to you or what you have chosen for yourself, in spite of all your former circumstances, you can choose what you will do with your life from here. Through your choices, you have the ability to determine whether you'll remain as you were in the past or become someone brand-new.

First, there are some false assumptions and "hope thieves" we have to clear out of the way. Consider some of the myths and faulty notions we have been taught about our past. They destroy our expectations and leave us in a condition of hopelessness and despair. Here are seven of the most common false beliefs we might have bought into that we need to dispel before we can move forward.

1. You made your bed, so now you must lie in it. Do you remember this all-but-worn-out cliché? Don't believe it! It's a lie. If you've made your bed by accidentally creating a situation that is now harming you in any way, get up, get out, and move on to a better place. For years, I bought into this myth and was convinced my mistakes had me in their grip forever. I felt I had paved my future path in cement and there was no way to reroute it. But guess what? You can break up that cement and chart a new course. You can trade that bed in for a new one. You can leave your past behind and start again. You have many options because *"all things are possible with God"* (Mark 10:27 KJV).

2. Opportunity only knocks once. Not true either! You may have missed an opportunity or two along the way, even botched a few chances to turn your life around, but there are always new prospects and possibilities opening up to you every day.

3. Your reputation follows you the rest of your life. Aren't you glad the twenty-third Psalm does not proclaim, "Surely my mistakes and blunders shall follow me all the days of my life"? While it's true your actions reap results and every choice has a consequence, buying into this false notion can keep you stuck in your past until your dying day. Whether it's poor choices you made during your teen years, an extramarital affair that became public, a drug or alcohol problem you've overcome, or the time you spent in prison, it is possible to redeem yourself. By your new choices, actions, and behaviors, you can go on to build a new life and make valuable contributions to your family, church, community, and the world.

4. There's no such thing as a second chance. In many ways, we've been persuaded to believe that if we mess up, it's for all time—there is no starting over. However, history books are full of stories of those who learned from their failures and went on to become successes. Many who may have thought they had flunked out of the school of life accepted the chance to enroll once again and ended up graduating with honors. Since the time of Adam and Eve, we have heard about a loving God who offers second chances…and third ones…and fourth ones… and on and on. Where your future is concerned, there are no limits in God's eyes. He sees your potential and never gives up on you. You'll never hear

Him say, "Oops, look what she's done now. Well, there's no hope for this one!" There is always another day, another week, another year, and another opportunity to begin again.

5. You may need counseling for the rest of your life. While counseling may be a correct path for you to follow for now, therapy shouldn't be a permanent condition. If you are seeing a counselor who has given you a "life sentence," get out quickly and find another. Seek out a therapist whose goal is to get rid of you! The idea of therapy is to get you standing on your own two feet, get the problem resolved, and have you move forward on your own.

6. It's too late to have a new beginning. Although it's true that you cannot literally begin anew, you can create a brand-new *ending*. What would you like the end of your story to look like? It's never too late to be what you might have been. I was being interviewed on national television for my book *5-Minute Retreats for Women,** and one of the other guests was a beautiful lady in her 80s named Ruby. She had just graduated from law school. Seven years earlier, when her family had said, "Mom, you'll be 81 by the time you're a lawyer," she'd replied, "I'll be 81 anyway. I may as well be a lawyer." What a woman!

7. You can't help who you are because you are a victim of your circumstances. Whether it's your upbringing, childhood trauma, peer pressure, societal expectations, cultural traditions, your boss, your spouse, your teenagers, or your mother-in-law that is to blame, you are ultimately responsible for the choices you make that have resulted in who you have become and how you behave. I cannot imagine standing before God on judgment day and being allowed to rhyme off the many people and situations that prevented me from becoming all I was intended to be.

Each of these "hope thieves" can be brought under control. Don't let them continue robbing you of the joy of anticipation. Hope is the seed of future delight. It is the enticement to trust, to risk, to try once more,

---

* Harvest House Publishers, 2002.

and to carry on. Robert Frost told us, "In three words I can sum up everything I've learned about life: It goes on." One thing *I've* learned about life is, often what I thought was the most terrible thing to happen has turned out to be for the best!

The Best–Worst Time of My Life!

Most of us have had what I refer to as "best–worst" experiences. While I was struggling through the darkest hour of my former existence, leaving an abusive marriage to go out and start over as a single mom earning a living just above poverty level, I probably would have described my experience as the worst thing I'd ever had to endure. (I'll tell you about this time in more detail in chapter 21.) With seemingly impossible odds to overcome, how could I see it as anything else? Living in a tiny apartment with barely enough money for food and rent, believing I would probably be alone and never marry again, there were many times when I would feel so hopeless I would collapse, weeping, onto the floor in the middle of the night.

One time I cried so hard I felt my insides might come out and my head might split open. Trembling, I called out to God, "Where are You, Father? You promised You would never leave me or forsake me." Gently, He came to me on that dark and dreary night and whispered into my heart, "*Be still, and know that I am God.*" (Psalm 46:10). My entire body relaxed and became still, and I knew God Almighty had come into that room to comfort me. Afterward, I went to bed and fell into a long, deep sleep. When I woke up, I was refreshed and tranquil, and never grieved to that extent again.

Now that time has provided me with new insights and fresh perspectives, I can truly say I believe those were the best of days because of where I am today and the woman I have become. Though I was also struggling with dreadfully low self-esteem, a life-threatening illness, devastating financial burdens, and the fear of being hunted down by a frustrated and desperate ex-spouse, I've come to realize that learning to triumph over those apparently unsolvable difficulties actually proved to be an open door to the chance of a lifetime. Through it all, I've discovered many of the principles for living a contented and fulfilling life that I can share with you now.

While we examine how your past has been hurting your present and what to do about it, and as you begin to see what's been holding you back, I'm sure you will recognize some of your own "best–worst" experiences. Perhaps, for the first time in your life, you will realize that what you thought was the most horrible thing to happen was actually the greatest. I pray you will gain a new hope that you can be set free from the harmful emotions, feelings, and thoughts of the past. You can find happiness whether or not your circumstances ever change. Whether it's a chronic illness, a devastating loss, the scar of an injury, or any other situation you have to live with, try to view the problems you face as gifts, perhaps brought into your life on purpose—designed to transform you and bring you to a better place.

Consider these examples of some women's best–worst situations—things that looked negative or hopeless at the time but turned out to be positive, advantageous, or profitable in some way:

- Sally failed in college and ended up taking a different course more suited to her unique natural abilities.

- Christine was stood up at the altar. Now, a few years later, she's involved in a much healthier relationship.

- Terry Lynne lost a corporate position and chose to fulfill a lifelong dream of opening an antique shop.

- Vicky's friend canceled a vacation they had planned together, providing her with the gift of some much-needed quiet time alone.

- Pat was passed over for a promotion and landed a position in a more stress-free environment.

- A couple was forced to sell their larger home for financial reasons and moved into a smaller one with less property to care for, freeing up time for relaxation.

- On a snow day, a busy mom had the opportunity to stay in her pajamas all day, playing board games with the kids and sipping hot chocolate by the fireplace.

- Alex moved away from old friends but now stays in touch more frequently.

- Lela is forced to wait at an appointment and has time to catch up on some reading.

- The car in front of you insists on driving the speed limit, making you late—and saving you from the radar trap up ahead!

In my life, I can relate to most of these. How about you? Not long ago, I was traveling around the globe full-time as a conference and retreat speaker, often booked to present sessions in a different city each day for several days per week. When my workload lightened drastically and much of my work was closer to home, I was disappointed at first. I enjoy what I do and also love to travel, so it took some time to adjust to my new schedule. I have to admit that I whined, crabbed, and complained to God, asking why He would do this to me. He gently reminded me that because I wanted to write more books, this change in direction was freeing my time to do just that. What seemed to be the worst turned out to be the best. I am now more relaxed, have the freedom to spend quality time with our family and friends, and am able to be involved with our community and church. I also enjoy being home to write in a peaceful atmosphere—rather than in airports, planes, and hotels, where my first books were written.

Spiritual Detours

More recently, I had an even more devastating detour that turned into a best–worst experience. After four months of serious writing for the book you're reading now, my computer crashed. The good news is, I have learned to save my work to a disk. The bad news is, the day the technician returned my repaired computer I was suffering with a severe throat virus and was taking strong medication for the pain and swelling. Not thinking straight, I made a mistake while working on the disk and deleted the whole thing. My entire book—gone!

Well, I cried to the Lord, asking, "Why me? How could this happen? Don't you like me anymore, Father?" Desperate to hear from Him, I opened my daily devotional book and read Isaiah 43:18-19:

> *Forget the former things; do not dwell on the past. See, I am doing a new thing!*

God is so good. He doesn't leave us alone, even when we're whiny, but comes to comfort and reassure us—and always with a better plan. Immediately, an outline for a new and improved version of this book came to me very clearly. What I quickly scribbled on the back of an envelope that day as ideas poured into my mind was so much more exciting to me than what I had been working on. The new version is the one you are reading right now. As the Psalmist proclaimed, *"As for me, I will always have hope!"* (Psalm 71:14).

Disturbances in our lives are like spiritual detours. At the time, they appear to be disasters—or frustrations at the very least—but they can end up taking us on more meaningful routes and redirecting our paths in ways we never expected. What appears to be an annoying deviation from our final destination turns out to be a much more pleasant journey, with less traffic, fewer stoplights, and a more picturesque view. Remind yourself that today's disruptions just may be heavenly gateways in disguise.

Our problems have a tendency to rob us of hope. My thesaurus tells me hope means to expect, anticipate, and look forward to. The opposite is to lose heart and feel despondent. When we have hope, we walk by faith and not by sight (2 Corinthians 5:7). A good friend says she loves the Bible verses that start, *"And it came to pass..."* In other words, it didn't come to stay! Eventually, misery, gloom, and anguish are replaced with confidence, belief, and certainty.

One day I was frustrated as I inched my way along a winding road with half a dozen cars in front of me. A slow-moving truck was leading the way, and no one could pass because it was impossible to see oncoming traffic. Until then, I had been right on schedule, but now it seemed I would be late. Suddenly, the road became straight, and although we still could not see ahead, the truck driver waved his hand signifying that all was clear for us to go around. Chances are no one knew this truck driver, yet we all trusted our lives to him.

This reminded me that after we have done all we can, we must trust the details to God because *"faith is the substance of things hoped for, the evidence of things not seen"* (Hebrews 11:1 KJV). How wonderful that we can rest in the hope and knowledge that our loving heavenly Father always has a clear view of the landscape that's ahead of us. When He waves you on, you know He will carefully direct you and never lead you astray. Even when all else is gone, you can still have hope in Him.

'Tis better to hope, though clouds hang low,
And keep the eyes uplifted;
For the sweet blue sky will soon peep through,
When the ominous clouds are lifted.

There never was a night without a day
Or an evening without a morning,
And the darkest hour, as the proverb goes,
Is the hour before the dawning.

AUTHOR UNKNOWN

Chapter 3

The Choice Is Always Yours

There are only two ways to live your life—
as though nothing is a miracle or everything is a miracle.
ALBERT EINSTEIN

This is the day the LORD has made;
We will rejoice and be glad in it.
PSALM 118:24 NKJV

HERE'S A STARTLING THOUGHT. WHEN A WOMAN who had been sick for 12 years with internal bleeding came up behind Jesus to touch His clothing, believing she'd be healed by doing that, He turned and spoke to her. *"Daughter,"* He told her, *"all is well. Your faith has healed you"* (Matthew 9:21 TLB). Later, two blind men came to Jesus to heal them. He asked,

> *"Do you believe I can make you see?" "Yes, Lord," they told him, "we do." Then he touched their eyes and said, "Because of your faith it will happen"* (Matthew 9:29 TLB).

I'm not sure about you, but those two accounts make me want to reassess my level of hope and trust in God. But they also make me aware of the power of our choices. Among other things, you and I have the ability to choose faith. These stories tell me that according to what we choose, we do have a certain degree of control over what's happening in our lives. To some extent, we can determine how things will turn out for us. Our future is not left up to chance. It isn't fate that determines our outcomes, but rather God—and the level of faith we choose to place in Him.

A number of years ago, I attended a seminar through my part-time job. The speaker announced, "Right now, you are a sum total of all your past choices. You are where you are today because of them. Your choices have determined who and where you are now." I couldn't believe what I was hearing. I know her comments were made to the entire audience, but at that moment I felt as though she were speaking directly to me. I wanted to stand up and say, "How ludicrous! If we are victims of someone else's inappropriate, immoral, or illegal actions, the pain and heartache we are now suffering did not have to do with our choices. I can think of many examples of things that happen to us that are beyond our control."

Beyond that, I wanted to add, "You obviously don't know what I have to cope with when I go home every night, or you wouldn't make such an unfair statement!" After all, who would choose the life I was living? At that time, as a victim of domestic violence, I believed someone else was responsible for what was happening. I felt trapped in my situation because I knew, realistically, I could not change another person or alter what had gone on in the past.

But what the speaker got me to see was that even though I was powerless when it came to those things, what I could do to regain control was choose how I would respond and react from that point on. As a mature adult, I could decide the actions I would take—whether I would stay or leave, and how I would think and feel about the person and the situation.

Your Choices—Past and Future

You might be reading this and having the same thoughts I did. Maybe no one knows the trauma you've experienced, whether it's the abuse you suffered growing up, the onslaught of destructive criticism you received at school, the betrayal or rejection you've endured in your relationships over the years, or the dreadful things that are still going on in your life. Of course you did not choose the cruelty you've had to bear, the losses you've experienced, or the violence you may have witnessed that continues to cause unbearable heartache. If you were victimized, these are choices you did not make.

In that case, how could it be true that you are where you are today because of your past choices? That day in the seminar, I knew in my heart I had not intentionally chosen to be married to an abusive partner or live in poverty. I also knew I wouldn't have chosen the rare blood disease I had recently been diagnosed with. So how could someone have the audacity to insinuate I was in this situation because of my own doing? I left the seminar blinking back tears and feeling infuriated, hurt, disappointed, and confused. I vowed to never again attend one of those programs if that's what they would be teaching. Ironically, today I present the same principle to my readers and audiences. Even though I walked out on that speaker, the concept she presented played a major role in my life's being turned around.

For days, I couldn't stop thinking about the words "You are a sum total of all your past choices!" They played over and over in my mind, like a tape on auto-rewind. Then, one day out of the blue, it all became clear and made sense to me. I realized this was *good news*. For the first time I understood I could alter the outcomes in my life by taking charge of my choices. I had always thought that in order to move on with my life, all the problems would have to go away, the past would have to be rectified, and other people would have to be different. That day I realized I had other options in the very midst of the chaos. Accepting full responsibility for my future choices paved the way for a new beginning. It was revolutionary. I realized I had more control of my life than I had ever imagined.

Out of Control

> You may not be able to control what happens *to* you, but you can control what happens *within* you.

In another experiment, two groups of people were given exceptionally complex puzzles to solve within a very short time. To make the test more challenging, the participants were subjected to background noises on tape, including doors slamming, telephones ringing, people speaking foreign languages, dogs barking, and children hollering. Can you put yourself in their place? Their dilemma sounds a bit like everyday life. With a crisis to be solved, time constraints and deadlines to be overcome, and lots of noisy disturbances and interruptions, I can imagine how they felt.

There was only one difference between the two groups. The first was told they could turn off the cassette with the irritating noises, but only if it became absolutely imperative—if they felt pushed to the brink. They committed to going as far into the experiment as they could. The second group failed miserably. Not only did they not solve the puzzle within the allotted time, they became convinced it was not humanly possible with all the racket. However, the first group completed the puzzle perfectly and within the time frame. You've probably guessed the most intriguing part—they did not have to shut off the noise. Simply knowing it was within their control was all that was necessary for them to accomplish the assignment.

I find this aspect of human nature fascinating. It reminds me of when I'm working in my office at home with my car parked conveniently in the garage, even though I probably won't need to drive anywhere. But can you guess how I feel on the day when the car needs to go in for an oil change or some repairs? It bothers me because I feel that I am no longer in control. It's not that I need to use the car or have to go anywhere. I just want to know it's available.

The same thing happens to us when challenges come into our life. It's not always necessary to have everything going our way or to be able to get rid of the problems in order to have a good life. Instead, we merely need a sense of control within the situation. Though we can't control other people or many of the situations we encounter, our control comes from knowing and understanding there are other options available to us. It's when we mistakenly believe we are stuck—with no alternatives—that our difficulties overwhelm us.

When it comes right down to it, there is only one thing God has given us complete control of in this life, and that is our power to choose. That's enough because it's always our choices, and not our past experiences, that determine our future. Our past can control today and tomorrow only to the degree we allow it. The past should not be a place where we dwell, but a place from which we learn all we can and then move on. What freedom we'll have once we have come to the place where we are *"forgetting the past and looking forward to what lies ahead"* (Philippians 3:13 TLB).

It's true there are many aspects of your life you do not get to control—your parents and siblings, where you were born, your facial characteristics, your height and bone structure, your personality traits, or how you were treated growing up, to name a few. But you always have the power to control your thoughts, attitudes, perceptions, and behaviors today. Certainly, even now, there are many circumstances beyond your control that can get you down, like bad weather conditions, traffic jams, the high price of gas and food, one-sided company policies, tax increases, or politics that go on behind the scenes at work—but you can choose how you will act in response to those things.

Nor are other people's thoughts, belief patterns, behaviors, or actions toward you yours to control—but you can decide how you will react and deal with them. Even though you did not get to control a lot of what went on in your past, and you may not always be able to choose your present or future circumstances either, you can always decide on your personal views, values, standards, ideals, and future goals. It's these choices that influence your actions and eventually determine your final outcomes. So even though we all may have a reason to be the way we are, none of us has a reason to stay that way.

You're Not Trapped

Everything in life asks for a choice from you. At the moment you wake up, you can say, "Good morning, Lord," or "Good Lord, it's morning." The psalmist said,

> *This is the day the LORD has made; we will rejoice and be glad in it* (Psalm 118:24 NKJV).

How you get up is an act of the will and a choice you make; then the day gets better or worse from that point, depending upon your choice. You can sit on the edge of the bed and think you're going to get a headache, and you probably will! You can go out into the world and notice only the heavy traffic and the thunderstorm, or you can observe how green the grass is after the rain and have a laugh at the funny message on someone's license plate as you inch your way through a traffic jam. If you see nothing as a miracle or everything as a miracle, it's up to you.

Whether you triumph in your troubles or crumble under the pressure of affliction, you get to choose. You can decide whether you will endure the difficulties you go through and develop maturity of character, or be crushed by your hardships and troubles. Although your past has been painful, devastating, or cruel, God has promised to be a Restorer and a Redeemer. He says He'll *"give us gladness in proportion to our former misery,"* and *"replace the evil years with good"* (Psalm 90:15 TLB).

When you are feeling trapped by your circumstances, start to see there are choices being offered to you each step of the way. Once you realize everything brings a choice and you don't *have* to do anything, it will set you free. You are not locked in. There are alternatives. The reason you've handled your situation the way you have in the past is because it's less scary than making a change, or it's more comfortable than moving in a different direction—even though you may have felt you had no other options available to you.

I heard about a tribe native to South America whose members had died prematurely over many generations from a strange illness. Finally, scientists discovered the disease was caused by the bite of an insect that lived inside the walls of the tribe's adobe homes. The tribe members were presented with several solutions. They could use an insecticide to kill the pests, they could demolish and rebuild their homes, they could move to another region where there are no such insects, or they could continue to live as they always had and die early. Can you guess what they did? They opted to stay where they were and die early. It was the path of least resistance and the one option that felt familiar, controllable, and comfortable. It required no change. We do the same thing. When we have come from damaged backgrounds or sordid pasts, we tend to shrink back when we are offered a chance at a better way. Even though our old ways are not doing us the most good, rather than put ourselves in an uncomfortable or risky situation, it's much easier to stay put, believing we have no other choice.

"But I *Have* To..."

The truth is, you don't have to do *anything*. Now that you are an adult, you have other options. In fact, nearly everything is a choice. To make a point here, let me get a little silly and exaggerate. You do not have to get out of bed each morning. No, you could just lie there, and most likely, after several days someone would come looking for you. Of course, they may take you away and put you in an institution, but you didn't have to get up. You don't have to go to work every day to earn a living; you can collect government assistance. There's no need to pay the rent; the other option is to live on the street. You do not have to raise your children because there are government agencies that will take them and place them in other people's homes. (When I mentioned this at one seminar I was giving, a woman raised her hand to ask if she could please have the phone number. I'm *certain* she was kidding... although I saw her jot something down!) You do not have to pay your taxes, either. The alternative is going to jail.

When we say we *have to* do something, it's generally because we don't like the alternatives, and not because we don't see the other options available. In most cases, we are not completely forced into any situation. There are nearly always other choices, but their outcomes may not seem very appealing to us. Perhaps our new options are scarier than what we are currently enduring, so we choose to continue with our old ways for a while longer. When I say, "I *have to* visit Aunt Mary," it's probably because I don't want to face the consequences of not visiting—not necessarily because it's mandatory. So even though I don't have to do most things, I think I'd rather get up each day, go to work, raise my children, visit Aunt Mary, and pay my taxes. The reason is because I don't like the price of not doing those things. I prefer doing what I do over any alternatives available.

Likewise, you don't *have to* stay in a job that is destroying you, a friendship that continually wears you down, or a marriage in which you may be in danger. If you are staying, it's because the alternatives are frightening or not appealing to you—not just yet, anyway. But begin to check out your options. I chose to stay in a devastating situation until the scary unknown became less scary than what I was enduring. Are you there yet? Remember, the choice is always yours.

Choices Include Taking Responsibility

The idea of taking responsibility for your own life is probably not new to you. It's a message many of us have been given throughout our entire lives. But I am not sure most of us understand what it really means. Some think being responsible is about getting a good education, finding a job, and earning enough money to support ourselves so we are not dependent on anyone else for survival. While that is part of it, accepting personal responsibility goes so much deeper.

Many of us think we are taking responsibility for our own lives when we try to change the people we believe have control over us. But in reality, this leaves us with a "victim mentality." Victim thinking says, *I am caught in my circumstances, with no way out unless someone else changes.* If you are playing the role of victim, it's not possible for you to assume responsibility for the direction of your future. When we see ourselves as victims of our circumstances, we are powerless for two main reasons. One is, we tend to look to outside sources for our happiness, and the other is, we blame other people for our lack of success. That's exactly what I had been doing. I believed that the good life was out there somewhere and that other people had the power to make it happen for me or the ability to prevent me from reaching it. The only way to regain power, though, is to accept total responsibility for what is presently happening in your life and to be 100-percent accountable for your future choices, actions, and behaviors.

Mary Ellen is a high-powered senior executive who exists in a perpetual state of nervousness. When she talked with me after attending one of my programs recently, she admitted she was anxious and fearful most of the time but rejected the idea of getting some professional help. She believed if the other people in her life would change, everything would be fine. While that may have been true, it left her living in the fairy-tale kingdom of "if only." *If only* her husband were more attentive and understanding; *if only* her boss would treat her with the respect she deserves and start implementing some of her ideas; and *if only* her teenagers would help out more around the house and quit fighting with each other, she wouldn't have these problems. She was convinced all of her frustrations were their fault and she isn't the one who needs help. Granted, if these changes took place, her life might be easier in many ways. But her emotional condition would still be subject to others' behaviors and actions. Because she isn't ready to accept responsibility for her past actions and her future choices, she is caught in a trap. She is inadvertently blocking the very changes she desperately wants and needs.

Jo-Anne is a single mother who never married. She constantly complains about her child's father, his lack of attentiveness to their son, his neglect when it comes to making support payments, and the way his traits and habits are being passed down to their child. She continually berates this man and blames him for everything that goes wrong in her home, even though they don't live together. Until she takes responsibility for her own actions, she is allowing this man to control her life and negatively influence her little boy's thinking, too.

Simone is a single woman who can't get past the betrayal she suffered when her boyfriend neglected to tell her he was married. She thought she had found her true love and was starting to trust him completely with her future. When she found out about his "secret," she broke off the relationship. But then she held him responsible for not being able to move forward with her life. She still believes he is to blame for her current insecurities and the inability to trust other men.

Each one of these women has given over her power to someone or something else. Granted, they have been wronged—but by playing the role of victim, they are becoming paralyzed with fear and are slipping further away from being able to move on with their lives.

If you are single and want to be married, if you're stuck in a job you can't stand or a relationship you want to get out of, if your teens are driving you nuts and giving you wrinkles, and if nothing seems to be working out the way you hoped it would, you may be playing the role of victim. No wonder you feel out of control—victims are powerless.

My friend, here is some good news for you. Through your past choices, you have determined who you are and where you are today, and now through your choices you can change all that. If for some reason you have chosen to stay in a harmful relationship, allow a domineering person to put you down, be in your lousy job, hate your single life, or allow your kids to give you gray hair, it's possible that you are choosing to sabotage anything good in your life because you feel it won't work out anyway.

Because I have been there, I realize it is very difficult to accept that you are staying in your current condition because of your choices. It is much more comfortable for us to lay the blame elsewhere for our pain and lack of joy. It is very upsetting when we start to see that *we* may be our own worst enemy. I want you to know this realization could turn out to be your biggest blessing ever! If you can create your own misery by your choices, then it stands to reason that you can also create a more joyful existence. Just because some of your past choices got you into a troublesome situation, don't let them become excuses for staying there. Make a decision to stop mourning the past and begin to overcome your former existence with a series of good choices.

We will never move out of the present and into the future with all God has planned for us if we cling to and dwell in the past. What freedom you will experience when at last you accept accountability for the rest of your life!

Chapter 4

Ready. Set. Let Go!

Drop the last year into the silent limbo of the past.
Let it go, for it was imperfect, and thank God that it can go!
BROOKS ATKINSON

Clear out the old because of the new.
LEVITICUS 26:10 NKJV

CLEANING OUT MY CLOSETS IS STILL ONE of the hardest things I have to do. Letting go just doesn't come easy for me. Even though part of my seminar business involves teaching organizational skills to others for their home and office, it's still tough for me to get rid of certain things. For example, the slinky black evening gown I know will never fit again still hangs in the back of the closet in the spare room. So does the 70s-style blue satin dress I wore on my first date with my new hubby, the pink angora sweater that's worn too thin at the elbows, and the matching red plaid dresses I made for our little girls to wear one Christmas. Whether it's an outdated item, the wrong fit, or something with sentimental value, I know I'm not alone when I have a difficult time releasing my possessions. (It's obvious when I see the huge numbers of attendees at my workshops called "Organized and Clutter-Free at Last!")

Because most of us have such a difficult time letting go, clutter is a growing problem in our culture—whether in our homes, workplaces, garages, attics, cars, handbags, wallets, briefcases, or garden sheds. I tell my audiences, that if they are serious about relinquishing their "stuff," they may want to listen to Engelbert Humperdinck's recording of "Please Release Me" while they attempt to de-clutter.

On the other hand, inner clutter is much more of a problem. We either hang on tightly to outdated thoughts and disturbing memories, or we cling to sentimental parts of our past we feel are too meaningful to abandon. Maybe you've had this happen—you're driving along listening to the car radio when a certain song comes on that instantly takes you back to a time when you were crushed, heartbroken, or devastated. Suddenly, all those dreadful emotions come flooding in once again. When that happens, we always have the choice of turning the dial, but we usually go on listening, and hurting, and sobbing.

Although being set free from the past can happen quickly, for most of us it is a step-by-step process. Sometimes there are "levels of liberty" we go through, and just when we think we're free from something, it rears its ugly head again. One step we can take toward letting go and releasing the pain is to change the station!

If you have a tendency to hang on to old memories, personal belongings, material possessions, viewpoints, opinions, and other clutter, join the crowd. Even though we understand that our baggage weighs us down and holds us back, it's often more painful to let it go. We know intuitively that letting go is the way to inner peace, yet it takes courage to quit hanging on. In closets and in life, holding tight to our past comes naturally. It's also what holds us back, keeps us stuck, and cripples our dreams for an exciting and meaningful future.

Making Room for the New

God said in the Old Testament that we must clear out the old to make room for the new. Women know if it's new furnishings we need, the best way to make it happen is to get rid of something old. When we want to add a new item to our wardrobe, something miraculous happens when we clean out our closet, letting go of items we no longer wear. We are making space for the new, and in doing so, we are allowing it to come to us.

The same is true when we desire a peaceful, liberated life. We must free ourselves to receive the prosperity, health, joy, and abundance we seek. The way we do this is to clear out whatever is not contributing to our betterment—whether it's old feelings and attitudes that have become outdated, or beliefs and viewpoints that simply don't "fit" anymore. The rule applies to relationships, too. Now I am not talking about clearing out your spouse, your toddler, your teen, your mother-in-law, or your friends (necessarily!), but there may be associations you have that aren't working or you've outgrown.

When we finally release our grasp and clear out the old, there's room for the new to flow into our lives. Start experimenting by letting go of a few material possessions and tangible items. I'm sure you will be surprised at how suddenly and effortlessly something new flows into your life. Once you have mastered the tangible, you'll be freer to move on to clearing out some of the more intangible things…sad or upsetting memories, hurts, regrets, and disappointments.

There is an ancient Egyptian proverb that says, "The marksman hitteth the target partly by pulling, partly by letting go. The boatsman reacheth the landing partly by pulling, partly by letting go." Think about it. A sharpshooter must first pull the trigger but then let it go. An archer starts off by pulling back on the bow, but nothing happens until he lets the arrow go. When rowing, it's that combination of drawing back and letting go that propels your boat forward. It's much the same with our lives. We can get a good start by pulling from the past with all its disappointments, regrets, and heartache, but then step out in faith and let go. These are probably the scariest two words in the English language, especially for someone who has a need to be in control!

If we know there is freedom in letting go, why is it so difficult to

Quote

release the problems and burdens of yesterday? We first have to acknowledge the reasons before we can even begin to muster up the energy to take the necessary steps. Here are a few of the most common hindrances when it comes to letting go:

- *Our memory keeps bringing it back to our mind.* We may try to let go, but the incident keeps coming back to haunt us. The more effort we put into letting go, the more persistent the memories become. In our thoughts, they keep hanging on…and on…and on.

- *We are conditioned to believe it's just not that easy.* Some of us have bought into the false idea that it will surely entail a lifetime of hard work and energy to relinquish the hurtful events of our past. We think if we're serious about letting go, it might mean we'll end up in therapy for years. We believe it will require tremendous struggles, and we are not sure if we are ready to devote that amount of time and effort to do it.

- *Letting go seems too simple an answer.* We think, *Surely it's more complicated than simply letting go!* We have a hard time believing that letting go will really help solve our problems. We are certain that if it's going to be effective, clearing out the old must be a complex undertaking.

- *We feel we'll be losing control.* By letting go we believe we'll be relinquishing power in our lives. In reality, the opposite is true—whatever you cannot release has control and power over you!

Letting go is one of the major cornerstones of being liberated from your past. If you are ready to be set free, make a decision to release whatever is holding you back. Don't hang on to anything that is not empowering you to move forward. In reality, you always have the option of choosing whether you will focus on a hurtful past or fill your mind with uplifting thoughts of the present and all its blessings. Your mind cannot focus on both negative and positive ideas at the same time. The Bible says, *"You will know the truth and the truth will set you free"* (John 8:32 TLB). When you choose to focus on today and all the possibilities that lie ahead, you automatically release your grip on yesterday. Layers of the past gradually fall away and you are soon set free!

There was an interesting study involving a monkey that couldn't let go. Now, I am not comparing you or me to monkeys in any way, but this experiment makes such a good point I want to share it with you. A peanut was placed inside a jar with a small opening. When the jar was presented to the monkey, he immediately reached inside to retrieve the treat. His hand went in easily enough, but once he grasped the peanut, his fist was larger than the opening and he was not able to get it back out. As long as he held on tightly, his fist was wedged. All he had to do to be set free was to release the thing that kept him trapped. To get *unstuck,* he only needed to *let go* of the cause of the problem.

Sometimes we are like that monkey. Whether what we are holding on to is the "good ole days" or some horrific memories from a sorrowful past, we know in our heart of hearts what is keeping us stuck. The result is, much as with that monkey, freedom eludes us.

How often do we clutch the burdens of our own guilt and regrets—or of another's violation in our life—when we have the option of releasing them? There are many things we need to release in order to experience true freedom. Here are just a few:

1. Let go of…past regrets. Remorse, shame, the guilt complex, and self-reproach are some of the most debilitating problems we must deal with in leaving a hurtful past behind. In every life, there will always be regrets, but they must not cause us to be governed by our past. Because we can't change the past, regrets will only destroy the power of the present. You are not your past. You have too many options in front of you to loiter in bygone days.

2. Let go of…"should have," "could have," and "if only." Condemning inner voices whisper to us that we *should have…* spent more time with our spouse or children, been a better wife, mom, daughter, or friend, taken a job to contribute to the family income (or stayed home with the children while they were small—moms just can't win!), gone back to finish our education, visited Grandma more often, eaten healthier, walked more, accepted the promotion, turned down the offer, joined the gym, entertained more often, said "no" to temptation, kept a cleaner house, or let the house go to look after more important matters.

We tell ourselves we *could have* tried harder, been more astute and discerning, tuned into another's needs, kept our cool, stayed calm, not fought back, learned better ways to handle a difficult situation, called a friend for support, stayed away, kept our mouth shut, saved up instead of going into debt, or prayed more.

Then we begin to live in the fantasy world of *if only*. If only I had listened to my parents, if only I had finished my degree, if only I hadn't married so young, and the list goes on. What a waste of effort, time, and energy, because you can never go back and change those things.

3. Let go of…putting life on hold. When we're not happy with what's happening now, we yearn for the future, putting our happiness on the back burner until conditions are "perfect." That's when you'll find yourself saying, "Someday I'll make a better life for myself," or "I'll be happy once I'm out of this situation." We think the longings will stop when we attain more material possessions, achieve our highest goals, take the right number of holidays each year, lose enough weight, get the right spouse, or have a better job.

See if this sounds familiar. When we're kids, we say "I'll be happy when I'm 16." Then when we're 16 and still not happy, it becomes "I'll really be happy when I turn 21, or once I get married (or divorced), or when the babies arrive." Then, "I'll really be happy when those babies sleep through the night, get potty-trained, have all their teeth, go to school, grow up, leave home, get married…." We are convinced we'll finally be happy once the mortgage is paid, when we are out of debt, or after we retire. We promise ourselves that's the time we'll start painting with watercolors, take tennis lessons, learn to play a musical instrument, write that book, buy a little antique shop, or open a bed and breakfast.

What a shame it is to put our life on hold until all the conditions are ideal and everything is lined up perfectly. It's as though we are waiting for God to call down from heaven telling us, "Your life is now in order. You may go ahead and start living!" Let me encourage you to go ahead—now! Quit stalling. Abandon all your excuses. Stop procrastinating and putting your life *on hold* and start living—today!

4. Let go of...yearning for the "good ole days." In society today, we notice a deep hunger for nostalgia. One way this is demonstrated is by the tremendous popularity of the "oldies" music stations, which are listened to by people of all ages. We're also seeing a resurgence of artwork that depicts the quieter, simpler times of days gone by. So many of us have a deep inner longing to return to those seemingly happier days. It's our heart's cry.

But were those days really as good as our memories present them to us now? There is a danger in longing for things to be as they once were, especially when it takes the place of anticipating and expecting an exciting future. We can become prisoners of our perception of a *positive* past, and that can affect us just as much as a *negative* past. I say "perception" because, whatever your picture is of the past, chances are it's not altogether accurate. If you have ever witnessed a car accident, you know that what they say is true. Talk to three different people who saw the accident and you'd get three different accounts. When you gather your siblings together to reminisce about the past, it can often seem as though you grew up in separate homes! You are thinking to yourself, *Who are these parents my sisters and brothers keep talking about?* because their memories of the good and bad about growing up are so different from your own.

We each see things through our own experiences. Consider this. If you were given a pair of blue glasses at birth and wore them continuously so that you always saw the world through them, what color would a lemon be to you? Green naturally, since that's the result when blue and yellow are combined. But that biased and distorted assumption is based on what you perceive because of the glasses that skew your world. It is not necessarily the truth.

Sometimes it's our false perceptions of the past that hurt us more than the troubles and heartaches we've come through. Exaggerated pleasant memories of the good times can shut out reality, too. When I left my abusive marriage, my tendency on lonely days was to reminisce about the fun times and loving moments, to remember only the good parts, the sunny breaks amid the storm. When that happened, I regretted my decision to leave, and I had to remind myself of the real reasons I was not in that situation anymore. Obviously, having a distorted view of the past is not healthy.

Interestingly, the human mind has a way of blocking out the *worst* of the good times. On the one hand, this can be beneficial. On the other hand, it can leave us with a false representation of what life was truly like. We need to be realistic when remembering times gone by. The best rule I know is, "Capture the best and forget the rest."

5. Let go of...believing it's your lot in life to suffer. Did you ever think to yourself, *Well, I guess I was born to have a permanent heartache. This must be God's plan for me!* Although through our own choices and the actions of others we may have to suffer some pretty heart-rending natural consequences, it is never God's plan to keep us down. He does not angrily punish us by stripping us of the things that matter to us in life. The Bible clearly teaches us that Jesus' death and resurrection finalized all God's anger against us. I now know the suffering in my first marriage taught me many valuable lessons and brought me to the place I am today. It may sound strange, but I wouldn't change one minute of my past. Although it was difficult at best and devastating at times, it was those experiences that gave me my two precious daughters, developed my character, and brought me to a place I never would have thought possible.

6. Let go of...the addiction to drama in your life. Chaos, confusion, and commotion can become a familiar and habitual way of life. It's easy to become dependent on an uproar-dominated lifestyle filled with turbulence and mayhem. If you are hooked on upheaval, disorder, and pandemonium, it could be that this "soap opera" existence has become your comfort zone and feels normal to you. When frantic, frenzied episodes are what you are used to and expect, in a strange way it becomes a dependable and reliable part of your life. When that happens, your need for turmoil seems to be the most natural condition, and it almost becomes an obsession or compulsion. When I moved away from my life of continual havoc and chaos, I suffered withdrawal symptoms until I adjusted to more serene and settled conditions. Living free from anxiety was unfamiliar to me, and it took some getting used to. Like me, you may have to wean yourself from this addiction.

7. Let go of...unproductive thoughts. Your thoughts are always producing results that are either helping or hindering you. Lord Halifax said, "A man may dwell so long on a thought that it may take him prisoner." Faulty thinking will do that. It will keep you locked up and trapped in the past. The good news is, *you* get to decide what you think about and focus on all day long. No one else can get inside your head and direct your thoughts. Only you are in control. When you change your thoughts, you change your world!

8. Let go of...unrealistic expectations. It doesn't work to expect to go through life without struggles, adversity, loss, and hardships. And it's unrealistic to expect to have the strength to go through those trials without God's presence, assurance, and help. You've had difficulties in the past, and you are going to have more troubles in the future. Jesus said,

> *In this godless world, you will continue to experience difficulties. But take heart! I've conquered the world* (John 16:33 MSG).

God will not leave you or forsake you. He promises you His presence; He promises to equip you with what you need to face every ordeal.

9. Let go of...setting impossible standards for yourself. We live in a world that promotes perfectionism and idealism. Women desperately want to prove we can not only bring home the bacon, but fry it up in a pan while homeschooling the kids, volunteering our time and talents, cooking great meals, staying fit, being a wonderful hostess, and keeping an immaculate home. (I read about a woman who did all that—plus she made her own pickles, jams, and jellies, modeled part-time for *Vogue,* and in her spare time shingled the roof!) We start comparing ourselves to nearly impossible images and then feel disappointed in ourselves and let down with our own performance. Avoid comparing yourself to impossible standards.

10. Let go of...feeling responsible for others' reactions. You are responsible for yourself—to be the best person you can be with the tools you have available to you. You are not responsible for the way others respond to you. They are responsible for their own actions, reactions, and behaviors. It is tempting for people to say to us, "See how I am behaving as a result of what you did!" In other words, "If you hadn't acted that way, I wouldn't be handling the situation this way." How ludicrous! When you stop to think of it, this type of response just doesn't make any sense. Let others think and feel what they want. Your responsibility is to keep doing the best you can with what you have at the stage you are at in your personal growth.

11. Let go of...pessimistic associations. Your own negativity can bring you down, but "negaholic" people will keep you there. You know who they are—they're the ones who brighten a room every time they leave! Not only do these dear people see the cup as half empty, not half full, but they complain it's chipped and now they've just cut their lip on it! A pessimistic outlook causes you to be depressed and will eventually make you sick. The Bible says to *"be transformed by the renewing of your mind"* (Romans 12:2). You can renew your mind by focusing on the hope that God gives by reading His promises over and over and committing them to memory. When you recognize the need to be uplifted, make a point of spending time with those who can encourage you, support you, and cheer you on in your new goals and dreams.

12. Let go of...wondering what other people think of you. Many of us were taught to always consider, "What will people think?" We were frightened into making that concern a prime consideration in our choices and decisions. It's no wonder that today we can get caught up in putting others' opinions of us before what God wants. Jesus said, *"No one can serve two masters"* (Matthew 6:24).

It's been suggested that we'd worry less about what others think of us if we would only realize that they're probably not! What they're thinking about is themselves—and they're wondering what you think of them. One of my sisters jokingly says, "Okay, enough about me. Now tell me, what do *you* think of me?" Most other people have enough to think about without concentrating on you. When I would say as a child, "I don't want to walk into school late because everybody will be staring at me," my mom would tease, "Who do you think you are, the Queen of England?" Good point! Besides, even if they are judging you, being controlled by the opinions of others is a sure way to miss all the unique plans God has for your future.

13. Let go of...trying to change other people. Face it...the only time you succeed in changing someone is when he's a baby! Think of the hours we can waste attempting to change another person. When you can see that change would be beneficial in someone's life, the best thing you can do is to be a positive example, a role model, a mentor, an encourager, and an effective influencer. Then accept others for who they are...learning, growing, and developing.

One of the best pieces of advice anyone ever gave me was this: "Stop expecting something from someone that they are not even capable of giving." If you want to drive yourself crazy, ignore other people's limits and keep expecting more from them. You will never succeed in changing another person, whether it's your spouse, your siblings, your in-laws, your friends, or your coworkers. So quit frustrating yourself. This includes your grown children. Although when our kids are young we are responsible to train them to make the right choices in life, as adults they are responsible for their own behavior.

14. Let go of...bitterness. Dale Carnegie said, "Wouldn't our enemies rub their hands with glee if they knew that our hate for them was exhausting us, making us tired and nervous, ruining our looks, giving us heart trouble, and probably shortening our lives?" The Bible says,

> *To worry yourself to death with resentment would be a foolish, senseless thing to do* (Job 5:2 GNT).

The bitter truth about bitterness is that if you insist on holding a grudge, soon it will hold you!

Many people hold on to old hurts and never get over them. Rather than relinquishing their pain through forgiveness, they mentally review the cause of the pain over and over. Bitterness, when internalized, opens the door to all sorts of unhealthy feelings and emotions, including resentment, animosity, antagonism, and even hatred. Some women clam up, while others blow up! Eventually, when those feelings are harbored long enough, they explode and lead to plotting revenge.

Bitterness always hurts you more than the person it's aimed at. Usually, the offender forgets the wrongdoing and goes on with life while you continue to seethe in your anguish, keeping the past alive.

The Best Way to Let Go

When we want to let go of a situation, no matter what it is, we must be able to "bless" it. When you bless something, you sanction it, giving it your approval and endorsement, freeing it to go forward with your cooperation and support. As one writer said, "Bless a thing and it will bless you. Curse it and it will curse you. If you bless a situation, it has no power to hurt you." So *let us throw off everything that hinders...and let us run with perseverance the race marked out for us"* (Hebrews 12:1). And let us discover true freedom through forgiveness.

Letting Go

To let go doesn't mean to stop caring;
it means I can't do it for someone else.
To let go is not to cut myself off;
it's the realization that I don't control another.
To let go is not to enable,
but to allow learning from natural consequences.
To let go is to admit powerlessness,
which means the outcome is not in my hands.
To let go is not to try to change or blame another;
I can only change myself.
To let go is not to care for,
but to care about.
To let go is not to fix,
but to be supportive.
To let go is not to be protective;
it is to permit another to face reality.
To let go is not to deny,
but to accept.
To let go is not to nag, scold, or argue,
but to search out my own shortcomings
and correct them.
To let go is not to criticize and regulate anyone,
but to try to become
what I dream I can be.
To let go is not to regret the past but to grow
and live for the future.
To let go is to fear less and love more.

AUTHOR UNKNOWN

Chapter 5

Forgiving the Unforgivable

If you hold a grudge long enough,
eventually it will hold you!
AUTHOR UNKNOWN

Never hold grudges.
COLOSSIANS 3:13 TLB

IT'S NOT EASY TO FORGIVE, WHETHER WE'VE been betrayed, wounded, heartbroken, or simply brought to tears. When someone hurts us unfairly and walks away without apologizing or repenting, it hurts. That hurt festers inside us until it turns into resentment, poisoning our thoughts and actions and making us bitter and miserable. There's only one way to end this downward spiral—with forgiveness. Those who have hurt you in the past cannot continue to hurt you now unless you hold on to the pain. You won't be free to let go of your pain without forgiving that individual, that group of people, or yourself. It may also mean asking to be forgiven by someone else.

The Choice to Be Liberated

Forgiveness is perhaps one of the most misunderstood concepts in the Bible. We think it's similar to saying, "Never mind, it's okay." This is a phrase we casually toss out when someone spills grape juice on our carpet, breaks a cherished trinket, or accidentally steps on our toe. But forgiveness is not the same as saying, "Never mind, it's okay," because sin without repentance is not all right. To be accurate, forgiveness on our part is being willing to let go of the pain we're experiencing even though what was done is wrong. It's choosing to relinquish feelings of resentment, bitterness, or hostility toward those who have wronged us or over situations where we have been injured or upset.

Forgiveness is not letting someone off the hook. Rather, it's deciding to let God deal with that person's wrongdoing rather than seething inside or trying to handle it our own way. After all, Hebrews 10:30 tells us vengeance is not our right, but His. Whether or not others are remorseful, have apologized, or have asked to be forgiven does not need to play a role. Although forgiveness can set another person free, it is not something we do for them, but a choice we make for ourselves as a means of being liberated. It's a catalyst, an act that allows us to relinquish harmful and toxic emotions that poison the deepest parts of our souls. Though forgiving an unrepentant person doesn't do much for that person, it purifies our heart and motives so we can stand before God and know He hears our prayers.

Stephanie came to speak with me at my book table after attending one of my seminars in which we dealt with forgiveness. With her sparkling eyes, warm smile, and delightful sense of humor she had already captured my attention by her participation in the audience. When we chatted privately, she confided to me that she and her husband had just celebrated their fortieth wedding anniversary and were, on the whole, very happy together. They had worked through a lot of their differences and truly enjoyed being with one another. But something hurtful had happened early on in their marriage, and it had left a deep wound she secretly continued to live with. Although she wanted to forgive her husband and actually thought she had, the memory of it would come back to haunt her unexpectedly, engulfing her like a gigantic tidal wave without warning.

Whenever this incident resurfaced, Stephanie admitted the biggest stumbling block for her was that her husband had never asked to be forgiven. In fact, if she mentioned it to him, he still held to his conviction that she had provoked the incident and he had been justified in his actions. He accused her of living in the past and thought she should get over it. What she wanted was for him to come to repentance, realize he'd been a total jerk, fall to his knees, and beg her to forgive him for being such a miserable slob. After 40 years, it was obvious that, short of a miracle, this probably wasn't going to happen!

Preparing to Forgive

So how was Stephanie to handle this? First of all, by knowing and accepting she could not force another person to own up to or admit any wrongful behavior—no matter how obvious she thought it was. As was the case with Stephanie, there may be someone in your life you feel should pay the price and doesn't deserve to be forgiven until he mends his ways. You might be thinking, *But you just don't understand. I can't forgive so-and-so until they are remorseful and apologize!* The truth is, you are not in charge of what another person does, or how others grow emotionally and spiritually; nor can you control how someone else thinks and feels.

I realize it would seem tough and insensitive to say, "Forgive and get on with your life." Yet my desire in this book is to provide ways for you to be set free from a past that hurts your present. I know from experience that bitterness and unforgiveness can cripple your dreams and harm your relationships faster than anything else. So here is the secret: You don't have to *feel* forgiveness—you just have to *do* it. Ask yourself how you would act toward a person if you had forgiven him. Then, with God's help, choose to act that way. (It's also called the habit of "acting as if"!)

It may help to write out your feelings in the form of a letter. Express how much pain and suffering you've experienced—then express that you have now chosen to forgive and let it go. Whether you deliver the letter or rip it up, it is the act of putting forgiveness into words that can finally allow you to move on. Perhaps you want to forgive someone who is no longer living and you think writing a letter wouldn't really do any good. Write it anyway—you might be surprised at the release it can bring to you.

Secondly, because Stephanie had chosen to stay in that relationship all these years in spite of that incident, and because she and her husband truly do enjoy each other's company, she began to recognize there must have been more pluses than minuses. She knew she could have chosen to leave if the situation was unbearable. There are always other options for us. When we make the decision to stay where we are, whether in a job, a relationship, or the neighborhood where we live, it must be because we'd rather be there then somewhere else. Then—as long as your life is not in danger—it becomes a matter of focusing on all the positives in the situation rather than dwelling on the ones that hurt.

Thirdly, Stephanie needed to understand that forgiving someone does not mean brushing off the misconduct as irrelevant. I am not suggesting you go around saying, "Really, it's okay you let the air out of my tires, poisoned my cat, and spread nasty rumors about me at work. I didn't need to drive anywhere that day anyway, the cat was getting on my nerves, and I'd been thinking about getting a new job in another town." Forgiving someone means knowing full well that the offense was inappropriate, improper, or out-and-out wrong—and then deciding to relinquish your feelings of being entitled to make the guilty person pay. We always have the choice of using our energy and emotions for retribution or resolution.

Finally, Stephanie came to the realization that we are obligated to forgive if we want to be forgiven. Can you think of anything you might like to be forgiven for? The Bible says, *"Forgive, and you will be forgiven"* (Luke 6:37). When we do forgive, we are not performing some great charitable act of generosity and goodwill. God tells us to do it; therefore, it is required of us. His Word says,

> *You must make allowance for each other's faults and forgive the person who offends you. Remember, the Lord forgave you, so you must forgive others* (Colossians 3:13 NLT).

However, we are not obligated to have warmhearted, sugary feelings toward that time in our life or the incident that caused the pain—just to relinquish it. It's been said that when you refuse to forgive, you allow the other person to control you. While that is true, it's not why we should forgive. The real reason is because we have been forgiven much. To know how much, simply look to the cross. Before Jesus died, He prayed, *"Father, forgive them, for they know not what they do"* (Luke 23:34 KJV). He looked past our transgressions, secured our forgiveness, and supernaturally enabled us to forgive others. It's up to us to repent and receive the forgiveness He secured, so we can establish a right relationship with God.

The Deadly Alternative

When you don't forgive, revenge is another route. That's when you start plotting ways to get even. The mere thought of the incident may cause you to be easily riled, annoyed, or provoked into doing and saying things you will later regret. There's only one thing to do with that kind of pent-up anger—let it go. And the way to let go is to forgive whoever and whatever it is that hurt you so much or made you so irate.

I know plotting revenge is more appealing than forgiving and can actually be invigorating in a crazy, twisted sort of way. It makes us feel all victim-ish and put-upon, which can be strangely gratifying. Our inclination is to cling to our righteous indignation and define ourselves as victims. The only problem is, victims are not free. When we forgive from the heart, though, it's an act of liberation. We not only free ourselves from the burden of being the "wounded one," but we set the other person free from the negative bonds between us. Forgiving can open up the way for a new and different relationship, one that has the potential of being much richer.

One main reason why forgiveness is such a tough thing to do is that it turns conventional logic upside down. In a society that places a premium on revenge, forgiveness is hardly a popular idea. By forgiving, it may seem as though we are condoning someone's poor behavior, or agreeing to tolerate what the person did while appearing to accept that they are innocent of any wrongdoing. We feel caught between excusing the person responsible and experiencing a compelling need to see justice done.

Forgiveness isn't about ignoring or dismissing the pain that has been caused. It does not mean we deny our injuries or lay aside all claims to justice. It is different from removing responsibility. We don't forgive because we believe the person is innocent or even because we feel like doing it, for that matter. (Most of the time we feel like making them pay big-time for what they did.) Rather, we choose to not let others' actions or behaviors have any more control or influence over our lives. By letting go of all feelings of resentment, indignation, hostility, and animosity, we are freeing ourselves to move forward. Holding others responsible for our sorrow, misery, or grief only keeps us ensnared in the grip of bygone incidents and stuck in the past. Although it is not our main motive, forgiveness is something wholesome and beneficial we can do for ourselves.

An old Chinese proverb warns, "Whoever opts for revenge should dig two graves." In other words, no one wins, and you'll end up burying yourself, too. The word "opt" signifies that revenge is a choice. It's something we can fix our minds on and act on. Or, we can choose to let it go. So often we believe if we could get revenge, if we could make the other person pay, we would somehow feel better about what has gone on in the past. But the truth is vengeance is bittersweet! It satisfies only temporarily, and then we revert to the same hard feelings we had in the beginning.

No matter how much we can rationalize our right to hold onto a grudge, being vengeful and vindictive can be the very root of depression, anxiety, and hopelessness. Even though we may be able to indisputably justify our bitterness and, with very little effort, manage to get others on our side and feeling sorry for us ("Poor woman...look what she's had to endure!"), nevertheless, our resentment will hold us back. By taking the stance of a victim and letting others know what has been done to us, we can often easily gain their support. But in the end, we are setting ourselves up for failure. With true forgiveness, what we are saying is, in a word, "Yes, I was seriously and severely hurt, but I am not going to let that pain continue to control my life. I am releasing it. I want the hurt gone so I can move forward."

Making the Choice and Carrying It Out

In the natural human state, complete and lasting forgiveness rarely happens. But what is impossible with humans is possible with God. When you pray, ask that the pain be released and that you will be free to move to a new place of compassion and empathy for those who have hurt you. It is unnatural to love your enemies, to bless those who curse you, to help those who hate you, and to pray for those who misuse you. Yet these are the commands of Christ. Would He tell you to do something that is impossible? No, but to do what He has commanded in your own strength is unachievable as well. To pass the love of God along to others, especially the undeserving, takes the power of the Holy Spirit and the deep knowledge of that love in the first place.

Forgiveness comes down to making a choice. The first step is to ask forgiveness for yourself—and then decide you are going to forgive. Trust that, through prayer, your heart will be softened toward the person by seeing him or her through the very eyes of Christ. Spend some quiet time forgiving that person who has wronged you in the past, then vow not to keep on victimizing yourself with private thoughts and remembrances of malice and cruelty or with plans of vengeance, which hurt only you. If possible, plan to meet, make a phone call to, or write a letter to anyone you have chosen to forgive, letting them know of your decision. Healing comes with making your thoughts tangible and also in getting them in writing. Only then will you be able to start afresh.

It's all well and good to talk about forgiveness, but how do we do it? If we have chosen to forgive and have decided to do it without looking back, what comes next? Here are some steps to get you started:

1. Make a deliberate decision to stop discussing the story with others. You may need to confide in one trusted friend or a trained professional for therapeutic reasons, but only open your heart to someone you know will encourage you to forgive. Even if you have told others in the past, make a promise to yourself not to talk about it in the future—other than for the purpose of supporting someone else in a similar position. Be uncompromising and strict with yourself. Reject the temptation to keep discussing the story. This is not easy, especially when we are still suffering the pain. If revenge is our goal, we know we can ruin someone's reputation by telling on them with statements like, "Can you believe what she did to me?"

2. Stop mentally dragging up the past. Rehashing hurtful and disturbing scenes over and over again in your mind can drive you crazy. We sometimes do this subconsciously, and other times we keep the anger fresh on purpose, but in either case, we are only hurting ourselves. Besides, the other person has no clue about what is going on inside our heads. We are suffering, yet it's not having any effect on them.

3. Be pleasant and congenial when you are in the company of those you forgive. This doesn't mean you have to go out of your way and conspicuously make an effort to be hospitable or sugary sweet. Simply don't say anything in reference to the event or do something that would cause them to feel ill at ease or apprehensive.

4. Avoid putting anyone on a "guilt trip." Guilt is most painful, and if we are truly ready to forgive, then we won't want others to have feelings of self-reproach, humiliation, or shame. Remind yourself of the Golden Rule—*"Do to others as you would have them do to you"* (Luke 6:31). In your mind, say a blessing over them. Mentally give them your consent to break from their own past and move forward.

One of the reasons others may have a difficult time apologizing or asking forgiveness is that they may have stopped growing—emotionally or spiritually. Pray that they will seek God's forgiveness for themselves and that they will thrive in their spirit, flourishing in every way. The opposite of blessing a person is wishing for his failure, or hoping for disaster to strike. That's when you want his success to be impeded in some way—or you are even hoping for the worst. You will know you have truly forgiven someone when you genuinely want the best in life for him and can sincerely bless him.

5. When a person is remorseful, do what you can to restore a sense of dignity. Allow others to feel good about themselves again by saying whatever you can (if it is true!) to restore their sense of worth, value, and self-respect.

6. Abolish any sense of self-righteousness in yourself. As long as there is even a trace of arrogance or condescension in it, or any finger-pointing, your attempt at total forgiveness will not succeed. Sometimes we can use false "kindness" to try to make the other person feel miserable.

7. Behave as though you don't even think they did anything wrong. This can be most difficult for all of us, but sometimes acting in a certain way helps us to actually experience the feeling. Remember the old phrase, "Fake it 'til you make it"? Actors do it all the time when they have to depict a certain emotion. It's an amazing attribute of human nature. You can act as if you hardly noticed the wrongdoing—and before you know it, the genuine feelings soon come along.

8. Make total forgiveness a lifelong commitment. Once you have chosen to forgive, keep it up today, tomorrow, and forever. Some days will be easier than others. You will have times when you think you have won a complete victory and are totally free from harboring any resentment, then WHAM!—the very next day, something happens to remind you of what someone did and of the utter injustice of the fact they will never be punished or exposed. That old temptation to "go public" or hold onto the bitterness will emerge once again. Not only will you have to make the commitment to forgive, but your pledge will have to be renewed periodically.

Even if I did not share with others what I was going through, there was a time when I felt justified in going before God and pleading my case. "He ought to be punished"; "She doesn't deserve to be let off the hook." Then, when I began thinking of God as my Father in heaven, I realized that, like most parents, He wants His children to get along and love one another. After all, no parent likes it when one child comes squealing on the other, demanding they be punished. But our Father loves all His children equally.

9. Pray for those who have wounded you. That's a difficult one to understand or put into practice. When you pray, be completely honest with God. If you feel angry, tell Him. Say, "Lord, nothing in me wants to pray for this person." Confess your anger, hurt, unforgiveness, resentment, and disappointment. Ask God to give you a right spirit and renewed sense of love. Trust Him to heal the situation. The Bible says, *"Let us not grow weary in doing good, for in due season, we shall reap if we do not lose heart"* (Galatians 6:9 NKJV). If you truly want to be set free from a past that is crippling you, desiring the best for your enemies is a powerful step. Something happens to our hearts when we pray for another person. The hardness melts away, and we become able to move beyond the hurts to forgive. Miraculously, we are even able to love the person we are praying for. It happens because, through prayer, we enter into God's presence—and He fills us with His own spirit of love.

10. Ask for healing for yourself. Memories of the situation can come back to haunt you when you least expect it. God's healing will release you from the hurtful recollections and the harmful emotions that go with them.

When you handle your resentment in these ways, you may get a sincere and heartfelt apology and a chance to restore the relationship. But even if you don't, you'll now have the freedom to let the situation go. When practicing forgiveness becomes a lifelong commitment, you will begin to genuinely want the best in life for those who have hurt you. You may even surprise yourself with your sincere desire for their success, health, and well-being. The freedom you experience will help you to overcome barriers that at one time seemed insurmountable. Forgiveness will become second nature.

In most cases, forgiving is an ongoing process. When Peter asked Jesus if he should forgive his brother seven times, Jesus answered, *"No, but seventy times seven"* (Matthew 18:22 TLB). We need the willingness to forgive as often as necessary. Whatever the situation, don't delay. It's too important. Far from leaving us weak and vulnerable, forgiveness is enlightening, empowering, and liberating both to the person who grants it and the one who receives it. In bringing true closure to the most difficult situations, it allows us to lay aside the riddles of retribution and human fairness, and to experience true peace of heart. Finally, it sets into motion a positive chain reaction that passes on the fruits of our forgiveness to others. There is a tremendous liberating power in forgiveness.

In every situation, ask God to forgive you and help you to forgive others. Focus on the forgiveness He has always so freely given to those who ask for it. Remember this little poem: *No forgiveness, no peace; know forgiveness, know peace.* This is the way to freedom. This is the path to starting over.

Chapter 6

Starting Over

*Though no one can go back and make a brand-new start, anyone
can start from now and make a brand-new ending!*
CARL BARD

*Old things are passed away;
behold, all things are become new.*
2 CORINTHIANS 5:17 KJV

ONE OF THE GREAT THINGS ABOUT LIFE is that you can start over.
With God, there are always new beginnings and second chances. He
specializes in giving people fresh starts. While you may feel overwhelmed at times and held back by painful recollections, haunting
fears, remorse, shame, or guilt, God's power in your present life is not
limited by what took place in your past. When you are being governed
and manipulated by your painful memories, you allow your past to
control your future. But when you choose to give God the controls, He
can do amazing things with the rest of your life. You can start now and
have a brand-new ending!

When Meredith shared her traumatic and gut-wrenching story with me, she admitted that, as she was going through it, she did not believe she could ever be free to start again. It all began when she was the general manager of a division of a financial institution. After several of her employees were found to have hidden millions of dollars in losses, she was held responsible. Eventually it came to light that, as a zealous perfectionist, her aggressive and sometimes confrontational leadership style had intimidated her subordinates and made her appear unapproachable. The result was, they were more willing to lie to her than let her know the bad news.

Meredith lost that position but was miraculously given a second chance when the corporation, recognizing her strong points and future potential, offered her the job of salvaging one of its smaller businesses. With her confidence crushed and self-esteem shattered, she almost turned down the offer. But after turning the situation over to God and through much prayer, asking for guidance from the Holy Spirit, she began to see this new position as her opportunity to change the way she related to others. Realizing she had to forgive her staff—and most of all, forgive herself—she began to take the necessary steps to amend her leadership techniques and employee relationships. She made a conscious effort to be more understanding and patient, and listen more closely and attentively in order to solicit negative feedback and bad news in a reassuring way.

Meredith went on to say that, a while later, through God's amazing grace, the way was opened for her to be promoted to an executive vice-president position. Through it all, she discovered failures, setbacks, and mistakes are not the end. Rather, they are the instruments God can use for our new beginnings and a better quality of life. They are opportunities to offer forgiveness and to be forgiven.

The Key to Starting Over

You really *can* start over. Indeed, the best starting point, after forgiving others, is to forgive yourself. New beginnings and forgiving yourself are strongly linked. In the Bible we are told, *"If we have bad consciences and feel that we have done wrong, the Lord will surely feel it even more, for he knows everything we do"* (1 John 3:20 TLB). It's impossible to have a bad conscience and still believe God will answer our prayers. After confessing our sin and accepting His forgiveness, then it's imperative that we forgive ourselves:

> *Once that's taken care of and we're no longer accusing or condemning ourselves, we're bold and free before God! We're able to stretch our hands out and receive what we asked for because we're doing what he said, doing what pleases him* (1 John 3:21-22 MSG).

God uses our conscience. He knows we can only start over when we are not condemning ourselves anymore.

The reason to forgive ourselves is not because we feel like it, or because we want to see ourselves as blameless, but because we limit what we can receive from God when we hold on to our past. He wants to do so much more than we could ever imagine. Forgiving yourself starts with believing in God's incredible love for you and accepting His amazing grace and mercy. If God Almighty can forgive us, who are we to hold on to what He has not only forgiven, but forgotten?

Yet in most cases, it's often easier to forgive someone else than it is to forgive ourselves. A woman I met, who admitted shoplifting for so many years that she's lost track of the value of the stolen goods, believes that even if God can forgive her, it's impossible for her to forgive herself. The mother who accidentally backed her car over her child in the driveway feels the same. The girl who earned money during her college years as a prostitute to support her drug habit; the woman who got pregnant while having an affair and then chose an abortion; and the one who maimed a family of four in a drinking-and-driving accident all think they could never be forgiven, let alone forgive themselves.

But not forgiving yourself often becomes the root of severe self-loathing, extreme self-hatred, and intense inhibitions. It will be next to impossible to truly start over when you feel unforgivable.

What do you have hidden in the back of your closet, behind all your suits, dresses, and shoes? Is there a skeleton so deplorable that you've never told even your spouse or closest friends? Is there a part of your past so appalling or sordid it causes you to cringe whenever the thought of it comes back to haunt you? If you were offered some remarkable opportunity to start over, to move your life in an entirely new direction or a direction that would suddenly put you in the public eye, would you shrink back and be tempted to decline in case you might be "found out?" Maybe you come from such a wounded background that you would be humiliated and embarrassed if others knew about it today. If so, you may be dealing with the disheartening consequences of too many secrets deeply buried and never resolved, secrets so distressing they contaminate your present life and cripple future possibilities.

Seeking Help

After confessing to God and accepting His forgiveness, you may find it easier to forgive yourself when you confide in a trusted friend. Usually we don't feel like doing this. When I need to forgive myself, my tendency is to avoid talking to others about it altogether. This is the worst thing we can do.

But choose your friend carefully, being certain she is one who will keep your confidence. Here's how a beautiful woman I met recently found healing this way. When Terry phoned to talk with me after attending one of my seminars at a corporate conference, she confided that she had always kept everything in. It was as if she had two lives— one she allowed outsiders to see, and one only she knew about. Because of a secret past and the parts of her life she kept to herself, she felt full of guilt, shame, and confusion much of the time.

After the conference where we talked about the consequences of not being able to forgive yourself, Terry decided to tell everything to someone close to her. She expected it to be especially painful to admit her wrongs. Instead, it was very different. The friend she chose to tell did not act shocked. She did not shame Terry or make her feel uncomfortable. She let Terry know she respected her for the courage and honesty it took to divulge her wrongdoings. She also opened up and felt free to share some areas of her life she had felt too ashamed to divulge to anyone. Afterward, Terry said, "Something inside me changed at that moment, and I knew I would never be the same."

When we admit our wrongs—first to ourselves, then to God, and then to another person—this three-step process can be a powerful, life-transforming experience. God wants us to know,

> *If we confess our sins, he is faithful and just and will forgive*
> *us our sins and purify us from all unrighteousness* (1 John
> 1:9).

Each of us has an innate desire to be fully known—to share our innermost secrets that, if not told, become like toxic pollutants to our very being. We long to be loved by someone who knows all our faults, yet accepts us anyway and looks beyond them. God is like that. He knows everything about us and loves us in spite of ourselves. Confession is a powerful spiritual discipline that allows us to experience His grace in realistic, feasible ways. The Bible says,

> *What happiness for those whose guilt has been forgiven!*
> *What joys when sins are covered over! What relief for those*
> *who have confessed their sins and God has cleared their*
> *record* (Psalm 32:1-2 TLB).

The God of New Beginnings

Could it be that, despite all your mistakes, blunders, and flawed decisions, you can truly start over now? Have you considered that a forgiving, loving, compassionate God can accept you just the way you are and wants you to have a new beginning? You may think you can never have a second chance. While that may be true in the sense that you can't actually take a trip back in time to make a brand-new start, you can

always have a second chance at your life…and a third…and a fourth…
and on and on. There are no limits when it comes to starting over. I cannot imagine God looking down from heaven and saying, "Oh, no—now
look what she's gone and done. She's really messed up this time, and
even I can't help. I guess there's just no future for this girl!" That can't
happen. I've always thought about writing a book called, *God Never says
"Oops!"* With God, there can always be another chance to start over.

I think that's what I have always loved about Monday mornings,
turning the calendar to the new month, the changing of the seasons,
New Year's Eve, and birthdays. To me, they all represent God's opportunities for starting over, for new beginnings. We all need the chance to
start over at one time or another. Whether you're disappointed in yourself because you stuffed your face at the smorgasbord last night after
promising yourself you'd eat "light," or you've failed at a relationship,
or made some unsuccessful business moves, or blew up at your spouse
in public, you always have the opportunity to begin again, to start over,
to try something different, and to move in a new direction. So instead
of feeling frustrated because you can't turn back the clock, why not
begin now to create a brand-new ending for yourself?

Here's the most extraordinary part of God's forgiveness, which
always enables a brand-new ending. His amazing grace and mercy
ensure He won't even remember the offense. The Bible says, *"As far as
the east is from the west, so far has he removed our transgressions from us"*
(Psalm 103:12). God says, *"I will…remember their sins no more"*
(Hebrews 8:12). I still find it incredible to know that if I referred to
something for which I have been forgiven and said to God, "Remember
that time I messed up so badly?" He would say, "No, I cannot recall it!"

As humans, we unfortunately don't seem to have that divine ability.
Yet even though we might still have the memory, forgiveness allows us
to assert our God-given power to let go. Then the events themselves can
no longer control or destroy us. Instead, they become experiences that
deepen the wisdom of our heart. They bring us to a place of empathy

and compassion for others. Whether or not we forget, forgiveness undeniably acts as a healing balm to the memories we carry.

Asking Forgiveness from Others

There may be times when you know you have hurt someone and sincerely want to make amends. You probably know intuitively that expressing regret and asking that person to forgive you is the only way to truly let go, to be set free, and begin making progress in your personal journey. However, communicating remorse over what we've said or done, apologizing, and asking forgiveness is often one of the most difficult things we ever attempt to do.

Allyson is a young woman who wrote to me and told me she was frightened when she decided to call her former friend Beth. She feared she would have the phone slammed in her ear. "We used to be such good friends, but I haven't talked to her for six years. She was deeply hurt by some things I said and false accusations I made against her during an exceptionally distressing time in my life right after my divorce. I asked her to meet me for a coffee so I could make amends for the hurtful things I had said and she agreed. I was floored! When we met, I said everything I had prepared to say, and afterward we talked and laughed and cried for hours. She seemed so understanding and assured me she has been in similar positions herself. I was delightfully surprised that our friendship was restored. Now I only wish I hadn't put off calling for so long."

Making amends may seem like an unattainable feat. It does involve a great deal of risk and effort. It is important to recognize we will not always be welcomed with open arms or rewarded with restored relationships as Allyson was with Beth. But our task is to offer to make amends and not to anticipate or depend upon the way others will respond.

Some broken relationships *can* experience healing. But regardless of how people act in response to your effort, it's the serenity that comes from saying, "I blew it—I hurt you and I'm sorry" that provides its own rich reward. Making amends can lead to growth in our lives—both emotional and spiritual—whether or not our course of action has any effect on others.

Each new step of growth requires us to return to the fundamental truths of life. The practical effect of those truths reminds us that we are powerless in ourselves to take this giant leap. We need to rely on God to give us the necessary strength to make amends to those we have offended, injured, upset, or harmed. Reconciliation and living in peace with others to the best of your ability is always a choice. You are responsible to put out your best effort, but you are not responsible for the way others receive it. Each person is responsible for the choices they make. You can only control how you handle things on your end.

> *If it is possible, as far as it depends on you, live at peace with everyone* (Romans 12:18).

Living in peace with others is a choice you make in your

- marriage
- relationships with children or parents
- family members
- friendships
- church community
- neighborhood
- workplace

To truly start over, make living in peace a priority in all those areas. Choose to seek it and you will find it. But even when you do, conflicts will continue to come up. Relationships can't remain permanently peaceful. So many times friends make the mistake of thinking that, if it's a good friendship, everything in their relationship should be fantastic all the time. Some married couples think the same. I have to say that my husband and I are very much in love and plan to stay married "'til death do us part"—but there isn't a week that goes by that we do not have to forgive each other for something!

Forgetting and Trusting Again

> They teach us to remember; why do they not teach us to forget? There is not a man living who has not, some time in his life, admitted that memory was as much of a curse as a blessing (Frances Durivage).

Forgiving and forgetting are not the same thing. Even though we may choose to forgive, the memory of the wound may stay with us for a long time. It might even stay for a lifetime. Some memories also have visible signs that serve as constant reminders—a child born as the result of an extramarital affair, or a physical scar from a severe beating or an attempted suicide—that make it even more difficult to put it out of our mind. Aside from these, our minds have a remarkable ability to recall everything we have ever heard, seen, and done.

But healing is still possible and here's why: Forgiveness changes the *way* we remember. The starting place for forgiveness is to transform the curse into a blessing. Once we forgive others for the wrong choices they've made—our spouse for being unfaithful, our parents for things said or done in anger, our children for their lack of consideration and gratitude, our friends for not being there for us during an emergency, or our physicians for improper diagnosis or inadequate treatment—we no longer have to play the role of victim of our circumstances.

How can we learn to forget once we have mastered forgiveness? First of all, it's one of those choices in life. Decide to put it behind you and choose to stop mulling it over or recalling every hurtful detail. Start focusing on other things. Make up your mind you won't bring it up again. It may cross your mind, but you can decide ahead of time that, when it happens, you won't dwell on it or mention it.

Trust is another part of forgetting when we choose to forgive someone. Sometimes we find it hard to forgive because we don't understand the difference between forgiveness and trust. Forgiveness is choosing to let go of the past by the grace of God, whereas trust is dependent on another person's future actions and behaviors. Starting over and building a new future with trust takes time and requires a track record.

Whether someone hurts you once or repeatedly, God commands that you forgive right away. However, you are not expected to allow that person to continue hurting or abusing you, or to use you as a personal whipping post for every angry whim. God does not require that of you. In fact, if you are in any kind of physical or emotional danger, leave the situation immediately and seek out a safe place where you can get help. You can pray from a distance while the abuser receives the counseling he needs.

Even when you are reunited, you are not required to trust immediately. Trust is based on performance. It calls for a fresh history of trustworthy experiences to be created. The other person must be willing to prove he has changed—and that happens over time. Trust then becomes active rather than passive. Without denying the pain or being naïve, you can begin trusting again based on the truth of what you observe and experience. When you are strong and insightful, and respect yourself, you can know when it is time to trust again.

Starting over with forgiveness in some situations may seem impossible, but with God, all things are possible. In my travels, I have met or heard about victims of violent crime, betrayal, abuse, bigotry, and war—and of more commonplace offenses including backbiting, gossip, strained family ties, marriages gone cold, and tensions or harassment in the workplace—who have come to forgive their victimizers and begin anew. These are people who have come to realize that whether you need to forgive or be forgiven, it's not the event but the unforgiveness that destroys. God who lives in you gives you the grace to move beyond your deepest wounds and say, "You are forgiven!" and, "I am forgiven." If you allow Him, He will give you a fresh start—right now.

Chapter 7

Reclaiming Your Inner Power

In everything you do, stay away from complaining and arguing.
PHILIPPIANS 2:14 TLB

ON THEIR WAY HOME FROM WORK one evening, Sara and Marcy stopped at a newsstand. The man behind the counter seemed grumpy and out of sorts, and after Sara paid for her newspaper, he snarled at her, throwing the change in her direction. Gathering it up, Sara smiled warmly and said, "Thank you very much, sir. Have a nice evening, and I'll see you tomorrow!" Marcy was taken aback and, as they walked away, asked why Sara would be so kind to the man in spite of his inconsiderate manner. Sara admitted that most every night he acted the same, but added, "A while ago, I made a decision not to allow other people to determine my attitude or govern my actions." She had discovered the secret to reclaiming inner power. It lies in taking responsibility for our own conduct, allowing the Holy Spirit to direct our words and deeds, and choosing not to complain and blame others for what we do, think, or say.

Reclaiming your inner power has nothing to do with gaining power over someone. In fact, it's quite the opposite. It's more about relinquishing all claims to power in and of yourself, and instead, relying on God's power to transform you, your circumstances, and the other people in your life. Your inner power is not a weapon to be used to destroy, but a tool for building and restoring. It is a way to invite God's power into your life to fulfill your potential and receive your greatest blessings.

In the same way, it's not about New Age self-help techniques, egotistical goals, or selfish ambitions. Because of this misconception, we might shy away when we mistakenly think women who are living for God shouldn't desire inner power or don't have a need to reclaim it. By talking about power for women here, I am not referring to women's lib, but rather women's liberation through Christ. While it sounds contradictory, reclaiming our power is something we can do only through God's enablement and our own surrender. We also have the ability to forfeit that power through our blaming and complaining.

In Genesis 3:11-13, God said to Adam, *"Have you eaten from the tree that I commanded you not to eat from?"* Adam answered, "Yes, but it was that woman's idea!" Then God said to Eve, *"What is this you have done?"* to which she replied, "It wasn't really my fault because that scheming serpent misled me." So, Adam blamed Eve, Eve blamed the serpent, and the serpent didn't have a leg to stand on! This was the original game of pass the buck. People have been playing this game and blaming each other ever since by failing to accept responsibility for their thoughts, feelings, and actions. What we don't realize is that in doing so, we are being robbed of the very power we need to get beyond our past hurts.

In coming through a painful past, you may have inadvertently relinquished your inner power by falling into the subtle trap of blaming and complaining. It can happen so slowly over time that we may not even be aware we've been ensnared. Now it's time to reclaim that power by stopping these two extremely toxic habits and taking back responsibility for our feelings, reactions, and future focus. You're going to need your inner power now that you're about to start over.

The Bible has much to say about our inner power. It tells us God can do more than we could ask or imagine *"according to His power that is at work within us"* (Ephesians 3:20). Imagine that—God's incredible power always at work in you! We also know that, rather than giving us fear and timidity, God gave us a spirit *"of power, of love and of self-discipline"* (2 Timothy 1:7). In fact, the power God gave us is the same power that raised Christ from the dead! In 1 Corinthians 6:14 we read, *"God both raised up the Lord and will also raise us up by His power"* (NKJV).

So how is it that we give our power away? Each time we complain or blame we take on a *victim stance*—and victims are powerless. Certainly we've all experienced times of devastation when we've been literal victims of crime or abuse, and were perhaps justified in complaining or blaming others for our heaviness and heartache. In the Old Testament, David experienced this personally and complained to God. In 1 Samuel 22, we read about the time he was stuck in a cave, hiding from King Saul, who wanted to kill him. His account in Psalm 142, written during this time when he felt surrounded by trouble, hemmed in by his circumstances, and immersed in danger, says, *"I cry aloud to the Lord; I lift up my voice to the LORD for mercy. I pour out my complaint before him."*

When we look at our own life's circumstances and all we have come through, it's not surprising we would have something to complain about. God understands our need to complain because He knows full well our weaknesses and human frailties. Sometimes lifting our complaint to God in prayer seems to help, and other times it doesn't appear to make a difference. What matters most is the mind-set we have each time we are tempted to blame and complain. If we give in, whether we're justified or not, we willingly give our power away and things tend to turn out horribly. If we choose to go through trials with an attitude of praise and thankfulness, as difficult as that can be, God promises to cause good things to result in spite of those trials.

We reclaim our power by accepting responsibility and choosing how we'll view each situation. The Bible says when your life is full of difficulties,

> *Be happy, for when the way is rough, your patience has a chance to grow. So let it grow, and don't try to squirm out of your problems. For when your patience is finally in full bloom, then you will be ready for anything, strong in character, full and complete* (James 1:2-4 TLB).

I have learned that when disappointing things happen, one way out of the "blame and complain" trap is to remind myself of all the good in my life. There are people I love and who care for me. I have my health, my home, and a career I enjoy. Most of all, I have God's love and protection and the assurance that I can talk with Him every day, knowing He's listening and will answer, and that He wants the best for me.

Before I discovered gratitude as a profound remedy, I used to be the world's champion complainer. I had a desperate need to tell others all about my problem, filling in every detail, letting them know whose fault it all was, and describing how terrible it felt to be in such a devastating and destructive situation. My personal motto was, "It's my pity-party and I'll cry if I want to!" I would gripe and grumble, and well-meaning friends would soon come to my aid feeling sorry for me. As much as I appreciated their support, none of that did me one bit of good.

In those days, one thing I could not tell you was what I planned to do about the problem or how I intended to move ahead with my life. Instead, I funneled all my energies into moaning, groaning, and fault-finding rather than focusing on becoming a problem-solver. All the "poor Sues" in the world were not able to pull me out of my predicament, so I continued to wallow in self-pity. Thankfully, I eventually got weary of knowing I was the dismal soul everyone took pity on. Then, a good friend gave me a suggestion that changed everything. She said, "Stop telling God about your big problems, and start telling your problem about your big God!" That's when I began to look for answers and solutions rather than concentrating on disasters and dilemmas.

Being solution-minded rather than problem-oriented is a mind-set you can develop. One of my corporate clients, the president of a large organization, taught me a valuable lesson. She has an open-door policy and has placed a sign behind her desk that employees can spot as soon as they enter her office. Printed on the sign are the letters *WDYR*. When I asked her about this, she told me the letters stand for *What Do You Recommend?* The message she is sending her staff is that they can feel free to come to her with any problem happening out there on the floor, as long as they can also suggest at least one potential approach to resolving the situation. Her ultimate goal is to be surrounded by solution-oriented people rather than problem-minded complainers. Her creative technique is working.

Granted, there is a time and place for valid and justifiable complaining, but if you nurture this toxic habit in place of being on the lookout for possible solutions, it will soon conquer you and do you in. If you let complaints rule your thoughts and govern your words, you will remain stuck in the mire of your past. This is why the Bible clearly states, *"Do not grumble"* (John 6:43 NASB). Before you realize it, complaining can take over your life. Even when you think you've got it under control, without warning, it rears its ugly head once again.

Complaining not only robs you of inner power, it destroys your life and leaves you all alone. After all, no one would choose to spend time with a complainer. Would you? I don't know anyone who looks forward to coming home to a complainer. No matter how justified one might be in grumbling, no one gets excited about dating a complainer, living with one, inviting one to a party, being a business partner or coworker of one, or even having one in the same room. In fact, grumblers can brighten a room every time they leave! They are usually miserable, edgy, and irritable, and their continual whining eventually destroys any relationship. Ask someone close to you about your own complaining habits and let them know you want them to be honest with you. You may not even be aware you have fallen into the trap. Then make up your mind to do as the psalmist did when he declared, *"I'm going to quit complaining!"* (Psalm 39:1 TLB).

If you want to know the effects of complaining, look at the children of Israel from the Old Testament. When they were slaves in Egypt, God performed a series of spectacular miracles to get them out. Once they had their freedom, they were headed toward the Promised Land, but sadly, they never made it. The reason is, right from the very first day, they started to complain. They grumbled about everything from the food that miraculously appeared (they were just freed from slavery and they're complaining about what's for dinner?) to the water in the desert (they *had* water in the desert and they still griped?). They complained about the weather, the terrain, and the distance. *It's too hot, too cold, too far, too grueling.* They whined and whined, and God finally had enough—He delayed the whole venture for 40 years.

Those Israelites' behavior would be typical of most of us if we were in a similar position today. It just happened that their story made it into the Bible. It goes on to say they never did reach the Promised Land. In fact, they died in the desert after all they had gone through. It seems there are a couple of lessons in their story. First, if you succumb to complaining about your past or your present long enough, you will eventually destroy your future—future opportunities, future relationships, and future goals. Second, it appears even God can handle only so much complaining!

I think you get the point. Complaining will not help you get past your past. It will not enhance the present nor will it increase your chances for a victorious future. You must focus on what you can control, not on what's beyond your control. Start to dwell more on the opportunities presented to you, and less on the difficulties you have faced. Remind yourself that God uses our trials for His purpose and often puts difficult people in our path to teach us valuable lessons and to help us discover our true purpose. We must not get in the way. George Bernard Shaw wrote,

This is the true joy of life: the being used up for a purpose recognized by yourself as a mighty one; being a force of nature instead of a feverish, selfish little clot of ailments and grievances, complaining that the world will not devote itself to making you happy.

Who's to Blame?

In my past, if I wasn't complaining, I was blaming. The old blame game was easy for me to play, whereas the opposite—accepting responsibility—was difficult to do. It meant acknowledging that, even if I was a victim in the past, I was now accountable to take charge of my present behaviors and choose my future actions. That's tough for most of us to do. In some instances, it could also imply that in some way we are at fault—and no one likes to take the blame. (Of course, here I am not referring to the true literal victims of crime or abuse.) To avoid feeling the pressure of taking charge and making different choices, and to eliminate all guilt or accountability, we automatically look for ways to place the blame elsewhere. We point our fingers at outside sources as a way of letting ourselves off the hook when it comes to making changes for today or new decisions for tomorrow.

George Bernard Shaw also said,

> People are always blaming circumstances for what they are. I don't believe in circumstances; the people who get on in this world go out and find the circumstances they want and if they can't find them, they make their own.

Imagine that...going out to find or create circumstances that would help rather than hinder you. Here's an example: Have you ever blamed someone for making you late by saying, "She talked my ear off and I couldn't get away," or "I couldn't get off the phone"? In reality, all you had to do was be honest, speak your mind, hang up, or get creative, but it seems to come naturally for us to lay the blame elsewhere. One woman

I know keeps a bell near her phone she can ring so long-winded callers think she has to get her other line. (I am just reporting, not recommending!) In the same way, we tend to say, "You made me angry," or "You made me happy," while neither statement is accurate. In both cases, we had a choice as to what emotion we would feel. Nothing can make us feel happy or sad without our consent. Even though something may have happened to prompt a certain reaction, the way we respond in the end is still up to us. It's always a choice.

Now, I have to be honest and admit that although I teach this and believe it, when I am upset, angry, depressed, or frustrated and find myself reacting inappropriately (I know you'll find this hard to believe, but it happens now and then), I am still tempted to blame my behavior on others rather than take responsibility for my choices. We never have to look far to find someone or something to blame our actions on. What is really difficult is to accept responsibility for our behaviors, conduct, moods, and attitudes from this day forward. While laying the blame brings bondage, true freedom comes from being accountable. We can't do this alone, but God has promised that "*in all these things we are more than conquerors through him who loved us*" (Romans 8:37). What we think, say, and do are all choices, and with the Holy Spirit, we can make the best ones.

Although circumstances in your past may have been deplorable and the actions of others toward you might have been reprehensible, where you are headed next will be the result of the day-to-day choices you make and will not be dependent on what's happened in the past. Because you can change only the present and the future, it's pointless to keep coming up with some of these typical excuses:

- It's my parents' fault.
- It's your fault.
- Society is to blame.
- The devil made me do it.

Now let's look at each of these areas of blame individually.

1. It's my parents' fault. A while back, I came across a sketch depicting a conference hall with a huge banner draped across the stage that read, *ACNP*. In smaller print below were the words *Adult Children of Normal Parents.* In the audience, there were two people! Well, that says a lot, doesn't it? When we are tempted to place all the blame for our current troubles on our upbringing, I say, "Show me a *functional* family!" Besides, as the old saying goes, "If it isn't one thing, it's your mother." I have a feeling every one of us could go back and find something to blame our parents for if we wanted to.

One research experiment involved a group of adults who felt their current despair, grief, or lack of success was caused by their past family life. They were asked to explain specifically why they believed this to be true. While some of the participants said it was because their parents were much too strict, stern, and serious, and they were raised with harsh rules and severe punishments, an almost equal number said their parents were too lenient or indulgent and they had not received proper training or guidance. Another group said they felt because their families were poor, they didn't have the same opportunities as children who were better off, while others said it was because they were so wealthy and given too much or spoiled rotten, so they never knew what it was like to work hard to achieve anything. A few more blamed their present troubles on the fact that they were the only child, while just as many said it was because there were so many children in their family. Some blamed their current difficulties on having religion forced on them, and others said it was because they had no spiritual teaching at all. Isn't human nature interesting?

Back in the Old Testament, people were blaming their parents, too. When the prophet Ezekiel wanted to get the Hebrew captives to return to their homes and their God, he was having a hard time. They complained, "You can't be serious about wanting us to repent. It's obviously our parents' fault." They defended themselves with a proverb: "*The fathers eat sour grapes, and the children's teeth are set on edge*" (Ezekiel

18:2). In other words, "Our parents sinned by eating the sour grapes, so now we have to pay the price." When they blamed their captivity on their parents, God said through Ezekiel, *You will not use this proverb any more in Israel*" (Ezekiel 18:3 TLB). From then on, each person would bear responsibility for his own actions.

What it boils down to is this: Your parents didn't have a chance. It wouldn't matter which path they took, you could still find a reason to blame them. Yet, I don't believe there are any parents who wake up in the morning and say, "Honey, how can we psychologically mess up our children's minds today so we can ruin their lives?" Most likely your parents did the very best they could with the tools they had available to them at the time, in the same way you do the best you can, and your children will continue the trend. When I started to see my parents as human beings like me, with their own troubled backgrounds, past baggage, quirks, inhibitions, and trials to overcome, it allowed me to be free from blaming. I realize you may have come from an exceptionally difficult, discouraging, or damaging background and you're still paying the price today, but choosing to let your parents off the hook will be a monumental step toward being set free.

2. *It's your fault*. In other words, "I wouldn't be acting this way if you hadn't done or said what you did." When I'm frustrated over another's actions or behavior, I am tempted to say, "Just look at what you made me do!" But I've learned that when you lay the blame on another person, you are ultimately giving your power away. Then, someone else has more power over you, and the way you respond than you do. The only way to reclaim your power is to take back total responsibility for your actions and behaviors toward the person and the situation.

3. *Society is to blame*. There are two main sources of power in our society: authority (what we must do by law) and influence (what we are convinced into believing is best). The more dominant of these is influence. When we buy into popular beliefs and messages sent by society, whether through other people, the media, or cultural traditions, we are opening ourselves up to being swayed in ways that keep us stuck in our past. Then we blame society for the way we've turned out.

Rather than making choices based on what is popular in the eye of the general public, try redefining a happy, peace-filled, successful life in your own terms. How would you describe a powerful life? What would bring you inner harmony and total freedom from the past today? Through prayer and meditating on God's Word, determine what future choices are best for you regardless of what is happening all around you. Run your own race. When we don't take charge, we are opening ourselves up to blaming and being manipulated by outside influences. If that's the case, the rules and systems of our society will always have more power over the direction of our lives than we do.

4. The devil made me do it. A woman was upset with herself because she had overspent her budget on a new dress. When she discussed it with her hubby, he couldn't understand how she could have let this happen after they had talked it over that very morning. Her only defense was, "It looked so good, the fit was perfect, it was in my favorite color and on sale. I tried to resist, but the devil made me do it!" He reminded her of Jesus' words in the Bible: "Satan, get thee behind me." She answered, "I tried saying that, but he told me it looked pretty good from back there, too."

Although it's a cute story, and there are times when we are genuinely tempted by evil forces, there are also times when we act out of our own selfish desires and ambitions and then blame the devil. When we really want to, we can come up with all kinds of targets for our blame. There's an old parable of a Cherokee chief sitting by a flickering fire with his grandson, who had just broken a tribal taboo. To help him understand what made him do it, Grandpa said, "It's like we have two wolves inside us. One is good and the other is bad, and both are fighting for our obedience." When the boy asked, "Which one wins?" the wise old chief replied, "Whichever one we feed!"

While there are two opposing forces, good and evil, incessantly struggling for your attention, the bottom line is that you are in charge of your will, your choices, where you focus your thoughts, and the decisions you make. When you have the divine wisdom of the Holy Spirit to guide you, you will make choices that are pure, wholesome, constructive, and profitable. When you don't, your choices can be harmful and detrimental, to yourself and others.

We've been given free rein when it comes to choosing. It was God's first gift to us, and it's the one and only thing over which we've been given complete control in this life. If you want things to change, you must reclaim power through choosing not to blame and complain. Because of this, I believe these to be the ten most powerful two-letter words in the English language: *If it is to be, it is up to me!*

In other words, if you want to be healthier and happier, it's up to you. If you want to move forward, you have to believe that your past is past and nothing is going to change it. You must choose to let go of all the hurt associated with those past events. It's up to you to develop a good attitude and to decide to enjoy your life, your work, and your relationships. You have to determine your future goals and decide if you want them badly enough to do whatever is necessary, within healthy parameters, to see them materialize. You have to trust that you can be set free from whatever has swept over you like a giant wave, such as abuse, infidelity, the death of a child, loss, poverty, a devastating illness, or a tragic accident. You have to choose to have faith that God is big enough to handle all this and more. Silently repeat to yourself, *If it is to be, it is up to me.*

On the other hand, the most dangerous words are, "If everyone and everything around me would change, my life would be fine!" Even though it might be true that changes in others' attitudes, actions, and decisions could make life easier for you, those things are beyond your control—and it's futile to place your hope in something so elusive.

Another trap we fall into is the belief that having enough faith is all that is required of us for God to work powerfully in our lives. Nothing could be further from the truth. Faith without action is dead. While faith is necessary and unlocks the door to miracles, inner power in our lives is not passive but active. According to God's Word, we have a very important role to play in altering the direction of our future. We must *ask* in order to receive, *seek* if we want to find, and *knock* for the door to be opened (see Matthew 7:7). And it's *"not because we think we can do anything of lasting value by ourselves. Our only power and success is from God"* (2 Corinthians 3:5 TLB).

Yet many of God's promises begin with the action required by us. For example, *"Don't be impatient. Wait for the Lord, and he will come and save you! Be brave, stouthearted and courageous"* (Psalm 27:14 TLB). In other words, we are the ones who must take action, being patient and bold. *"Don't worry about anything; instead pray about everything; tell God your needs and don't forget to thank him for his answers. If you do this you will experience God's peace, which is far more wonderful than the human mind can understand"* (Philippians 4:6-7 TLB). Again, it's up to us to forgo worry, express our needs to God, and thank Him. The same is true when Paul says to *"fix your thoughts on what is true and good and right"* (Philippians 4:8 TLB); *"work hard and cheerfully at all you do, just as though you were working for the Lord"* (Colossians 3:23 TLB); and *"be kind to one another, tenderhearted, forgiving each other, just as God in Christ also has forgiven you"* (Ephesians 4:32 NASB). All these verses indicate there are steps we must take in order to see God at work.

Sometimes it can take a while, but eventually we discover that the greatest hindrance to receiving supernatural blessings in our life is not others or outside circumstances, but ourselves—our lack of understanding when it comes to reclaiming our inner power through choices as they are linked with divine principles. It's not until we give it all up— our worries, doubts, weaknesses, habits, hurts, and hang-ups—that we can truly experience the freedom we yearn for. That's what refusing to blame and complain is all about—taking spiritual responsibility by deciding to completely surrender our past, present, and future into the hands of a loving God.

> *If we are living now by the Holy Spirit's power, let us follow the Holy Spirit's leading in every part of our lives* (Galatians 5:25 TLB).

On this journey, we've discovered that each one of us has a choice in most matters. We can choose to accept the things we can't change and learn to act on those things we can change. We have found that, through our choices, God has granted us power over many more aspects of our lives than we've imagined. We've learned ways to use our choices to let go of the pain of our past, whether it was caused by actions committed against us or by our own doing, and we've found that it's possible to be set free through forgiving the unforgivable, in others and ourselves. When you choose at last to relinquish the blaming and complaining, just watch and see what God can do!

Dear God,

Please take away my pain and despair of yesterday, and any unpleasant memories, and replace them with Your glorious promise of new hope. Show me a fresh Holy Spirit-inspired way of relating to negative things that have happened. I ask You for the mind of Christ so I can discern Your voice from the voice of my past. I pray that former rejection and deep hurts will not color what I see and hear now.

Help me to see all the choices I have ahead of me that can alter the direction of my life. I ask You to empower me to let go of the painful events and heartaches that would keep me bound. Thank You for Your forgiveness that You have offered to me at such a great price. Pour it into my heart so I can relinquish bitterness, revenge, and resentment that have no place in my life. Please set me free to forgive those who have sinned against me and caused me pain, and also myself. Open my heart to receive Your complete forgiveness and amazing grace. You have promised to bind up my wounds (Psalm 147:3) and restore my soul (Psalm 23:3).

Help me to relinquish my past, surrender to You my present, and move into the future You have prepared for me. I ask You to come into my heart and make me who You would have me be so that I might do Your will here on this earth. I thank You, Lord, for all that's happened in my past and for all I have become through those experiences. I pray You will begin to gloriously renew my present.

In Jesus' name, Amen.

Part Two

Renew Your Present

I tell you, now is the time of God's favor; now is the day of salvation!
2 CORINTHIANS 6:2

Everyone's life lies within the present, for the past is spent and done with, and the future is uncertain.
MARCUS AURELIUS ANTONIUS

One of the most tragic things I know about human nature is that all of us tend to put off living. We are all dreaming of some magical rose garden over the horizon—instead of enjoying the roses that are blooming outside our windows today.
DALE CARNEGIE

To renew...

Synonyms:
Rekindle, restart, get a new lease on life, restore, put back into working order, replenish, revitalize, rejuvenate, recharge, refresh, invigorate, enliven, energize, brighten up, stimulate, rouse, awaken, ignite, breathe life into

Antonyms:
Deteriorate, weaken, wear out, drain, exhaust, deplete, run down, fade, falter, wreck, spoil, mess up, destroy, diminish, fade out, break down, stop from working

Chapter 8

Today

*Today a new sun rises for me; everything lives,
everything is animated; everything seems to speak
to me of my passion, everything invites me to cherish it.*
ANNE DE LENCLOS

*Live neither in the past nor the future, but let each day's work
absorb your entire energies, and satisfy your wildest ambitions.*
WILLIAM OSLER

HERE YOU STAND...POISED BETWEEN THE past and the future. Yesterday is over, and tomorrow stretches out before you—full of promise and possibility. Today comes flooding in, overflowing with possibilities and brimming with potential. In spite of what's gone on in our past, God tell us that *"all that happens to us is working for our good if we love God and are fitting into his plan"* (Romans 8:28 TLB). Now, as you are being transformed day by day, you no longer need to be haunted by the past. You're free to follow new paths with a fresh purpose and renewed determination. You are a woman with a destiny. Not running from the mistakes and failures of yesterday, nor avoiding decisions that seemed too difficult to make, you can look ahead toward a full and prosperous future based on a newness of heart. Today, you can have a new beginning.

Beginning with Endings

The real problem with starting over is, it usually means something must end. Although we truly want to grow, develop, and move forward, most of us are not fond of endings because it normally means giving up old habits, past thinking patterns, former relationships, comfortable conditions, familiar attitudes, or established behaviors. However, endings are a part of life. As soon as we are born, we start to die. (And you're thinking, *This is supposed to be encouraging?* But stay tuned, because this is simply the way it is.) It's not necessarily good or bad, it just is. It's the way of the whole earth and everything on it. Everything comes to an end, and every ending leads to a new beginning.

Living for today is all about endings and starting over. It's about beginning again after facing loss in our lives and turning the page to the next chapter. Not only do we ultimately face the end of life in this human body and begin a new life in eternity, but we must also confront endings continuously throughout our earthly lives.

For example, one stage of our lives is continually replacing another. As children, when we go off to school, we experience an ending to the total security we had being with Mom and Dad all day. As young adults, if we decide to move out and set up housekeeping in our own place, there's an end to the familiarity of what has always been home. When we get married, we face another ending as we leave our family and begin life with our spouse. Some of us deal with endings through separation or divorce, the loss of a job, stolen possessions, or the death of a loved one. We also face endings when it comes to money, status, careers, power, and our identities as we grow and evolve. Things come and go, and the way we respond to them is crucial to our mental and emotional health.

Endings are ongoing. They are constant, and they're going to continue. As soon as you are over the hurdle of dealing with one ending, another is on its way. Now, that might not seem to be very motivating, but the important thing is the way we think about endings. Some of us handle them better than others. We can respond with sadness, disappointment, bitterness, hostility, irritation, spite, or other feelings of ill will that can eventually bring on depression, anxiety, or despair. Or, we can refuse to hold tightly to our past, relinquishing all reactions that will harm us, rob us of joy, and put us into a state of distress.

When we see endings as bad or negative, they can hinder our future growth and development. Endings don't mean going from having something to not having it. If that's how it was, even *I'd* be getting depressed! What they are really about is passing naturally from one phase of your life into the next, closing one chapter so you can open another. The challenge is not to fear endings, but to embrace them as a time of renewal. This is the only way you will discover your new beginnings! The Bible says,

> *If anyone is in Christ, he is a new creation; the old has gone, the new has come!* (2 Corinthians 5:17).

Once you are a new creation, the old things don't have the power to keep affecting your new life.

Today—Not "Someday"

When you're weary, afraid, and feeling all alone, how do you embrace endings and begin renewing your life? Someone once said that the only way to eat an elephant is one bite at a time. The best way to renew your life is to do it one step at a time, one day at a time, and to start today. It doesn't matter whether it's a broken heart that needs healing, a physical condition you must live with, an exam you are preparing for, or all the projects you have on your list to accomplish, you can manage one at a time. It is so easy for us to put off taking action today and get caught in the trap of procrastinating. With our full lives and schedules packed to the brim with responsibilities, pressures, and perpetual, never-ending to-do lists, no wonder we are tempted to say, "Someday I'll get serious about making some powerful, positive choices that I know will transform my life!"

Life is not like your VCR. There is no pause, stop, or rewind button. You can never go back and do it all over, or see it again. There is only forward. In fact, usually there is only "fast forward"! Everything just keeps hurriedly moving ahead. But most importantly, none of us knows how many more opportunities we'll have to do things differently. Our situations change quickly. Children grow up and leave home. People we love to be with die. If you want to renew your life, you'd better begin today.

Today is a brand-new experience—fresh and untarnished by what has gone on before. There's an old adage that says, "Tomorrow is not promised." In that sense, neither is the very next moment. There is only *now*. Today, the hindrances, heartaches, anger, guilt, and shame of the past have no place unless you choose to bring them with you. Likewise, anxiety, worry, doubt, and fear of the future cannot affect you in this moment if you don't allow them. While society may expect you to walk in disappointment, grief, shame, or guilt forever, you no longer have to go through life with your head held low. You do not have to conform to what others expect of you or to what the world dictates. When you know Christ as Savior, your mind has been renewed and your heart changed forever. You are not chained to past beliefs and programs, bound by remorse, constrained by bitterness, or held back by regrets. You are renewed moment by moment.

Being in Today

To live in the moment is a challenging thing to do. On my desk, I keep a little placard with the phrase *Be here now* as a reminder. How often are we somewhere in body, but somewhere else in mind and spirit? I remember being at work when my children were young and thinking, *What am I doing with my life? It's all work, work, and more work. I should go home and take my family on a picnic.* So when I got home, we packed our wicker basket, a few folding chairs, and some badminton rackets, and off we went to the park. Then, with the family seated around the picnic table and a lovely meal spread out before us, can you guess what I was thinking about? Work, of course. I felt guilty taking time out to enjoy a picnic, knowing all that work was back there waiting for me. Sometimes we are never where we are. It's no wonder we don't really get full enjoyment from this present moment. We bypass the joy of today when we center all our focus on yesterday or tomorrow.

Are you here now, or are you recalling some upsetting details from an unpleasant past event? Are you in the present moment enjoying the beauty right outside your window today, or are you putting off living while you envision some mysterious future paradise over the horizon? Are you feeling frustrated by focusing on all that was on your to-do list yesterday that you didn't get around to, or are you here, living in the present, today?

With the past gone, today is all you need to invigorate and ignite the present. Allow the Holy Spirit to breathe new life into you. Now is your chance to be restored, revitalized, rejuvenated, and recharged.

How to Be Happy When You're Miserable!

"Most people," said Abraham Lincoln, "are about as happy as they make up their minds to be!" Today, you may not be satisfied *with* your situation, but you can find joy and contentment *in* it. One of the biggest lies we have been fed is that you cannot be happy if your circumstances are not ideal. The next biggest lie we believe is that once you get your life in order, you will automatically be happy. The truth is that you will probably never get all your circumstances lined up perfectly, and even if you did, it would not assure genuine happiness.

Here's some good news for you today. You can be happy even if you are not in a happy place! To some people, this may be a revolutionary thought, but it is really quite basic. Just as success and prosperity do not ensure instant happiness, your difficulties, dilemmas, problems, and predicaments do not have to guarantee you'll be miserable. Happiness is a state of mind, and so is unhappiness. Neither depends on anything tangible or concrete, including your existing circumstances. Happiness comes from a place deep within your heart, and only God can provide it.

Even when life is throwing you a multitude of troubles, there are ways to find happiness in the midst of it all. I don't know about you, but when troubles hit, I am tempted to cry out, "God, where are You now? How could You leave me when I need You most?" The Bible tells us,

> *Friends, when life gets really difficult, don't jump to the conclusion that God isn't on the job. Instead be glad you are in the very thick of what Christ experienced. This is a spiritual refining process with glory just around the corner!* (1 Peter 4:12-13 MSG).

True joy comes from trusting that God in heaven has something magnificent just around the bend and knowing He is taking care of every detail as you journey through. The Psalmist said, *"Oh, the joys of those who put their trust in him"* (Psalm 2:12 TLB).

You might be thinking, *That's easy for her to say.* After all, I get paid to talk (isn't that every woman's dream?), travel the world, speak on cruise ships in tropical climates, share the platform with some of the world's greatest motivational speakers, write books that are now being translated into other languages, have a happy marriage, a terrific family life, and great health. Why wouldn't I feel joyful? I often hear, "Do you know how many people would love to do what you're doing?"

The part they don't know about is the number of times I've said goodbye to my hubby and family at the airport with tears in my eyes, dreading being away from them one more time. They don't know the times I've boarded a plane exhausted, with my inner reserves depleted, knowing I'll miss yet another family get-together, a special celebration with friends, or other meaningful event. They're probably not aware of the times I have been so distraught or heartbroken over a personal challenge or some devastating circumstances my children or grandchildren were facing that I could hardly stop the tears or get words to come out of my mouth, let alone stand on stage in front of hundreds of people to be an encouragement to them. They never hear about the times I have gone backstage during the break to cry my eyes out, heartsick and broken before my God, then splash cold water on my face, put on fresh makeup, and get back out there to finish the program.

You might think my professional accomplishments would result in the happiness we all yearn for. Maybe you feel you're being denied some of your dreams and think that's what is robbing you of your joy. But those things are not where true happiness and joy come from. For me, even the thrill of my work comes from having a purpose and a mission, and from hopefully making a worthy contribution and a difference in people's lives. I used to think that maybe if I got as successful as "this speaker" or "that author," I'd be content. I thought if I could earn the respect of others in my profession, or win an industry award, I'd feel fulfilled. I felt that if I had a full calendar and sold a certain number of books every year with a few bestsellers thrown in, I'd really be successful—or at least I'd *feel* successful.

What I have learned is, what I really want more than anything is to make a difference in people's lives—and that I don't have a thing to offer apart from the life of God in me. All I have to share that's of lasting value is His love. The Lord has allowed me to speak to thousands of individuals—to both secular and Christian audiences. When I am on stage, I see people's needs and the pain on their faces. I recognize it because I have experienced it and continue to do so. We are never exempt from heartache, or free from suffering. We can only know that God is right there in the middle of it, ready to hold our hand and take us through.

My desire is to impart courage and a message of hope through being transparent and sharing my own struggles. I have found that we are all comforted in some strange way by knowing someone else has shared our sorrow. When I look out on my audiences, I see the "hungry" faces of those who have come to be fed. What they hunger for is encouragement, hope, and strength to carry on. I sometimes feel as though I am the waiter, the server, who has been given the awesome opportunity to dish up what God has prepared for them. What a privilege and a joy in spite of the ongoing challenges!

True Happiness

We tend to get caught in the trap of believing that happiness, contentment, and joy are not possible as long as we are struggling with some problem, dealing with some crisis, or have a major decision to make. This outlook only weakens our ability to hear the voice of God in the situation. It destroys our ability to be creative problem-solvers and unnecessarily prolongs our pain and sorrow. The choice is always ours. Optimism and pessimism are learned behavioral attitudes and not the result of whether we have or don't have everything we think we need. Perhaps you believe you will be a more optimistic person once certain conditions are met—once you're with the right person, have a bigger home or better job, earn a promotion, have a baby, get the kids grown and on their own, win the lottery...or any one of a hundred other desires.

These are not where happiness comes from. We cannot expect things to make us happy, nor can we expect another person to meet all our needs. First of all, it's not fair to saddle others with such unreasonable expectations. The job of making you happy is quite a responsibility. Secondly, true happiness can only come from within—when you're satisfied with yourself and the life you're living. It comes from learning to like and appreciate who you are and what you are doing with your life from this day forward. And even if that list of happiness items suddenly materializes for you, there is no guarantee they will bring the pleasure you are searching for. Quite often, those things will leave you feeling strangely empty and continuing to yearn for inner fulfillment. Until you realize that happiness can be found only within yourself, you'll never discover the lasting kind that brings peace and contentment.

When you find yourself in an unhappy place, it's possible to push yourself into further disaster with your thoughts. If you wake up in the morning, sit on the edge of the bed, and feel a little headache coming on, you can imagine yourself right into a migraine. If you make the mistake of reading the medical journal, before you know it you'll realize you have all the symptoms on page 43. When you start out the day with the dread of something bad happening, sure enough you'll back out of the driveway and right into the neighbor's car. Look to the day with fear and doubt, and you'll end up reaping the results.

It's time to quit predicting disaster for your world and yourself. Begin the morning with new hope. Wake up to your favorite music. Sing in the shower. Have a morning coffee with a person you like, someone who is an optimist. Listen to motivational messages on CD during your morning walk or the drive to work. Read inspirational books and articles periodically throughout the day and again at bedtime. Memorize God's promises, uplifting scriptures, and inspirational quotes. When you are feeling sad, sorrowful, or dejected, choose a meaningful goal for the future and fill your mind with thoughts of hope, anticipation, and positive expectancy.

If you are in a situation you cannot get out of or are not ready to leave—at least for now—it's possible to create your own safe haven and joy-filled existence within your unhappy circumstances. Surround yourself with comfort—good and reliable friends, happy events, and light-hearted fun. Enjoy great books, some hearty laughter and good clean humor, a loving pet, your favorite soothing music, calming scents and candles, and photos of fun times and special people. Decorate with colors you find tranquil, furnishings that are snug and comforting, and artwork that inspires you.

Plan something special to look forward to every day, each week, and once a month. Practice innocent pleasures and simple indulgences regularly. These are affordable luxuries that don't take up much time, like a candlelight bubble bath, an evening stroll, breakfast in bed, or a funny video. Use your best china mug for tea and get yourself a gold pen for journaling. Buy some pretty lingerie and wear perfume to bed. Once a year, plan something big you can get excited about and anticipate with joy. Keep your life as uncomplicated and undemanding as you possibly can until you are ready for new avenues, choices, and relationships.

In his book *The Achilles Syndrome*, Dr. Harold Bloomfield says,

> Many of us live the first half of our adult lives postponing satisfaction and the last half with regrets. Fulfillment seems always to be just over the next hill.

Life will always have its share of difficulties—and in the midst of them, you can choose to be a fulfilled, caring, loving, healthy, and balanced person. Learn to choose happiness in this moment in spite of your current circumstances. Instead of concentrating on why you can't be happy, focus your attention on all that is good. It's possible to find happiness where you are when you put your mind to it! The apostle Paul said it best:

> *I've learned by now to be quite content whatever my circumstances. I'm just as happy with little as much, with much as little. I've found the recipe for being happy whether full or hungry, hands full or hands empty. Whatever I have, wherever I am, I can make it through anything in the One who makes me who I am* (Philippians 4:11-13 MSG).

There's an old familiar quote that reminds us, "Today is a gift—that's why they call it the present!" Your life is a gift. So take your present, unwrap it carefully, open it gently, and live it intensely!

Chapter 9

From Problems
to Pearls

When it gets dark enough, you can see the stars.
ANONYMOUS

Dear friends, do not be surprised
at the painful trial you are suffering as
though something strange were happening to you.
1 PETER 4:12

YOU'VE PROBABLY FIGURED OUT THAT ALL your problems are not going away, at least not all at once. Problems come and go, and troubles are a natural condition in this life. Jesus warned us that here on earth we will have many trials and sorrows (see John 16:33 TLB), and we can expect them to continue. The only time you and I will be completely problem-free is when we get to heaven. Be certain that, once your existing problems are solved, more will show up.

Sometimes the new problems are worse than the ones you could hardly wait to get rid of. As Lily Tomlin put it, "Things are going to get a lot worse before they get worse!" But the Bible tells us that each of our trials is like the purification of gold, which when *"put in the fire comes out of it proved pure"* (1 Peter 1:7 MSG). There is a purpose behind every problem, and God can use our uncomfortable circumstances to develop our character. But if we aren't aware of this, we tend to put off living until we are problem-free.

Do you know people who continually put their lives on hold and place their happiness on the back burner while they wait for all their problems to go away? They assure us that once they get through this financial catastrophe or that family disaster, or when they get their marriage straightened out, survive their children's toddler or teen years, move into a better neighborhood with a bigger house, make it through menopause, buy a better car, or get transferred to a different department with a more agreeable boss, they'll start to have a good life. They're convinced they couldn't possibly experience true happiness or fulfillment until they are completely free from troubles. It's as though they're waiting to hear a voice resounding from the heavens informing them, *Your life is now perfect. You may go ahead and enjoy!* Let's face it, that's simply not going to happen. Our problems will never clear up entirely. What a waste of precious energy and effort to be perpetually waiting for a problem-free existence.

It's no secret that our lives often fall short of our expectations. Some of us seem to have times when we struggle with one disappointment after another. These times may follow a critical fall in our personal walk with God and in the standards of conduct we hold for ourselves. Often, though, we've been crushed by circumstances. Job or family pressures have become unbearable, or we've suffered abuse at the hands of another. For each of us, there are times when we feel downhearted, wounded, and defeated, and we simply can't take it anymore. These are times when we know we need God's grace and mercy. (The truth is, we need them all the time.)

Instead of allowing problems to take you by surprise, be prepared to meet them head on. Each of us is in one of three places: We are right in the middle of working out a major problem, we've just finished handling a critical problem, or we're headed toward the next big problem. It's true for everyone. So, if you are not dealing with a serious predicament right at this moment, don't be concerned. I assure you it's on its way!

Sometimes we are granted a reprieve, a little space and time between problems. It's a chance to coast a bit, riding on the wings of God's love so we can catch our breath, recoup our strength, regain our perspective, and salvage our sanity. You might be enjoying a plateau like that right now. But regardless of who you are or what stage of life you are in, it's certain that more problems are on the way, whether big or small, and they will eventually reveal themselves.

When problems do come into your life, you will either grow strong under the pressure, or the force will crush you. As the old saying goes, troubles will make us bitter or better. They'll either make or break you. But what is it that makes the difference in the way people handle challenges? Generally, it's what comes from us and not what happens to us that matters most. When you get bumped, it's whatever you're full of that spills over!

Pearls Don't Hurt!

When I have problems to deal with, it helps to remember how the pearl is formed. It's the only precious gem that's produced as the result of a whole lot of pain and discomfort. When a tiny grain of sand slips inside an oyster's shell, its jagged edges hurt so much that the oyster begins to secrete a substance that will coat that tiny, prickly particle. It keeps coating and coating the hurtful culprit until the cause of the horrible irritation has finally been enveloped in a lustrous substance. At last, the irritant's cutting spikes are no longer exposed. The satiny-smooth gem that results is not capable of causing any more pain. Even more astonishing than that, this incredible source of pain has now become a rare and precious jewel.

Your life can be like that depending on how you choose to respond to your problems. They can irritate, aggravate, and exasperate, causing nonstop pain and heartache for years—or you can begin to "coat" your difficulties with God's grace, new hope, complete forgiveness, a balanced outlook, a healthy attitude, and a positive perspective. Allow the restorative touch of the Master to coat your wounds with His healing salve and because *"he heals the brokenhearted and binds up their wounds"* (Psalm 147:3), you will soon become that priceless pearl.

Expect a Miracle!

When life is full of problems, the last thing we tend to do is to look for a miracle. However, miracles have a habit of happening in the midst of trouble, especially to those who believe in them and expect them. We normally anticipate the worst, and that is generally what we get. As Job said in the Old Testament, *"What I always feared has happened to me"* (Job 3:25 TLB). Life has a strange way of giving you what you expect from it. There's an old adage that says if you refuse to accept anything less than the best, life will often oblige.

So keep your eyes open and look expectantly every day for great and wonderful things to happen. Always expect the best, and you will be amazed at what you'll experience. Practice the habit of *confident expectation* and notice how answers to your greatest problems begin to come your way. Miracles will become a daily occurrence and not a rare incident. A miracle is not necessarily some mysterious phenomenon, unexplainable in the scientific realm. If you look it up in the dictionary, you will find that a miracle is described as some wonderful and marvelous condition that can be brought to pass. We might think of miracles in the context of being something magical or accomplishing the impossible. I once saw a plaque with the motto of a service-oriented business that said, "The difficult we do immediately; the impossible takes a little longer." In other words, what seems to be impossible is actually doable and achievable.

Look around and study those who expect miracles, and you will see they consistently seem to have great things happen in their lives. I know a delightful lady who describes herself as an "inverse paranoid." While others are anticipating problems and expecting things to go wrong, she is convinced that everything and everyone is working toward her happiness and success. And guess what? Everywhere she goes, that is exactly what she experiences. She finds a parking space exactly when and where she needs it. The one designer dress in her size and favorite color is on sale for half-price. She always manages to get in the fast-moving lines at the bank, gas station, and grocery store. When she accidentally knocks a crystal goblet off the countertop, she manages to catch it just in the nick of time. Here's a lady who goes through life believing there's a conspiracy out there—everyone is scheming to make her life easier—and that's just what she finds. Our expectations do play a role in what happens to us.

How then can you go about expecting miracles and believing they will happen? The number-one answer is to look to the One who is the originator of all miracles and develop a deep faith in Him—one so intense and positive that it rises above the doubts that set in. Doubt is bound to happen, and it is the chief enemy of faith. When you doubt, it robs you of your miracles before you get to experience them. But choosing to have faith in Almighty God releases an astonishing power in your life to conquer doubt.

You can start building your faith by becoming solution-oriented rather than problem-minded. Alter your attention and be on the lookout for answers rather than problems. What you focus on and expect is most likely what you will get. If you have ever driven a new car, or at least one that is new to you, you've probably noticed that you start to see the same car everywhere—the identical make, model, and color! It's as if a voice came down from the heavens, instructing, *She bought one, so go ahead and bring out all the others!* Now, we know they were there all the time, right? But did we notice them before? Not until we had the same one, which brought our attention and focus to all the rest. The same thing happens with problems and solutions. Whichever you choose to dwell on and expect is exactly what you will notice.

We tend to see more with our brain than we do with our eyes. For instance, have you ever known someone with a mustache who shaved it off, then asked you if you notice anything different? If you are like most of us, you probably did not. My hubby and I once spent an entire weekend with some family members. On our way home we commented that there was something different about our brother-in-law. That's when it dawned on us that he had shaved off his beard and mustache, which he'd had since we'd known him. Can you imagine how silly we felt, knowing we had spent a few days together and hadn't even commented on it during our entire visit? We tend to see what we expect to see. The same goes for problems and predicaments, answers and solutions. Which are you looking for?

When you're having problems, or have a dire need, the question is, How deep is your faith? Is it deep enough to look for a solution and genuinely anticipate a miracle? I remember a time when my children and I had first moved to our little apartment after leaving the abusive situation we were in. At that time, we were suffering from "malnutrition of the bank account," but I was not too concerned, because I was expecting two checks to come in the mail at the end of the week. Our cupboards were bare except for a jar of peanut butter and some crackers. We knew once the checks arrived on Friday, we would be grocery shopping to replenish our bare shelves.

Well, Friday came and went, and so did the postman, but there were no checks. After making a few phone calls to investigate, I discovered that because of our change of address, there would be a further delay of a few weeks. So there I sat—with my two hungry children, no food, and no money. When I contemplated what to do, I knew without a doubt I could go to family and friends and they would be glad to help out, or we could pray and trust God for a miracle. After we talked it over, the children agreed we should pray and it would definitely have to be a miracle. With their simple childlike trust, they knelt beside me as we held hands, looked up, and asked God to provide for us. I am certain the girls expected the ceiling to open up so groceries could fall into our laps right then and there. What faith my little ones had! (Sadly, I must admit, I had a backup plan and decided if God did not come through for us by Monday, I would call my mom!)

Although nothing happened just then, we were able to satisfy our hunger with peanut butter and crackers for breakfast, lunch, and supper over the next day-and-a-half. On Sunday morning, we went to church as usual. After the service, the girls went to the car while I chatted with a friend. They quickly returned and told me the car was packed with boxes with the words "God Bless You" on them. With my heart pounding and tears in my eyes, I ran to the car, saw the boxes full of groceries, and began to sob.

When we got home and unpacked everything, we noticed the brands that had been chosen were what we would have picked if we had purchased them ourselves. Almost everything came in giant-size packages. As we placed the food, along with paper products and cleaning supplies, into our cupboards, the girls teased me that I would use up all the new boxes of tissues drying my tears. We had no idea who would have been so generous toward us or how anyone could have possibly known our need, because we had decided not to tell anyone.

I sometimes wonder what our heavenly Father feels in His heart when He sees His children with an urgent need, praying and believing for a miracle, and someone else answering the call to fulfill that cry for help. It must be a wonderful thing! A number of months passed before we discovered that a caring young couple in our church had felt God nudging them to buy groceries totalling a certain dollar amount to place in my car on a Sunday morning in two weeks time. How comforting it was for us to know that our prayer had been answered before we even knew we had a need. The Bible says, *"Before they call I will answer"* (Isaiah 65:24), and Jesus told us, *"Your father knows what you need before you ask him"* (Matthew 6:8).

It's amazing what can happen when you manage to get your faith strengthened to the point where you can fight off the doubt that attempts to take over. You are more likely to experience miracles when you believe in them and expect to see them. Remember, your life is full of potential miracles put there by your Creator, the one who knows you better than anyone. Why not allow those miracles to come forth and live?

Don't Turn Back!

It has been my experience that when I am about to reach my target, complete a task, or achieve some major goal, problems seem to hit full force with a vengeance. Without realizing success is just around the bend, it's tempting to throw in the towel or turn back, believing I must have made a wrong turn somewhere. At those times, it seems I'm fighting my battles alone, but the Bible says,

> When life gets really difficult, don't jump to the conclusion
> that God isn't on the job...this is a spiritual refining process,
> with glory just around the corner (1 Peter 4:12-13 MSG).

This makes me think about what happened when my present husband and I moved to our home on a winding country road in the days before cell phones. We would invariably get a phone call from the clerk at Country General Store down the road, saying our guests were lost. Later, when they would finally arrive, we would ask them just how far they had driven before they went back to call us. In almost every case, we discovered they were just around the bend. Thinking they had gone too far or taken a wrong turn, they went back. If they had simply continued on and driven around the very next curve, they would have found us! How often do you and I do the same thing? Maybe if we had simply persisted a little longer, we might have achieved glory around the next bend. Instead, we got frustrated and turned back too soon, or we called out, "Why me, Lord?" and God answered back, "Why not?" Sometimes the battles we face are gifts from above designed to strengthen us, bolster our confidence, increase our faith, and prepare us for the next exciting endeavor.

Problems as Gifts

Charles C. West was right on the mark when he said, "We turn to God for help when our foundations are shaking, only to learn that it is God who is shaking them!" Could it be that the very discomfort that caused you to pick up this book in the first place was a gift? While we are going through challenging or upsetting circumstances, it is difficult for us to believe they may have come into our lives for our benefit. Pain and heartache can often motivate us to seek out new directions and better ways to fulfill our life's purpose. It's when we are hurting the most that we have the greatest desire to learn how to be strong. We may not be thankful at the time, but neither would we be grateful for the pain caused by taking a sip of hot coffee or stepping into a scalding bathtub.

Pain, anguish, grief, and sorrow often serve a purpose, preparing us to reconsider our options and actions. God's Word encourages us:

> *Consider it a sheer gift, friends, when tests and challenges come at you from all sides. You know that under pressure, your faith-life is forced into the open and shows its true colors. So don't try to get out of anything prematurely. Let it do its work so you become mature and well-developed* (James 1:2-5 MSG).

The purpose of problems is to cause change; the purpose of change is to bring growth; and the reason for growth is to become better. To change, grow, and become better requires that we do things differently. When problems hit, we must ask ourselves, *What lessons can I learn, and what can I do differently next time?*

I believe Helen Keller was right when she said, "The richness of the human experience would lose something of its rewarding joy if there were no limitations to overcome." Remind yourself that today's disruptions just may be heavenly gateways in disguise. Problems that seem to be the worst thing to happen may turn into the best after all. When God is in it, we can say with the apostle Paul, *"We are troubled on every side, yet not distressed; we are perplexed, but not in despair; persecuted, but not forsaken; cast down, but not destroyed"* (2 Corinthians 4:8-9 KJV).

Chapter 10

Resiliency—Bouncing Back After Adversity

There is in every woman's heart a spark of heavenly fire which kindles and beams and blazes in the dark hour of adversity.
WASHINGTON IRVING

He restoreth my soul.
PSALM 23:3 KJV

IT IS AMAZING HOW MUCH RESILIENCY THERE is in the human spirit. One thing that amazes me about those who beat the odds and come through their trials is that they get up again. No matter what, they rise back up to tackle a new day again and again. According to *Webster's*, resiliency refers to the tendency of a body or material to return to its original shape or position after deformation that does not exceed its elastic limit. Did you know God never causes you to exceed your elastic limits? He will not give you more than you can bear or stretch you so far beyond your limit that you cannot spring back. He knows your limitations. He will not force you where you cannot safely go and rebound. God never demands of us work which will crush us beyond our strength and ability to recover.

Do you feel you have been stretched out of shape or compressed beyond recognition? Having elasticity and the power to recuperate requires some suppleness and flexibility on our part. How adaptable you are determines whether you will have the knack to spring back! We've all faced setbacks or losses in our past that have thrown us for a loop and left us reeling. While some women are able to not only stabilize but spring back with renewed hope and fresh enthusiasm, others continue to stagger and stumble long after the adverse experience has passed. So what separates women who manage to rebound after a crisis from those who find they are overwhelmed by the wounds, heartaches, difficulties, stumbling blocks, failures, and ever-changing complexities of life? Why is it that some bounce back from life's setbacks and come through stronger than before, while others never seem to recover? It's been said that the *ABCs* of growth could stand for *Adversity Builds Character*. Oswald Chambers took it a step further when he said, "A crisis does not make character; rather a crisis reveals character."

When we study the character or nature of women in crisis who have what we might call *survivor personalities,* we see one common trait above all others: resiliency. Women who have developed the capacity to rebound after adversity have a greater probability of full recovery. Even after they have been tried and tested by their traumatic or heartbreaking circumstances, they seem to experience a resurgence of energy that enables them to retain their confidence, a positive self-image, and an optimistic view of the world. Resiliency is the ability to get up and over the trials, to thrive after trauma and tribulations have struck.

A Skill to Learn

Fortunately, resiliency is a skill you can learn. Not only that, it's a vital ingredient to your survival, happiness, and an emotionally healthy life. When your faith is tested in times of adversity, you have the choice to see yourself in one of two ways—as a victim or a flexible-change agent. A crisis always presents you with the options to dig deep for courage and tap inner strengths you never knew you had, or to get so stretched out of shape that you stay that way. My crisis situation presented me with both danger and opportunity. I had to choose to focus my attention on opportunities even though I had to make changes in the face of danger.

Did you ever play with a toy called a "Slinky"? My sisters and I each got one in our stocking every Christmas morning, and we'd play with them for hours at a time, giggling as we watched our new playthings stretch and bounce their way down the stairs. Sometimes we would have Slinky races! Today, I keep a bright, multicolored Slinky on my desk as a constant reminder to stay resilient in order to bounce back. When I stretch that little toy out to the max, it still has an amazing capacity to rebound to its former state. You and I have been blessed with an inborn ability to be stretched and then return to our original condition—as long as we stay pliable and supple, that is. Think of the elasticity of a new rubber band. Even when that band has been stretched to the limit, it springs right back to its initial shape.

So why do some women develop the skill of resiliency, while others stay rigid and snap? One reason is that instead of asking, "Why me?" or, "Why do bad things always happen to good people?" resilient women focus their time and energy on devising the best ways to overcome bad events and damaging situations. They treat difficulties much like they would handle learning a new craft, hobby, or sport. They start out doing their very best, and then they pause for a bit to reflect on what happened. If they're having some challenges, they ask themselves, *What can I learn from this?* And, *What will I do differently when I try again?* Then they get a clear mental picture of themselves improving next time. Resilient personalities see disturbances and difficulties much like puzzles to be solved rather than forces that will surely impede their progress.

Flexibility

When I sought out and interviewed resilient women while writing this book, I discovered that, more than any other trait, they value being flexible and adaptable. They don't put themselves in a box or allow others to label them either. These women have discovered we each have an amazing innate ability to be both one way and the opposite. Similar to the way opposing muscles in your body contract and extend, there's a time to be trusting and a time to be cautious. There are some occasions when you'll be playful and others when you'll be more serious. In the same way, it's beneficial to be rigid in some circumstance but pliable in others. Once you learn the skill of resiliency, you will know when to take action and when to go with the flow.

There are many ways you can hone this skill. If you have a problem and there is something you can do to proactively make positive changes, then take action. Get out of that destructive relationship. Move away from a potentially dangerous situation. When you believe strongly in a worthy cause, take an interest and make a contribution. Involve yourself in community affairs. You can always vote or sign a petition. Give to your favorite charity. Make a difference by volunteering at a women's shelter, sitting on a board of directors, fighting an injustice, or taking a stand against prejudice.

Being adaptable, flexible, and quick to recover doesn't mean you look the other way, refusing to stand up for what matters to you. Nor does it mean you'll become a doormat for others to wipe their feet. Resiliency is something you choose to do for yourself as a shock absorber to lessen the effects of failures, setbacks, uninvited change, distressful circumstances beyond your control, and unsettling conditions that you cannot change anyway.

Being rigid and unbending is setting yourself up for frustration and disappointment. Not that long ago, when I'd be planning a dinner party, for instance, I would have such high expectations about the outcome of the evening that I was sure to be let down. I expected that everyone should arrive on time, no one would cancel at the last minute, the meal would turn out perfectly, nothing would get spilled, and after-dinner conversation would be fascinating. I also expected that after dessert and coffee, I'd get out the board games and everyone would be as excited about playing as I was! As you can see, the greater the number of requirements I had, the greater the likelihood I would be let down if things didn't go exactly as I had planned. Learning to be flexible and go with the flow has always been a difficult thing for me to do. Resiliency is a learned skill that takes time to develop.

Wouldn't it be nice if everything always went your way? Imagine what life would be like if everyone treated you with respect, handled your possessions with consideration, and received your ideas with sheer delight. What if no one ever lied to you, stole from you, spoke to you in a demeaning tone, or mistreated you in any way? There would never be a need to be flexible. If only life were that fair.

While your world may seem at times to be an intolerable, frightful, or disappointing place on any given day, and other people's behaviors, or your own, may not meet up to your expectations, you do have the option to rebound. Just as skyscrapers are built to flex in the middle so they won't snap when the storms come, and a willow tree sways effortlessly in the strong winds to keep it from breaking, so must we bend and sway and give a little when hard times hit. Adaptability is the pathway to life; inflexibility is asking for trouble. While flexibility and adaptability don't come naturally to most of us, there are ways they can be developed.

Here are some steps you can take to build up resilience, strengthen your coping skills, and make adversity work for you:

*1. **Practice failing.*** Look for opportunities to put yourself in difficult situations where you might fall flat on your face. Resiliency develops when we acknowledge our weaknesses and flaws. If you are in an environment where nothing challenging happens, you won't have the motivation to learn how to bounce back.

*2. **Take small risks.*** Don't allow the fear of failure to keep you from trying something new. Seek out challenges and look for new ways of doing things. When you bounce back from the small catastrophes, you'll be strengthening the coping skills to rebound from the big ones.

3. Shake off the victim stance. Give yourself a set amount of time to feel sorry for yourself or grieve a loss, then move on. When you're invited to a "poor me" personal pity-party, you can agree to show up, but don't stay long. Instead of moaning, "What a loser I am!" or, "Everything happens to me," tell yourself that just because you *have* a failure doesn't mean you *are* a failure. Don't take it personally and refuse to let it define who you are.

4. Check your explanatory style. The way you explain problems, hitches, complications, and the world around you affects your adaptability. Optimists have the ability to attribute difficulties to transitory, nonpermanent conditions rather than to personal inadequacies, enduring weaknesses, or inherent flaws. They recognize that everything is temporary and nothing is permanent. To them, it was simply a demanding customer or a computer glitch or a bad-hair day! Pessimists, on the other hand, think it's a lasting condition and assume personal responsibility for every failure. Even when they achieve success, they see it as sheer luck, a fluke, or a coincidence.

5. Regain your perspective. You'll have a better chance at bouncing back if you can step away from the situation and get a view of the bigger picture. Detach yourself and ask what this will mean to you in five or ten years. Positive reframing will give you a fresh perspective with which to evaluate what has happened to you and decide whether it is worth losing inner peace over it.

6. Become flexible. Do you remember Gumby, the little animated green-clay character? You may have watched his adventures with Pokey and the gang on television. Well, the thing about Gumby is that he is so bendable and pliable. This little guy is as supple as you can get. He can be stretched all out of shape and then spring right back into form again. Does that sound like you? If you don't have some flexibility or know how to give a little when you're stretched, you will eventually break in two. Being rigid causes you to crack when difficulties and hardships strike.

7. *Quit recycling old emotions*. You can easily get caught in the rut of developing one long, drawn-out excuse for why you still have problems years later. We could all find a reason to be the way we are; none of us has a valid reason to stay that way.

8. *Make the best of the worst*. People who bounce back from past setbacks and move confidently into the future believe that whatever the problem, they'll make something good come from it. At a large corporation where I presented one of my workshops, employees Deanna and Shelley were both notified that their company was downsizing. They knew they would lose their jobs. Shelley's first thought was, *This is the worst thing that could ever happen to me. I can't see myself ever pulling through.* Deanna, although initially devastated, eventually came to the place where she thought, *I've always wondered what it would be like to turn my hobby into a business. Now it looks like I'm going to have the chance!* Decide to first assess the new reality and then look for innovative ways to adapt.

9. *Learn to curb emotions and keep them in check*. Most of us react emotionally to a major crisis, or even a minor setback. Feelings of anger, sadness, anxiety, or fear are appropriate and normal. But people who recover from misfortune don't wallow in those emotions. In the face of conflict or crisis, resilient people exercise self-control. They don't ride out feelings of intense anger and anxiety. They also don't lash out and burn bridges—rather, they maintain relationships and keep doors open. Women who focus too much on their feelings about a situation do not cope well with life's challenges.

10. *Develop a flexible thinking style*. Being able to recognize the opportunities within a setback takes a special kind of open-mindedness. All of us have a unique thinking style, our own way of processing the information that shapes and defines our perceptions. The problem is that our perceptions, especially in the midst of adversity, are often inaccurate. Whether true or false, our thoughts and perceptions drive our emotions and behaviors. Practice getting out of your habitual way of thinking and be flexible when you look at problems.

11. Choose to be positive. People who consistently make the best out of difficult circumstances tend to be optimistic. No matter how bad things get, they are usually able to say, "Bad things aren't going to be bad forever." Rigid people tend to believe things will never change. Survivors imagine possibilities that aren't anywhere in sight right now. They can envision a way out of a dead-end job or an abusive relationship. They tend to believe, "If anyone can do it, why not me?"

12. Find the humor. A sense of humor is a wonderful coping device and a main ingredient in resiliency. It's been said that she who laughs, lasts! Seeing things from a funny standpoint helps you have some emotional distance and view the situation from a new perspective. Lighten up and have a good laugh at yourself while you're at it. (By the way, if you haven't laughed at yourself lately, somebody else probably has!) People who can laugh at themselves and their mistakes will never cease to be amused! You'll be healthier for it, too. As the Bible says, *"A merry heart doeth good like a medicine"* (Proverbs 17:22 KJV).

13. Build a strong support network. Be brave enough to seek help and encouragement from others. Although I always felt that self-sufficiency went hand in hand with being resilient, it wasn't until I began reaching out to others for positive support that I gained the strength to recover and the courage to make constructive changes. Look for family members, friends, other survivors, or a support group where people are trustworthy, available, and willing to rally round you in your darkest hours. They can pray for you and with you, coach you through your experience, and also be there to celebrate in your recovery. An old Irish proverb states, "It is in the shelter of each other that people live."

14. *Rely on faith, not fate*. Trust in God to bring you through. Your life is in His hands and is not dependent on fate, chance, or coincidences. When you believe in fate, you are trusting outside circumstances and external influences. Instead, believe in "divine intervention" and watch for miracles to happen. My own personal transformation happened when I first became aware that you and I are not human beings trying to discover our spirituality, but rather we are spiritual beings having a human experience here on earth. Life's challenges have a way of bringing us face-to-face with our Creator and the realization that there is a divine plan for our lives:

> *The God of all grace, who called you to his eternal glory in Christ, after you have suffered a little while, will himself restore you and make you strong, firm and steadfast* (1 Peter 5:10).

15. *Be a giver*. Get involved in a worthy cause. The Bible says, *"Let us not love with words or tongue but with actions and in truth"* (1 John 3:18). See where you can volunteer your time, talents, and energy. Resiliency comes with finding ways to make a valuable contribution. The more you get connected to the bigger things in life, beyond yourself, the more pliable you will be. Being involved with your church, community, or a larger cause helps put your personal problems into perspective. People who live self-absorbed, "me-centered" lives have greater difficulty finding meaning in their life and don't weather trauma as well. As Lucy Lucom said, "If the world seems cold to you, kindle fires to warm it."

Life's changes offer us the opportunity to move beyond our small-mindedness, to walk out of our past through the doorway of wisdom and into the light of the truth, to discover who we really are at the center of our very soul, and then to realize how resilient we have become. Then, from that realization, we become equipped to offer the best of ourselves to others. Well-known author and pastor Henri Nouwen wrote,

> In the giving it becomes clear that we are chosen, blessed, and broken not simply for our own sakes, but so that all we are about, all that we live, finds its final significance in its being lived for others.

Hurts from the past don't have to last forever when you are resilient. Don't let the past rob you of today. The knack to bounce back can help you to close that door so you can successfully move into the future.

Chapter 11

Unpacking Your Emotional Baggage

Do not be anxious about anything.
PHILIPPIANS 4:6

*I have only two emotional flare-ups per year.
The only problem is they each last six months!*
AUTHOR UNKNOWN

EVER SINCE EVE STRUGGLED WITH TEMPTATION, women have been wrestling with their emotions, and we probably always will. Let's face it, you and I were created with some pretty complex and intricate feelings. When I first read the psalmist's words, *"Thank you for making me so wonderfully complex! It is amazing to think about. Your workmanship is marvelous"* (Psalm 139:14 TLB), I thought to myself, *This has to be a man's view.* I don't know one woman who would choose the words "wonderful" or "marvelous" to refer to this complex roller-coaster ride of fiery feelings and intense moods we seem destined to experience. But what that verse does tell me is that our intricate feelings are not a mistake. They are not an accident—and you don't need to be fixed or repaired, even though you (and others) may think so at times. Thankfully though, God, who created us this way, is also the One who lives in us and speaks to us about learning new ways to handle our emotions and deal with our unique design.

It's Up to You

For starters, here's a revolutionary idea. You were never meant to be controlled by your emotions. Yet, if you're not on guard, they can dominate your life and unnecessarily keep you dwelling in a sorrowful or painful past. As you go through the various stages of relinquishing your past, you'll undoubtedly experience a myriad of emotional ups and downs. When that happens, will you manage those moods and feelings, or will they manage you?

One day a few years ago, I passed a mirror and saw my eyes red and swollen from crying tears of sorrow, disappointment, heartache, and loneliness. At that moment, I was terribly tired of feeling sad and sorry for myself. As I glanced at my reflection, I had a divine revelation. For the first time, I realized I did not have to be ruled by my emotions. I could choose how I would respond when those emotions rose up and attempted to take over.

When this reality hit me, I felt "righteous rage" well up inside of me for all the years my emotions had held me captive. I stared at my reflection in the mirror and shouted, "I'm not doing this anymore. I've had it with being controlled by my feelings." That was the day I woke up to the understanding I had been given a choice in the matter. I had always accepted that emotions "just happened" and believed we were bound to tolerate them. The truth is, until we are aware we're able to manage our emotions, they will continue to govern our actions and behaviors.

Did you know you actually get to decide how long you will experience any emotion? Although your initial reaction to an unpleasant, sad, or hurtful situation may be natural and perfectly understandable given your circumstances, what you do with that emotion and how long you experience it is up to you. You can say, "Yes, I'm feeling depressed right now, and I plan to stay that way until tomorrow. Then I'll get on with what has to be done in my life to change it." Or, you can decide to release it right away. When you're outraged about a situation or infuriated with someone, you can tell yourself, *It's no wonder I feel angry after what happened. I think I'll continue to be angry for an hour, and then I'll try to make amends or just let it go.*

If you are feeling guilty or being hard on yourself for choices you've made in your past, and you're tempted to berate yourself over and over again, it's up to you to say, "I can either continue to feel bad…or shameful…or guilty…or disgusted with myself," or, "I can go to God, ask for and accept His complete forgiveness, forgive myself, and begin to let it go." You might have to do it more than once, but keep reminding yourself that you are human, and we all make mistakes. God knows we're far from perfect, and He promises to love us—weaknesses and all. If you still can't seem to shake your feelings, it sometimes helps to talk them over with someone you trust. Then, chances are with a more balanced perspective you can start to focus on some of the more promising aspects of your life.

When the enemy comes to remind me of my past mistakes and failures, I am tempted to bury myself in those old feelings, mull them over to the tune of some sad memory music on the radio, and loll around on the sofa all day in my old, tattered, "Help me, Lord—I'm a total failure" bathrobe with matching slippers. However, I have also found that, when I choose to, I can reroute my thoughts in the same way I would change the channel if I were watching a scary movie.

Likewise, you hold the remote control for *your* emotions. Unless the emotions you're experiencing are caused by certain chronic conditions such as clinical depression or a chemical imbalance, you can always take control and decide to switch to a different station. No one can determine which emotion you will focus on. It's all up to you. Often anger, depression, worry, fear, jealousy, and other negative emotions are merely habitual ways of thinking that have been given place in your mind over time. We tend to believe these patterns are part of our character that can't be changed, but they can be broken. Don't accept being manipulated by your feelings. Freedom from your troubled emotions may be just a prayer away.

Who's in Charge?

There's one emotion that will keep you miserable more than any others—and that is feeling like a disappointment in God's eyes. Believing you have let God down will certainly hold you back from receiving His best—love, mercy, grace, and forgiveness. Let me encourage you right now—you are definitely not a disappointment to God. He made you, and He understands your human emotions, passions, and frailties.

How comforting it is to know He was there when you were being formed in your mother's womb—strengths, weaknesses, intense feelings, gifts, talents, limitations, and all. According to Psalm 139, He scheduled each day of your life before you began to breathe, and every day was recorded in His book. He knew about the choices you would make, with their victories and their blunders, along life's journey. Whether you have a fragile and sensitive disposition or a powerful and dynamic temperament, those things don't come as a surprise to your heavenly Father. Regardless of how you've handled those traits in the past, you can say with King David,

> *He lifted me out of the pit of despair, out from the bog and the mire, and set my feet on a hard, firm path, and steadied me as I walked along* (Psalm 40:2 TLB).

While negative emotions are not wrong in and of themselves, they can lead us into sin if they are not dealt with. When our feelings govern our actions, they can affect our health, peace of mind, and relationships.

For women especially, there is a direct parallel between the way we feel about ourselves and how we relate to others. It's not easy to admit that our emotions often rule our attitudes, moods, and responses to people and God. However, unresolved feelings can surface when we least expect them and often result in sarcasm, cynicism, or accusatory comments to our spouse, family members, friends, or coworkers. Everything from feeling anger, apprehension, and anxiety to being plagued with frustration, jealousy, depression, guilt, and shame, or being overcome by the "hormonal crazies" that come with PMS or menopause, can rob us of our sense of joy. Who is in charge of these feelings anyway? To be honest, most of us are not capable of fully controlling our emotions at all times, but the Holy Spirit can and God wants to use our deepest passions in ways that will bring Him glory.

There are three unique areas affecting the emotions you experience each and every day that you can control, and they have the ability to either open the door to future blessings or keep you focusing on former adversities, heartaches, and difficulties. Your ability to get beyond your past is greatly influenced by your thoughts, your words, and your frame of mind. Let's consider each of these three areas.

Your Thoughts: What Are You Thinking?

God's Word has a lot to say about what you think. Jesus commanded us to *"love God with all our mind."* He placed great importance on where you should focus your whole mind because it's mentioned several times in the New Testament. One practical reason your thoughts are so critical is because all emotion begins in your mind. When a situation arises, right away you begin to have an opinion and make a judgment about what's happening. Any negative thoughts will be evident through what you say to yourself concerning the situation. Your self-talk then produces your moods and feelings, which in turn create a physical reaction, including muscle tension, clenched fists and jaw, and a rise in blood pressure, to name a few. Those changes affect your energy levels, immune system, and general health. When you don't feel well physically, more negative thoughts are triggered, followed by the subsequent emotions, and this becomes a vicious cycle.

Your thoughts are very real and powerful. Researchers tell us that when people's thoughts are monitored, more than 80 percent of what they think about on any given day is negative. That's on an average day. Can you imagine what that percentage becomes on a *bad* day? Here's an exercise for you to try. Put yourself on a 21-day positive mental attitude diet. For the next three weeks, don't allow yourself to think negative thoughts about anything or anyone, including yourself. You may have to stop and start over again, but that's okay. After three weeks, it will become a habit.

Beyond that, an even better way to be transformed from the inside out is by fixing your thoughts on God and being *"transformed by the renewing of your mind"* (Romans 12:2). One powerful way you can alter your thinking patterns is through continual meditation on who God is, what He has done, and who He says He is in His Word. I used to think of meditation as some mysterious ritual practiced only by mystics, monks, and New Age gurus. I pictured them sitting on a mountain top, hands folded and fingers pointed heavenward, while chanting some strange-sounding mantra.

True meditation simply means to focus your thinking—to choose what you will dwell on and decide which thoughts you will concentrate on. When you dwell on your troubles over and over, whether real or imagined, that's called worry and fear. So if you have ever done that, you have already had practice meditating! Switch your attention from troubles and trials to God's love, goodness, and mercy and decide to focus on His promises to you. Because emotions are a direct result of what we think about all day, I assure you that when you perfect the skill of meditating and spend your days reviewing what God has to say, you will never be the same again! After all, as believers, *"We have the mind of Christ"* (1 Corinthians 2:16). But just as a musician must practice every day and an actor must rehearse regularly, we must consistently train ourselves to focus on God.

Your Words: What Are You Saying?

If you find you're still facing difficulties or challenges in overcoming a hurtful past, it's probably time to take inventory of what and how you speak. Your words are the evidence of what you have been thinking about and meditating on. Remember, your words have incredible power, *"for by thy words thou shalt be justified, and by thy words thou shalt be condemned"* (Matthew 12:37). So decide to make your words work for you.

Start by examining your own speech habits. For one thing, you may be speaking when it would do better to be silent. I had to chuckle when I read what Elisabeth Elliot said about our words: "Never pass up an opportunity to keep your mouth shut!" Over the years, I have learned to pray, "Lord, walk beside me with one hand on my shoulder and the other over my mouth!" On days when my emotions threaten to rage out of control, my family members often overhear me hollering, "Oh, Lord—please shut my mouth before I say what's on my mind!"

Our spoken words are very impactful. In fact, the Bible tells us that life and death are in the power of the tongue. Yet, beyond anything you could say to someone else, it's the things you say to yourself that can be the most damaging. Those are the words that influence your emotional responses to people, situations, and God.

Do you ever talk to yourself? You do if you are like most of us. That's pretty normal. Here are some of the things we say to ourselves when something upsetting or disturbing happens. See if they sound familiar:

> *Life's not fair.*
> *I guess I'm not meant to be happy.*
> *I could just scream.*
> *I'll never have anything nice.*

Everyone's getting on my nerves.
I can't believe how she treated me.
What's wrong with people?
I feel so confused.
This world is crazy!
I always mess up; everything's my fault.
It's going to be one of those days.
How dare he treat me that way?
She has a lot of nerve.
I don't get paid enough to take this!

These are words that surely provoke harmful emotions and stir up destructive feelings. You may be able to add a few of your own to the list. When you catch yourself talking this way, try stopping yourself and replacing negative statements with positive responses. Think of your words as seeds and begin to plant the results you'd rather see happen. God promises you will always reap what you sow. When you're feeling angry, discouraged, let down, anxious, or fearful, why not choose to plant some of these seeds instead?

Every day in every way, things are getting better and better.
I now enjoy my life, my job, and my relationships.
I am happy, healthy, and energetic.
All I need is being provided for me.
I stay calm and composed in irritating circumstances.
New opportunities are opening up day by day.
There's no barrier I cannot overcome.
Everything that happens in my life is serving a special
  purpose.
I'm certain there's a lesson to be learned here.

You may chuckle at first, especially if what you are proclaiming is so far from the truth that it's hard for even you to believe. But keep on planting more of the positive results you hope to grow and you will be amazed at the miracles you will experience.

Even more effective than positive self-programming is quoting God's promises to you throughout the day. The Bible instructs us to *"pray without ceasing"* (1 Thessalonians 5:17 KJV), and this is one way you can do that. When you find yourself using self-defeating words like "I won't ever be able to forgive and forget" or "I can't seem to get beyond what's happened in the past," change them to, *"I can do all things through Christ which strengtheneth me"* (Philippians 4:13 KJV). When you're tempted to talk about what you've been lacking, say, *"My God shall supply all your needs according to his riches in glory by Christ Jesus"* (Philippians 4:19 KJV). Rather than dwelling on the anger, fear, or worry you can't seem to overcome, remind yourself that *"God always causes me to triumph in Christ Jesus"* (2 Corinthians 2:14 NKJV). Instead of focusing on the frustrations you've experienced on your life's journey, say that you are *"casting all my cares on him who cares for me"* (see 1 Peter 5:7) and *"We know that all that happens to us is working for our good if we love God and are fitting into his plans"* (Romans 8:28 TLB). When you are feeling confused, bewildered, or panic-stricken as you move from old comfort patterns into new territory, tell yourself, *"The Lord God will help me; therefore shall I not be confounded: therefore have I set my face like a flint, and I know that I shall not be ashamed"* (Isaiah 50:7 KJV). Write these verses out and post them where you can read them regularly. Commit some to memory. As believers, by thinking more positively and speaking the Word, we are affirming that all things are possible with God.

Your Frame of Mind: What Mood Are You In?

Your thoughts and words influence your attitude, which plays a major role in determining your moods. When many women come to the place where they are praying and fully trusting God, they believe their unhealthy outlook and pessimism will simply disappear. But a positive frame of mind is a choice. It's something that requires intentional effort. Fortunately, optimism is something that can be learned.

Although today I can say that I'm generally an optimistic person with a fairly balanced perspective and healthy attitude in most situations, it wasn't always that way. At one time, as a doom-and-gloom person, I thought life was unfair and I learned to expect little from it. It's only by God's grace I have been able to transform the way I view life. I grew up with a tendency toward pessimism, and as a child, felt sad about a lot of things. I cried easily, and puddles of tears seemed to hover just behind my eyeballs, waiting for any reason to gush down my cheeks. From the earliest time I can remember, my mother was constantly asking me, "What are you crying about *now?*" Although I couldn't explain it appropriately at that young age, it always seemed to me that life was not fair. As a child, I often cried for the hurts of others and wept over the injustice I observed happening in people's lives. Sadly, my genuine empathy eventually turned into perpetual pessimism.

What I had to learn was that when we are bogged down with negativity, we seem to attract tragedy. That was the case with me, and eventually I came to expect the worst in life. "Oh, woe is me" became my motto. I grumbled and complained a lot, and in school I became known for my dark cynicism and sarcastic sense of humor. When I was in grade 10, a new boyfriend (tall, dark, handsome, and captain of the football team!) broke up with me to begin dating Sandi, an older woman (she was in grade 12) who always seemed to be smiling. Unfortunately for me, she had a delightful way of looking at the bright side of life, which made me, in comparison, look like a most miserable and wretched soul. She was one of those bubbly girls, fun to be around and always excited about her future. Like a magnet, she attracted the same type of friends and went around with this entourage of supporters following her.

Later, I had the opportunity to get to know this "rival" of mine, and she let me in on a little secret. Sandi confided that she had not always been an optimistic person and often had to battle negativity herself.

Then, one day she simply made up her mind that she would be more positive and upbeat, and not allow the petty annoyances of life to get her down. She decided to focus on being happy and contented, choosing to be helpful and encouraging, uplifting others who were feeling down. (I think I was one of her projects!)

Through her, I discovered that having a positive perspective and optimistic outlook was possible through deliberate action and conscious effort. It also meant looking beyond myself to the needs of others. Although some people seem to be born with this optimistic nature, for most of us a cheerful disposition doesn't just happen, even when we come into a relationship with God. But it is encouraging to know that whatever your nature, with a little intentional effort, a lot of prayer, and complete trust in the Lord combined with a clear picture of the person you'd rather be, it is possible to see your moods transformed!

Maybe you've tried to have a positive outlook and you've discovered that optimists and idealists are often accused of being naïve and unrealistic. Yet, when we study those who see life through rose-colored glasses, we notice they tend to be more prosperous, stay healthier, enjoy more meaningful relationships, and live longer. The truth is that life will always have its challenges, but if we want to, we can choose to see the up side of every situation.

Thoughts and words produce your moods and attitudes, but in order to completely unpack your emotional baggage, bring your thoughts and words in line with God's Word. Healthy moods and positive attitudes will follow, and you'll see harmful emotions begin to fall away.

A Natural Path to Emotional Fitness

Aside from our thoughts, words, and attitudes, there are some physical reasons you and I have such intense mood swings as well. When I notice my feelings are starting to get out of control, one of the ways I can rein in emotional responses and curb my behavior is to be sure I am at my physical best. That means establishing some positive health habits like proper diet, regular exercise, and timeout with suffi-cient rest and relaxation. It also means recognizing the emotional ben-efit of laughter and tears. Let's look at each of those individually:

Please, Lord—not my sugar and caffeine! Do you ever feel as though you are two people? I don't mean those days when you're multitasking and getting so many things crossed off your to-do list that you amaze even yourself. What I'm talking about here are those times when it seems as though you're standing outside your own body, looking over at this crazed woman who's gone totally bonkers.

You're thinking to yourself, *What a wacko! She should shut up before she gets herself into a lot of trouble. Just listen to her saying all those stu-pid things she's really going to regret later on. Oh, now she's slamming doors and having visions of throwing her favorite antique porcelain fig-urine or the dining-room table or both across the room at something or someone. She's going to be sorry. Will she ever learn?* If you can't relate or have never been there, bless your little heart. Actually, I wish I could say you'd never see me acting that way, but if I told you that—and if my hubby and kids ever got hold of this chapter—they'd roll on the floor laughing (or crying!).

At a time when my hormones were raging with PMS and my emo-tions were way out of control (I'm not blaming, just reporting!), God showed me some things about my health habits that you may think are insignificant but can make a huge difference in how angry, annoyed, frustrated, or depressed you get. First, He revealed to me that I ate far too much sugar. In fact, I had become a sugar-holic! On some days, sweets were all I ate. At that time I fully understood the woman who said a balanced diet to her meant one cookie in each hand. (My family was aware of my problem and tried their best to help by monitoring what I ate, which annoyed me even more.)

My sugar cravings got so bad that I was forced to have candy hidden in every room of the house, plus in my desk, handbag, and car, so that if I had a sugar attack at any given moment, I could get my fix. (I even unwrapped it first, so no one would hear the crinkle and get suspicious or, worse yet, want me to share!) Eventually, sugar began to have such an adverse affect on my body that at night I would shake in bed so much it would wake up my husband. When you have too much sugar in your system, one common symptom is that you can usually go to sleep easily enough but then wake up suddenly in the night feeling jittery. Then no matter what you do, you just lay there staring at the clock, telling yourself, *Okay, if I fall asleep this very moment, I'll still get four hours of sleep!* Even worse, overdosing on sugar causes mental confusion, affects your memory, and plays havoc with your emotions and energy levels. Not only do your *moods* swing, but *you* may be swinging from the rafters one minute, and lying in a wretched, sobbing heap on the floor the next.

With too much sugar in my system, I was always apologizing because of displays of temper: yelling at my husband, screaming at the kids, throwing things around, and slamming a lot of doors—all the while blaming someone else, of course. If this sounds like you or someone you know, there is help. While sugar may not be the entire source of the problem, cutting back or going off it completely can't hurt and just may be the solution. Start by cleaning house of all the culprits and refusing to buy more. To break the cycle, keep your blood-sugar level even by eating snacks that are high in B vitamins and complex carbohydrates such as whole grains and fresh vegetables, or a combination of fruit with a solid protein or starch food, such as crackers with cheese or peanuts with raisins. I have found I can safely splurge and treat myself with sweets on special occasions without experiencing too many symptoms. The time I won't indulge is when I know I'm going to be under added stress or dealing with a conflict situation or a difficult person.

God also dealt with me about the amount of caffeine I consumed on an average day. When I actually counted the number of cups of tea, coffee, and cola I was having, I was so alarmed that I went off caffeine completely. Naturally I suffered terrible withdrawal symptoms (don't try this at home) and nearly drove myself and everyone around me crazy. These days when I want a cup of coffee, I choose water-processed decaffeinated. Most of the time I'll drink plain water that's been puri-fied, cold or hot with lemon. I'll also enjoy a cup of mild tea or one of the many herbal varieties available. At bedtime, chamomile is soothing and helps me to drift off naturally into a deep sleep.

The gift of tears. Another way to physically handle emotions is to let yourself cry. This week alone I ran into three friends on separate occa-sions who all told me the same thing—they had recently come through an emotionally trying time and the one thing that helped was giving themselves permission to have a good cry. Why we think we need permission from anyone, let alone from ourselves, in the first place is a good question. How sad that society discourages tears, espe-cially in boys and men, so much so that we see crying as a weakness. Then we deny ourselves the comfort of indulging in this natural, healthy form of emotional release. I encourage you to let the tears flow when you have something to cry about. Don't believe anyone who tells you that crying shows lack of faith or that tears are the work of the devil.

From a biological viewpoint, new research sheds fascinating light on crying. We now know there's a difference between biological tears—the type produced when we get something in our eye—and emotional tears that come when we are distraught. The emotional ones have been found to carry toxic poisons from our bodies that biological tears do not. These chemicals would otherwise build up and eventually cause various diseases. Crying as an emotional response when letting go of the past helps to cleanse and purify our bodies, helping keep us free from illness and restoring a sense of balance in our lives.

When you cry, let yourself moan, sigh, and wail. These instinctive groans are your body's voice and can actually be a form of prayer, pro-viding astounding relief from emotional pain. The Bible says the Holy Spirit helps us if we don't know how or what to pray—"*He does our praying in and for us, making prayer out of our wordless sighs, our aching groans*" (Romans 8:26 MSG). Allow your body to speak in this way. It's an effective, simple, and natural way to pray and relinquish the pain of the past. So go ahead. Cry and moan until you have emptied yourself. Crying and groaning are not weaknesses to be overcome. They are gifts to alleviate the negative effects of pain and suffering. Besides, God says He saves those tears in a bottle, so stop bottling your emotions inside!

Lighten up with laughter. Similar to tears, laughter acts as a calming, healing, soothing balm to your frazzled nerves and frayed emotions. The gift of laughter gives you the ability to find humor in even serious situations. With its mood-altering qualities, a good laugh works like a tranquilizer, but without the side effects. When you laugh, your brain releases endorphins and other biochemicals that provide you with an overall feeling of well-being and comfort.

So rather than waiting for laughter to happen, jump-start your funny bone by planning to integrate humorous activities into your life regularly, whether it's reading joke books, playing board games, watching funny movies, attending wholesome comedy theatre productions, or looking at comics and cartoons. When you choose to experience humor each day, you heighten your appreciation for the funny side of life. And even when you're feeling out of sorts, laughter will have a way of reviving and invigorating your soul. God promises He will give us the *"oil of gladness instead of mourning"* (Isaiah 61:3), and in Proverbs we read, *"A cheerful heart does good like a medicine, but a broken spirit makes one sick"* (17:22 TLB).

Following these steps and ideas will bring change into your emotional life, but they won't guarantee you'll never fall prey to your intricate moods and feelings of anger, frustration, envy, or doubt. There is no simple formula or magic wand to unravel the web of our emotions. When you understand the complexity and depth with which God created you, you'll begin to grasp and appreciate the beauty of your emotional makeup. Although our emotions can frustrate us and set us back in our relationships with others and God, the unique emotional sensitivities built into each of us are also serving as stepping-stones to greater spiritual maturity. Regardless of what you're feeling, when you decide to take your eyes off your circumstances and trust in the Lord, you won't have to be controlled by negative emotions.

Chapter 12

Oh Courage, Where Art Thou?

Courage is being the only one who knows you are afraid.
ANONYMOUS

Cheer up! Take courage if you are depending on the Lord.
PSALM 31:24 TLB

HAVE YOU EVER THOUGHT THAT THE BEST WAY to handle life's risky trials and frustrating difficulties might be to leave town, change your name, and start all over? I have to admit I've considered this more than once when my courage has suddenly disappeared. I've imagined dying my hair blond, getting all new ID, and beginning a new life as somebody else, even though I knew deep in my heart that wasn't the answer. It just seems so much easier when I'm lacking the courage to face and deal with whatever is going on that's causing my misery and heartache.

While running away may seem like a good way out, you'll never outrun what's going on inside of you. Thankfully, God has a different plan for you. When you've decided to face the heartaches of your past and leave your comfort zone behind to venture out into new territory, God's Word says,

> *Be strong and courageous. Do not be terrified; do not be discouraged, for the LORD your God will be with you wherever you go* (Joshua 1:9).

According to my thesaurus, other words for courage include "spirited bravery, boldness, daring, fearlessness." Earnest Hemingway described courage as "grace under pressure." It's often when we are under pressure, feeling weak, vulnerable and fatigued, and need courage the most, that it has a way of disappearing. That's when God's grace, mercy, and compassion take over. He tells us His grace is sufficient when we're feeling frail because His power is made perfect in our weakness (see 2 Corinthians 12:9).

"It Doesn't Have to Be This Way Anymore"

It takes courage to step out and make the changes we so desperately want to see happen. We'd be so much more comfortable doing things the way we've always done them. Even when we know courage is the answer, we'd rather choose the path of least resistance. When we've been defeated over and over again, our courage has a way of dissipating. After we've been trampled on too many times, we get worn down in our spirit. We eventually lose our enthusiasm, our push, and our drive to leave our comfort areas, and we become less willing to attempt the new and the challenging.

If you put a frog in a pot of water and very gradually turn up the heat, the frog won't notice the change and will remain in the pot until it eventually boils to death. However, if you drop the frog into a pot of water that's already boiling, it will leap out instantly. If you have had years of slowly rising temperatures—circumstances where you've experienced defeat, despair, and disappointments—you may have become conditioned to accept failure. You've been robbed of the courage to believe in a new tomorrow. When we live with defeat for a long time, we begin to tolerate predictable patterns of suffering and loss and see them as normal. Eventually we lose the bravery to leap out of the pan and say, "It doesn't have to be like this anymore. There must be a better way."

The frog in the pot feels safe and secure, but only because it's become accustomed to the heat little by little. We can get conditioned, too, with a perceived sense of security. Most of us long for a sense of certainty in our lives and many times, to get that feeling of safety and security, we will tolerate inexcusable acts by others—which have become our reliable and dependable patterns. But any security we think we experience here on this earth is only a myth. As Helen Keller said,

> Security is mostly superstition. It doesn't exist in nature nor do the children of men experience it. Life is either a daring adventure or it is nothing!

There isn't any true security here in this world. Aside from God and His love, nothing is 100-percent certain. So having courage means we will act in spite of that lack of security.

True Risk

The mystery of courage is that it grows when you step out and take a risk. Each time you have the boldness to venture beyond your comfort areas, it becomes easier to do. That's because risk-taking further reinforces your confidence, builds your self-esteem, and provides tangible confirmation that you can indeed succeed, regardless of the failures, setbacks, or mistakes. Theodore Roosevelt summed it up when he said,

> Far better it is to dare mighty things, to win glorious triumphs even though checkered by failure, than to take rank with those poor spirits that neither enjoy much nor suffer much because they live in that grey twilight that knows neither victory nor defeat.

Normally, I want to step out in faith that way. I long to have the courage to attempt daring ventures and aim to win glorious triumphs! Really, I do. Living in that grey twilight has no appeal for me. But then when I make the move and take a chance at a new venture, something strange happens to my courage. There I stand, trembling, feeling all naked and exposed, and wondering what on earth ever made me think I could do this in the first place.

Have you found yourself in such a situation? It's like waking up in the middle of a nightmare only to find the nightmare continues. Maybe you agreed to take a position on a committee, or give a presentation at a staff meeting or before a large audience. Maybe you said yes to performing in a live recital on stage or acting in local theatre. Perhaps you volunteered your services in your community or offered to go the extra mile on a project at work. You went there acting as if you knew what you were doing, but inside you were screaming, *What am I doing here?*

I have been there myself, and those were the times I had to learn that, even though I wanted to run away, I had to stay and act in spite of my fears and doubts. By staying in a situation and seeing it through, my confidence grew and so did my trust in God and all that He can do. To my surprise, I found that, not only was I scared silly, but I was excited at the same time.

True risk is like that. It has two elements—it's both frightening and exhilarating at once. I find it interesting that, as human beings, we can experience both of those emotions simultaneously. On Easter morning, the Bible tells us that when the angel spoke to the women at the empty tomb, they ran off to give the disciples the message Jesus had risen from His grave and they were *"badly frightened but also filled with great joy"* (Matthew 28:8 TLB). Imagine their incredible fear combined with the extraordinary thrill in their hearts!

Think of times when you have been afraid but excited at the same time. Was it when you were a kid riding a roller coaster at an amusement park, jumping off the diving board into the deep end, or later when you were learning to drive? Perhaps it happened when you decided to go back to school as an adult or start a job after being out of the workforce for a while. Maybe it was the time you moved to another neighborhood or a different part of the country. How about the first time you flew in an airplane, played in a piano recital, or spoke before an audience?

Risk means something different for everybody. For some, it's risky eating a meal in a restaurant alone and for another, it's attending a national conference. For someone else, it was a risk getting married, having a baby, or investing in a new car. Risks come in all shapes and sizes. What is risky for one may not be for another. We are all unique, and God can use individual risk situations for personal growth. Consider some of these areas of risk we encounter:

- *physical*—riding a bike, parachuting, rollerblading, ice-skating, white-water rafting, bungee-jumping, deep-sea diving

- *emotional*—learning to trust others, opening up to let someone know your true feelings, being willing to let go of bitterness and resentment, relinquishing past hurts and disappointments

- *intellectual*—learning new computer programs, how to operate a digital camera, or record a TV show on the VCR!

- *social*—planning a retirement party, arranging a family reunion, attending networking meetings, serving dinner to guests in your home

- *financial*—investing in insurance, saving for your retirement, buying your first home or any major purchase

- *spiritual*—giving up total control to live entirely by faith, trusting God for all your needs, committing your life to Christ

Make a point of observing yourself and how you respond in risky situations. You may be surprised by some of the limits you have set for yourself, especially when you catch yourself saying, "I'd never be comfortable doing that," or "I wish I had the courage to do this."

Risk Letting Go

What can happen is that our dread of doing something can ruin the experience. When we look back on it later, we find ourselves wishing we had enjoyed the ride. This happened to me the first time I flew in a helicopter. My husband Cliff and I were vacationing in Hawaii, and he really wanted to take a tour into a volcano, but I was against it from the beginning. I heard about a couple who had taken a similar tour just weeks earlier, and their helicopter crashed, killing the pilot and all passengers.

Although I felt my concerns were legitimate and justified, I also knew I could trust the Lord for our safety and protection. I decided to step out in faith and go with my husband. Cliff still teases me to this day because I wasted the first half hour crying from fear, and then spent the last half in tears because of the incredible beauty and magnificent view of paradise all around us. How often have you finally done something that took great courage, only to find yourself wishing you hadn't waited so long?

For most of us, it's risky to let go of our past and to move out from a comfortable place into the scary unknown. It takes courage to forgive, relinquish old hurts, and give up bitterness and resentment, especially if those have become our comfort patterns over the years. Do you know someone who continually walks through the same problems and stumbling blocks year after year? This person usually handles her past in one of two ways: Either she seems stuck and prepared to go on and on, griping about the same old issues without ever moving forward—or she desperately tries one more technique, attends yet another seminar, sees a different therapist, or checks out a new religious approach.

But either way, she remains hopelessly bound and never seems to gain the courage she needs to make the necessary changes. Maybe you know this woman. Maybe you know her personally! Whether that woman is you or someone close to you, there is hope. You can move forward. It can begin with becoming a positive risk-taker and letting go of the false security of living with the familiarity of your past wounds.

Opening up to tell someone of your true innermost feelings, wounds and all, is another form of risk. Ginny was ready to do this. She invited me for tea when she heard I was in her part of the country speaking at a conference. We had known each other for quite some time, but she had never shared with me certain parts of her past that still hurt her today. This particular crisp, spring morning we sat in her sunny kitchen at a beautifully laid table enjoying freshly baked biscuits with homemade jam and a large pot of English breakfast tea. Not only was Ginny an ideal hostess, she was an exceptionally attractive woman with impeccable style, and it would be hard to tell that this beautiful lady was nearing her eighth decade on earth!

After we'd chatted for a while, it was even more difficult for me to believe she had been harboring such deep resentment, bitterness, and ill feelings toward members of her own family for many years. She had been deeply wounded in her childhood by her siblings, and after years of extremely hurtful comments and rejection in subsequent relationships, she still had not recovered, even though most of those who had hurt her were no longer living. Tears came freely and cascaded down her cheeks as she told story after story of how she had been poorly treated, rejected, and abused, and she admitted she had never felt loved through her entire life, not even in her marriage.

As she shared her story, she was sobbing, and her words poured out in a deluge of pain and anguish. Soon I was weeping with her. I didn't preach to her. I didn't quote Bible verses on suffering. I simply went over to where she was seated and held her and hugged her, and cried some more. I felt God was allowing me to be His arms in the flesh. Afterward, I reminded her that, even though we can't go back and remake the past, one thing we can do to recover is to ask God to fill us with His love and take away the painful memories and heartache. And so we prayed that Jesus would come into her heart and heal her of all those past hurts. It had been a risk for her to open up and share all this with me. Apparently it was worth it. I saw her face change as the sobbing subsided, and she was truly born again into the family of God. After all, He promises to be there for us when our earthly family forsakes us.

When I arrived home from my tour and spoke with her a few weeks later, she said that sometime during our morning tea and prayer time, God had filled her with His love and Holy Spirit. She said she awoke the next morning a new person, and from that day on, Scriptures began to leap off the pages when she studied her Bible and a new love for Christ filled her being. It was only a few months later that Ginny left this earth and went to be with Jesus. I am ever grateful I was given that wonderful opportunity.

If, like Ginny, you keep letting your past experiences and future fears rule your life, you are never going to have the courage to risk letting go. You will never feel good about yourself either. The past will keep coming back to drag you down and keep you from the possibility of new dreams and hopes, until you turn it all over to the One who cares for you more than anyone here on earth ever could.

Learning to Like Change

There is no safe haven on earth where we will no longer have to suffer with the trials of this life. Although we have this intrinsic need for some sense of certainty, complete safety is an illusion. Being lifted from our troubles to be planted in a calm, serene place of total security is not going to happen. Besides, it wouldn't build in us the endurance and stamina we need to stop from crumbling under pressure. It takes courage to get up each morning, face the day, and make the necessary changes to handle whatever obstacles we find in our path.

Most of us would like life to improve while we stay the same. That simply cannot happen. In order for your life to be different, you must do the changing. Here are some suggestions for learning to risk and love change:

- *Get used to change—gradually.* You can break with the familiar in some small way each day. Change your morning routine, drive a different route to work, or wear your watch on the opposite wrist. It's not only okay to do things differently, it's necessary if you want to strengthen yourself to handle those bigger changes, especially the ones that come into your life uninvited.

- *Get out of your rut.* If you always read novels, try biographies or a history book. If you dress conservatively in traditional colors, shop for one outfit that is more colorful and glitzy. Rather than your favorite country music, switch to classical or jazz. If you've never thought you'd enjoy live theatre, opera, or the ballet, you may be pleasantly surprised.

- *Watch for opportunities to do things differently.* Try putting the toilet paper roll on upside down! If you always fold the towels in thirds, start folding them in half. In a restaurant, order something you've never had before.

- *Get a new perspective.* Try taking a different path if you run or walk around the block. If you normally jog in the evening, try going at sunrise. Change the direction of your desk, and you will be surprised at how even the most familiar surroundings will appear fresh.

- *Learn to do something new.* Sign up for a night course, lecture, workshop, or seminar. Take up a new hobby or learn to play an instrument. Look up new and interesting words in the dictionary and practice using them in conversation. Take golf lessons or join a sports team.

Break away from the routine of everyday living. Refuse to be satisfied with an ordinary, no-name brand of life. Why settle for vanilla when there are 31 flavors? You can't experience a miracle if you stay in a safe place. Our most rewarding and fulfilling moments seem to occur when we have chosen to put ourselves into situations where we must stretch to our limit in order to accomplish a worthy and challenging goal.

When was the last time you did anything so thrilling that it took your breath away? Can you think of something you willingly chose to do that you knew would take courage? Those experiences, both scary and exhilarating, give us the sensation of being free at last. These are the cherished moments of utmost fulfillment and contentment we wish could last forever. If you choose the path of least resistance instead, you'll never have the chance to see what God is able to do for you. The only way to live with the miraculous every day is to continually be in situations where, if God doesn't come through, you won't succeed. That does take courage, but as the psalmist said,

> *Oh, put God to the test and see how kind he is! See for yourself the way his mercies shower down on all who trust in him* (Psalm 34:8 TLB).

Start to see life as a breathless voyage of discovery and begin each day filled with boundless expectations.

Chapter 13

Conquering the Fears that Keep You Stuck

*Now you don't need to be afraid of the dark any more,
nor fear the dangers of the day; nor dread the plagues
of darkness, nor disasters in the morning.*
PSALM 91:5-6 TLB

Fear is pain arising from the anticipation of evil.
ARISTOTLE

FEAR IS ONE OF THE MOST NEGATIVE EMOTIONS we can experience. It acts almost like prayer in reverse. Your fears may be the result of a traumatic experience, unrealistic expectations, growing up with a controlling parent, perfectionism, or perhaps an inherited or genetic tendency. Whatever the source, fear can cause you to miss great opportunities when you play it safe, afraid to embark on a new journey out of the past and into the unknown future. Fear is a self-imposed trap that will cripple your dreams and prevent you from becoming all God intends you to be.

Hazards and Potential

As little girls growing up, most of us learned to be afraid of a number of things. Through our early experiences, we learned to fear embarrassment or looking silly. We dreaded being alone or being the center of attention. Because of our past programming and conditioning, many fears from our past continue to keep us stuck. What is it for you?

Is it the fear of…

- the unknown, if you are changing jobs, ending a relationship, starting a business, or going back to school?

- rejection when building a new relationship, stating your views, asserting yourself, or confiding in someone?

- being taken advantage of by someone you trust?

- the future, when you contemplate all that is going on in the world?

- failure when attempting something new, making major life decisions, speaking in public?

- impending success, because you lack confidence and think you don't have what's required to maintain your achievements?

- being alone, aging, dying, or losing a loved one?

These are just a few common fears. You can probably add your own to the list. If fear is something you have struggled to overcome, you may be surprised—and encouraged—to know you don't really have to conquer it! You may always experience some fear when you are facing difficult, demanding, or dangerous situations. In fact, some fears are healthy. It's fear that can cause you to jump out of the way of an oncoming car that is veering out of control. Fear can prompt you to take the elevator rather than the stairwell when you are alone in a strange building or a covered parking area. It's fear that can cause you to be apprehensive about trusting someone questionable.

There are times when fear can be a good thing, acting as a warning signal and a great protector. In some ways, it's an innate gift you've been given to warn you of danger and lead you through hazardous situations. We will explore this more in chapter 17.

Getting Unstuck

The fear we're talking about in this chapter, however, is that panicky feeling that becomes unreasonable, sweeping over us like a giant tidal wave and holding us back from attempting regular, everyday opportunities. Once we discover that fear is simply a fact of life and a normal response to a potentially threatening situation or an overwhelming condition, we can look for new and improved ways of handling it. Instead of trying to eliminate fear or waiting until it goes away, we can choose to determine whether it is acting as a danger signal alerting us to change our direction, or if we should go ahead and take action in spite of being afraid. One main principle of many diet programs is that it helps to get used to the feeling of hunger. Rather than hoping to come to the place where you have conquered hunger, know that it's okay to feel that way at times and you will not die if you refuse to give in to it. The same is true with fear—it won't kill you! In fact, there are times when it just may save your life.

A turning point in my life came when I realized that people who step out to achieve outstanding successes as well as those who hold back from attempting great feats both walk in trepidation and experience the same fears. We've been taught to believe that fear is an obstacle to be conquered and that we cannot move on to a peaceful future until we get rid of it. But by transforming our thoughts and renewing our minds, we can come to the realization that feeling fearful can't keep us prisoner.

In my past, I held on tightly to many things that were undeniably not working for me because I normally made choices based on my fears. Part of the problem was my inner voice that kept reminding me,

Don't take chances or make waves.
You'd better hang on to what you have.
You shouldn't change a thing because there's nothing else
    out there for you.
You don't have what it takes to make it.
You'll probably try and fail, and then you'll be sorry.
You'll end up wishing you had stayed where you were!

Does any of that sound vaguely familiar? If it does, there is hope for you. One day I changed my focus and started to speak God's words of power, love, joy, and peace over my life. Eventually, in Jesus' Name, I conquered the thinking that had been hindering my progress—and you can do the same. Today, it's not that I never experience fear, but now I know what to do with it.

However, many people are frozen in fear. It seems to be epidemic in our society and the number-one crippler of our dreams. We fear endings and beginnings. We fear change and being stuck. We fear failure, and success. We fear dying and we also fear living. Whatever the fear, this chapter will give you the insight and tools to vastly improve your ability to handle any given situation. You can move from a place of pain, paralysis, and depression (feelings that often accompany fear) to one of power, energy, confidence, and excitement.

Some of the most common fears that keep us stuck are the fear of the unknown, fear of accomplishment, fear of rejection, and fear of failure. Let's take a look at each one of these.

Fear of the Unknown

It's understandable that you might be tempted to feel trapped in fear of the unknown when you think about your future. This life is full of negative possibilities, things that *might* happen. As long as we are choosing a path of personal growth, we can expect to face apprehensive situations and to be led through unfamiliar territory and uncharted paths. New opportunities and challenges bring unknown, fearful situations we must deal with.

Acknowledge your fears and be honest with God. You may also want to seek help from experts in areas of concern, or talk over your fears and anxieties with your spouse or a trusted friend. Determine which aspects of a situation you can control and which ones are beyond your control. When you choose to go ahead and step out in faith, trusting God, believing His promises and making faith-filled choices, it may feel risky and extremely frightening. But it's much less terrifying than coping with the underlying fear that comes from staying in a position where you feel helpless to make a difference. Putting yourself in a position where you have to face those fears will feel impossible and gut-wrenching at first, but it will be worth it in the end.

Fear of Accomplishment

Although we truly want to achieve success, there is always a cost to fulfilling our mission and accomplishing our purpose in life. As sincerely devoted as we are to finally discovering God's purpose for us on this earth, we sometimes get scared off when we realize there's a price tag attached. The biggest price and most important thing required of you is that you abandon your personal ambitions in exchange for God's agenda. Rather than simply including His will along with all your private dreams, plans, expectations, and all the other things you'd like to do with your life, it's a matter of praying, "Lord, Thy will, not mine." In essence, you give God a signed blank check and ask Him to fill in the amount. That can be scary! However, once you've surrendered your hopes and desires and committed to fulfilling God's will for your life regardless of the cost, you'll experience a freedom like you've never known before. God will begin to bless you in ways you never imagined. The Bible says, *"If they obey and serve him, they will spend the rest of their days in prosperity and their years in contentment"* (Job 36:11).

In addition to that, a great part of our fear of accomplishment comes from doubting ourselves and wondering if we are really equipped, or have what it takes, to do what God calls us to do. The enemy wants you to have misgivings about your competency and focus on your own abilities, but God wants you to trust in Him. His Word has promised, *"The one who calls you is faithful and he will do it"* (1 Thessalonians 5:24). He never leaves you to do it on your own, so there is no need to fear. The Bible reassures us, *"God hath not given us the spirit of fear; but of power, and of love and of a sound mind"* (2 Timothy 1:7 KJV).

Fear of Rejection

Rejection can come in many forms, from being abandoned as a child by your father to being turned down continually when applying for job after job. It can also come from losing a good friend over a misunderstanding, or being left alone in a marriage when your husband chooses someone else. When rejection happens more than once, you can begin to feel like you've been discarded and cast off like a second-hand garment. Then, lonely and hurting, you put on a mask to hide and cover up the pain. Eventually when you've experienced rejection or abandonment enough times, you give up trying. The butterfly that has been trapped in a jar, after making numerous efforts to escape to no avail, no longer attempts to fly away even when the lid is finally left off.

Rejection can also come in the form of criticism. It helps to remember that the most critical people are usually ones who don't feel good about themselves, and they mistakenly believe that if they bring others down to their level, they'll feel better. But they never do, and so they keep trying. Even so, it's often hidden pain of our own past that is at the root of our hurt feelings, because it makes us supersensitive to criticism. Ask God to search your heart and bring to light any area where you need His healing touch or forgiveness.

Most of all, when you are being criticized continually, adopt a posture of curiosity. Develop the habit of saying to yourself, *Isn't it interesting that someone could have something negative to say about me!* Perhaps there is something positive you can learn from what seems to be a hurtful comment. On the other hand, maybe the person doing the criticizing is miserable and negative about a lot of things and you just happen to be one more. In that case, the worst thing you can do is to take it personally. Criticism is almost inevitable whenever you step away from the crowd and attempt to accomplish something out of the ordinary. Know that you will be setting yourself up as a target for criticism. If you want to change the direction of your life, brace yourself and refuse to let it throw you off guard.

Fear of Failure

If you want to grow, you can never escape failure, no matter how hard you try. Every person who has ever attempted to do anything at all has failed at one time or another. It doesn't matter how intelligent, talented, or privileged you are—the only way to avoid failure is to hide out and do nothing.

It might surprise you to know how many people fail before they reach their goals or experience success. Some of the most influential people in history were considered failures at some point in their lives. For example, Coco Chanel, of fragrance fame, was orphaned at an early age and raised by nuns. When her dreams were shattered after she attempted an unsuccessful singing career, she quit to go to work as a hatmaker and eventually began designing daring new fashions for women in the 1920s. That's when she created and introduced her first fragrance, Chanel No. 5. Then there was Charles Darrow, who was an unemployed heating engineer before he developed the game of Monopoly. He introduced his first version of the game to a toy company in 1935, and it was rejected for containing 52 "fundamental errors." Today the game is so successful that its publisher, Parker Brothers, prints more than 40 billion dollars worth of Monopoly money each year. (That's twice the amount of real money printed annually by the United Steates Mint.) What a successful failure that turned out to be!

Here is a list of a few more people who may have felt like failures or were told they were:

- Fred Astaire was described at an early screen test with the words "Can't act. Can't sing. Balding. Can dance a little."

- Elvis Presley was fired after just one show at the Grand Ole Opry and told, "You ain't goin' nowhere, son!"

- Anita Roddick pursued her idea for The Body Shop with all-natural hair and body products only after a restaurant and hotel she had invested in with her husband didn't get off the ground.

- Albert Einstein was four years old before he could speak and seven before he could read. He performed badly in almost all of his high-school courses. He flunked his college exams and was advised by a teacher to drop out of school. She said, "You'll never amount to anything, Einstein."

- Louisa May Alcott, who authored *Little Women* and numerous other novels, was told by an editor she'd never write anything that had popular appeal.

- The legendary tenor Enrico Caruso was told by a voice teacher that he couldn't sing at all.

- Leo Tolstoy (author of *War and Peace* and *Anna Karenina*, among others) flunked out of college.

- At age ten, famous artist Pablo Picasso stopped going to school because he was barely able to read or write. His father yanked him out of school and hired a tutor for him, but the tutor soon gave up and quit in disgust.

- A newspaper editor fired Walt Disney, saying he lacked creativity and good ideas.

- Steven Spielberg dropped out of high school. He did

return later, attending a class for those with learning disabilities, but after only a month, he dropped out again.

- Admiral Richard E. Byrd had been retired from the navy as "unfit for service" until he flew over both poles.
- Henry Ford barely made it through school, novelist F. Scott Fitzgerald flunked out of college, Isaac Newton was a poor student in grade school, and Michael Jordan was cut from his high-school basketball team.

Had enough? The list could go on and on. What does all this mean to us? It means we are in good company when we have a flop or produce a dud every now and then. It also means that mistakes, failures, and setbacks are not the end of the world. They certainly don't signify that we aren't capable of going on to accomplish great things.

Once failure comes your way, it's up to you how you handle it. Do you ever get down on yourself when you've failed? Maybe, like so many others, you tell yourself you're useless and you'll never amount to anything. For some of us, it's as though we carry around a big invisible baseball bat, poised and ready to give ourselves a few whacks over the head whenever we've fallen short. We say things like, "How could I be so stupid?"; "What a dummy I am! I can't believe I allowed that to happen"; or "I guess I'll never amount to anything anyway." What you say to yourself after a failure is critical. Failures, setbacks, and mistakes are a part of life. Instead of smacking yourself over the head with that bat and convincing yourself there's no hope, use this two-step strategy. Ask yourself,

1. What did I learn from this experience?
2. What will I do differently next time?

When you're tempted to put yourself down, choose instead to say, "Here's how I will handle the situation if it happens again, based on the lessons I've learned." Chances are you will be in a similar situation sometime down the road. Failure isn't a crime, but failure to learn from it is. By contemplating the answers to these questions, you are mentally setting yourself up for success when you encounter the same or similar setback again.

Whenever I organize a large event, speak on a new topic, or attempt anything for the first time, I now know how important it is to keep a "Next Time" file. In it, I record all the changes and improvements I might make. Someone asked, "Sue, isn't that like expecting to fail?" Instead, it's that I expect to learn new and better ways of handling similar circumstances. That way, when the next time comes around, I simply open my file and there outlined before me is my recipe for success!

Sometimes if we are not beating ourselves up, there is someone else in our life who will gladly take our invisible bat from us and give us a few whacks, accompanied by words such as, "I can't believe you allowed that salesperson to talk you into buying that," or "What were you thinking, parking the car there in the first place?" That is when we can hold our heads high and say to that person, "I can't go back and change a thing. If I could fix it, I would, but I can't. Here's what I've learned, and here is what I plan to do differently if there is a next time!" If you are dealing with someone irate, you may have to use the "broken record" technique. Just keep repeating the same phrase until the message gets across, being sure that both your voice tone and volume do not escalate. You can do a fine job beating yourself up over your failures, and you don't need someone else pitching in to help!

The "Oh, Well!" Strategy

When my children were young, they would get as flustered over misplacing a school library book, messing up in a piano recital, or not getting chosen for the volleyball team as I might get if I misplaced my flight tickets for my next vacation, got fired from my job, or had to have a limb removed. In their young minds, these concerns were genuine catastrophes. My way of being an encouragement was to advise them to say, "Oh, well!" and not to waste too much energy getting upset—

because this was probably not the worst thing that was ever going to happen to them. "Golly, Mom," they would say, "you're supposed to be a motivational speaker!" They obviously did not find comfort in my words of wisdom.

What I was suggesting was that they always do their best, go back and fix whatever mistakes could be corrected, and then say, "Oh, well!" to the rest, saving their energy for the "really big one," which could strike at any moment. I call it "positive procrastination"—putting off undue concern until it's absolutely essential. This assures that you never allow yourself to be distressed, because you are always holding off just in case it *really* becomes necessary.

The "Oh, well—this is not the worst thing to happen" theory has helped me through many otherwise horrendous and potentially demoralizing situations. "Oh, well—I broke the family heirloom vase and nothing's going to bring it back. After all, it's not the worst thing to happen." "Oh, well—someone ran into the brand-new Chrysler in a fender-bender this morning and now it has a huge dent. But it can be repaired. It could have been worse—and after all, no one was injured." "Oh, well—the cat just used the leg on the antique dining-room table as a scratching post, but worse things have happened."

Whether I've lost a $20 bill or been conned out of my life savings, this theory brings things back into perspective once I've done all I can to correct the situation. If I've dropped a bag of sugar all over the kitchen floor, my hubby is two hours late for the roast beef dinner I spent all afternoon preparing, there's a run in every pair of pantyhose I own and no time to shop for new ones before the meeting, the kids decide to float their Popsicle stick sailboats in the toilet, or a guest has just spilled grape juice on the white carpet, I can always think of worse things that have happened or could happen. It causes me to stop and think about what really matters in life. And it sure beats getting flustered over matters I cannot alter anyway. If I could go back and change it I would, but in most cases I can't. So, in the end, if I still have my health, my family is alive and well, and we have a roof over our heads, then life will go on and we will surely survive in spite of the calamity.

Our older daughter called one day sounding frantic and crying her heart out. When I answered the phone, all I heard was an unidentified person sobbing and obviously in a panic. I made sure to find out if she was all right and if everyone with her was okay. Then once she calmed down, I asked, "Who is this?" When I found out, our daughter explained that she had just managed to successfully put out a small kitchen fire after getting her three children out of the house and calling 9-1-1. Although she had managed to get through the ordeal in a composed manner, it was afterward that she broke down—a common reaction for many of us when confronting disaster. Then she confessed that the one disconcerting thought that kept coming to her mind through it all was that her mother would not be able to say, "Oh well, dear. Never mind, this is not the worst thing to ever happen." This time would have been "the big one"!

Something else you can do is use the "next time" method for all those little annoyances and petty irritations. *Next time*, I will buy kitty her own scratching post from the pet shop so she doesn't use the table. *Next time*, I will keep a heavy-duty carpet cleaner on hand, provide the kids with a tub of water for sailing their handmade boats, and have a good supply of extra pantyhose in the drawer. Rather than crying over spilled milk, stop hammering yourself over the head with that invisible bat and putting yourself down for making a mistake or having an accident. Then choose how you will handle similar situations in the future.

It's true that you can learn more from your failures than you will ever learn from your successes. You can see failure as your enemy and allow it to defeat you, or you can view it as your teacher. Face your future head on and with courage in spite of failures and setbacks. Most of all, accept God's divine protection for you. He wants you to be free from your fears. The choice is always yours.

Chapter 14

It's Okay to Be Assertive

*We teach others how to treat us
by what we will or will not tolerate.*
AUTHOR UNKNOWN

*Whoever has no rule over his own spirit
is like a city broken down, without walls.*
PROVERBS 25:28 NKJV

ASSERTIVENESS HASN'T COME NATURALLY TO ME. It's been a gradual process. I'm actually a recovering softy, otherwise known as an easy target. Ms. Pushover you might call me. It's so bad that I've been known to say I was sorry to an empty chair after bumping into it. When someone called and woke me up at 2 AM thinking I was Joe of Joe's Taxi Service (I blame my nighttime voice!), I apologized that I wasn't, then volunteered to get the phone book and look up the correct number. When I'm in merging traffic, I always let in other drivers and then wave and smile nicely at the ones who wouldn't think of doing the same for me. I've always been a telemarketer's dream come true—my chimney and carpets are now the cleanest in the neighbourhood. And I do my best to attend every fundraising circus that comes to town. After all, I wouldn't want the callers to say anything nasty about me when I hang up just because I didn't take advantage of their unbelievable offer or contribute to such a worthy cause!

It doesn't take much for me to feel guilty. I've been known to occasionally say "yes" to things I really didn't want to do. Not only would I feel guilty for not wanting to do the thing, but then I'd feel bad because the person asking would have to try to find someone else to do it. How could I cause havoc for so many people? Why...I'd suffer with guilt for days if I let them down like that.

I know I'm not alone. Guilt seems to be a natural condition for many women. I heard about a woman who is so proficient at assuming guilt for anything that goes wrong in the entire universe that when she got called for jury duty, they had to send her home. She kept insisting *she* was guilty!

A licensed counselor I know tells me that much of the guilt we suffer stems from the "disease to please." It's deeply rooted in insecurity and connected with the fear of other people's opinions. We would do well to remind ourselves that when we're worried about what others think of us that they're probably not thinking of us at all. Many of us grew up hearing our parents concern—"What will people think?" Someone once wisely stated, "I don't know all the keys to success, but one key to failure is to try to please everyone." All of this contributes to passive or aggressive behaviors, which are the opposite of assertiveness and cause a lot of unnecessary distress in our lives and relationships.

I remember years ago, early in my speaking career, spending several months trying to contact one of my seminar attendees, hoping to get her to like me. After reading the participant evaluations after one particular program, I had found that nearly all of the comments were positive. But the one that had stood out in my mind, of course, was from this woman, who said she had found my session bland and boring, and a total waste of her time and money. Besides that, she added that she felt my nail polish and pantyhose did not coordinate with the rest of my outfit!

While I could ignore the fashion observation (with a chuckle!), her words about the seminar hung like a heavy gray cloud over my head. I just couldn't shake the disturbing feeling. Truthfully, I was devastated. I wrote her letters, sent cards, left messages on her answering machine, offered to send her one of my autographed books as a gift, and gave her the opportunity to attend a different program free of charge. I was tempted to offer to buy her a new car and pay for a trip to the Caribbean. I think I remember actually inviting her to my house for a five-course home-cooked dinner. I just couldn't handle the thought that someone didn't think highly of me. As an up-and-coming speaker, I wanted desperately to make every attendee happy and have the whole audience like me. I never heard back from the disgruntled lady, and thankfully, after many sleepless nights, decided she wasn't the kind of person I needed to impress anyway.

What Is Assertiveness, Really?

In all of our insecurity, we fear rejection most of all. We've come to believe that if we act in a certain way, become all things to all people, always say "yes," and smile even when our heart is breaking, everyone will like us. Instead, the opposite is likely to happen. We open ourselves to becoming a doormat for others, giving them the opportunity to walk all over us and then, without warning, we either turn into "silent statuettes" or get a case of the "screaming meemies"—neither of which anyone can comprehend at the time it happens.

My personal motto had always been "peace at any cost." I took being a peacemaker seriously. What I didn't know was, while peacemaking is one of the most important skills we can develop, allowing others to always walk all over us is not what Christ had in mind when He taught the peacemaker principle. Peacemaking is not about running from conflict situations, pretending they don't exist or being afraid to confront the other party to discuss it. Jesus stood firm on certain issues and refused to back down in the face of evil resistance. Sadly, most of us have not been encouraged to stand our ground or given any instruction on how to resolve conflicts.

Conflict management does not mean appeasement, and peacemaking is not about avoiding controversy. At one time, I would go to any length in order to avoid a confrontation or an argument. On the flip side, being ignored or having someone turn away in the middle of a dispute was something else I wasn't able to tolerate. Because I couldn't stand to be on the receiving end of the "silent treatment," I was easy prey. Others knew I would cave in, so it became a weapon to get what they wanted. It took me a long time to learn that the best approach to the silent treatment was to assertively go about my business as though everything was normal.

If you notice others can make you feel guilty, chances are someone has used guilt to manipulate you in your past. Maybe some people in your life are still using it, as in: "Oh, go ahead and spend the evening with your girlfriends (sigh). I'll just sit here and have supper alone (sniffle). Don't worry—I'll manage somehow without you."

If you always passively agree to anything to avoid friction, it means your needs are probably not being met, and that's unhealthy. If you can't stand disapproval, you'll likely end up doing what someone else wants to stay in their good graces and not what you know is right for your own good. Maybe you say "yes" when you are being nagged just to silence the other person, when the best way to handle it is to announce that there will be no further discussion and then simply ignore the protests. Remember, the mighty oak is simply an acorn that held its ground!

If you have not been taught to be assertive, it can be difficult to begin to stand up and speak your mind. We try halfheartedly to get our point across without actually coming out and saying it. In spite of my God-given ability to be a communicator, I know I've been guilty of talking all around my feelings without stating the facts clearly, hoping the other person will get my vague message.

Sometimes women are known for belaboring irrelevant details that cause our mates' minds to wander. Even when we know a situation is getting to the crisis point, we mumble our way through, never making our case clear. The men in our lives want the bottom line, and they don't easily pick up on vague clues or backdoor approaches. It's important to be able to state the problem clearly, firmly, and assertively without attacking.

Assertiveness simply means being able to honestly and openly communicate your thoughts, feelings, opinions, wants, and needs in a direct and respectful manner. In other words, it's a way of speaking up to assure you will get what you sincerely need and want without resorting to being mean, cranky, confrontational, or antagonistic.

You have a right to stand up for yourself. God did not create you to be someone's doormat, to be walked all over and treated like dirt. Not only is it okay to be assertive, it's absolutely essential. Assertiveness is one of the most desirable behavior styles you can develop. If you place assertiveness on a continuum, it would be right in the middle, with passivity at one extreme end and aggressive behavior at the other.

<PASSIVE   ASSERTIVE   AGGRESSIVE>

When you are not acting assertively, your manner will be either passive or aggressive. Running from a problem, pretending it doesn't exist, or being afraid to talk about it is one opposite of assertiveness. Another is exploding into an emotional tirade to get your point made or your needs met. Sometimes, women stay in a passive mode for so long with no results that eventually they are left seething inside. Then without warning, they suddenly bypass "assertive" altogether and, for no reason apparent to the outside world, jump directly over to "aggressive." When that happens, the people we live or work with can't understand why this meek and normally compliant woman is suddenly on the warpath!

How many of our harmful past experiences happened because we responded in a non-assertive manner? Try to remember an event where you felt frightened or fragile, or a time when you were violated in any way, and ask yourself if practicing assertiveness might have made a difference. Make a decision to assert yourself in any future situations.

Assertive Behavior in Action

When you are not assertive, you will almost always feel like a victim of others' actions. Jennifer discovered this when her marriage dissolved and she moved back in with her parents. She attended one of my seminars for some inspiration, encouragement, and direction, and told me about some difficulties she was having. She was 31 years old with two children and a full-time corporate position, yet her parents began treating her like they did when she was a teenager. Because she did not know how to confront them assertively, she allowed the anger and frustration to build up until she felt ready to blow up.

I recommended she start by writing three letters to her parents explaining how she felt—the first one to get everything off her chest, and the second to revise what and how she wanted to tell them. These two were rough drafts only and not to be sent! The third letter, with all its edits and revisions, was the one she would actually give them. The idea was not to be angry and bitter, but to explain her feelings firmly and in the most sincere way possible. I suggested she start off on a positive note by letting them know how thankful she was for their support in welcoming her and the children into their home. She was truly grateful she could always count on her parents and they should know this. Then I recommended she go on and explain to them how she felt about some of the challenging areas. By being assertive, rather than passive or aggressive, she was allowing her parents to respond positively. It turned out that the rest of her time with them was pleasant and congenial.

In order to move beyond a past that is hurting your present, assertiveness is one of the most advantageous behaviors you can develop. When it comes to taking charge of your life, it means you won't be letting others determine what is right or wrong for you. Being assertive often marks the difference between being a victim and a victor.

But what comes to your mind when you hear the word "assertive"? For many, it conjures up images of a woman adamantly standing her ground, pushing to get her own way, and refusing to give an inch. Others think of a person who may be generally agreeable but unreasonably stubborn on certain issues.

Let's strip away our negative connotations and see what an assertive woman is really like. Most people do not understand that assertive behavior allows you to respect, honor, and be true to yourself without injuring or causing harm to others. It means being self-assured, confident, poised, and composed—enabling you to decisively handle difficult situations without going off the deep end. While there may be times when it's necessary and even appropriate to confront someone, assertiveness basically means being direct, honest, and respectful of others while having the ability to search out and attain all that you want and need to live with personal integrity. A genuinely assertive woman is one who is unwavering and determined to achieve her highest needs and goals while remaining calm, cool, and collected.

<PASSIVE	ASSERTIVE	AGGRESSIVE>

You can see the contrast between being assertive and being either passive or aggressive if you take another look at the continuum. My thesaurus tells me being passive means to be conforming, apathetic, unresponsive, and indifferent. Perhaps you know this woman. She takes great pleasure in knowing she is thought of as long-suffering, tolerant, and willing to accept almost any treatment by others. But being resigned to her lot in life is not bringing the joy she so desperately desires. On the other hand, you know the aggressive woman, too. She tends to be forceful, insistent, uncompromising, and rigid. She's often antagonistic and intimidating, always ready for a debate but won't be budged when it comes to her strong opinions.

Assertive women, however, confidently stand up for their rights, establish boundaries, and maintain limits while showing consideration for others. They earn respect and admiration without demanding it. In a conflict situation, they confront the behavior without attacking the person.

Scripting Your Assertive Answers Ahead of Time

It's a good idea to rehearse ahead of time a tentative script of some of the answers you can use to assert yourself. At one time, if Cliff wasn't interested when I wanted him to go to the ballet with me or take a romantic picnic to the lake, I would cry the blues and tell him if he really loved me, he'd go along. Now, I let him know that I have two tickets to the ballet or that the wicker picnic basket is packed, and I'd like him to join me. If not, that's okay, too. If I really want to go, I have friends or family I can ask to join me, or I can go alone—and I am prepared to do this. Nine times out of ten, when I put it this way, he'll come along! Even if he doesn't, I have other options and still get my needs met. Here are some other script ideas to get you started:

- When someone asks you a question you don't want to answer, smile and ask, "Why would you like to know?"

- When you are asked to donate your time or services and you know your schedule is already full, say, "Thanks for asking—but it's really not going to work for me at this time. Please try again in the future." Practice saying "no" without justifying yourself or giving reasons. (Usually our excuses don't sound good enough, so we start exaggerating to be more convincing. In other words, we lie. Don't allow yourself to be forced into that position.)

- When someone talks to you in a demeaning tone or inappropriate manner, say, "I don't appreciate being spoken to like that, and I won't continue the conversation until you can talk to me in a more dignified manner."

- If someone makes a belittling comment, say, "Ouch—that hurts!" You might add that it's tough enough to have healthy self-esteem and that their comment doesn't help. There may be times when you have to go further and say, "That sounds like a put-down. Is that how you meant it?" Then let the other person respond. Whether it's yes or no, either way, you'll know where you stand.

If you are being treated disrespectfully or are the victim of verbal abuse, here are four assertive steps you can take:

1. Name the behavior: *"You're yelling at me."*

2. Express your feelings: *"I don't like it."*

3. State the action you expect: *"I want you to stop it now."*

4. Identify how you'll handle it otherwise: *"I will leave until you can cool off."*

If the mistreatment continues after your assertive responses, use the "broken record" technique. Restate your answer over and over without escalating in your emotion, tone of voice, or body language. Remain calm—and after a number of repetitions, eventually your message will sink in. If not, carry out the actions you expressed.

What do you do when a person responds to your assertiveness in an aggressive manner with verbal hostility? For starters, refrain from answering with counteraggression. Then quietly and firmly declare that you will not respond to those hostile words and actions. When your assertiveness comes from a pure desire to show respect and courtesy, then you can firmly hold your ground. There is no need to apologize or back down. The same is true for those who look hurt and respond with pouting, crying, or expressions of self-pity or poor health. You may let those people know you "regret" they are upset while continuing to affirm your position.

At times, someone will be so shocked by positive assertiveness that they will deny what they said or that they meant it. They might even say, "Can't you take a joke?" In those cases, it is appropriate to apologize for your possible error while reasserting your original position.

There are cases when the other person is so sensitive or vulnerable that an assertive response only causes further agitation, adding to the problem. You never want to compound the hurt or intensify the confusion of someone who is already wounded. If your assertiveness devastates them, apologize and say, "I am sorry for the pain you are suffering. Perhaps I should have waited for a better time or put it in another way."

Genuine assertiveness is a divine virtue when it operates through the power of the Holy Spirit. It will always bring honor to God, His people, and His causes. When done in our own strength, it is usually felt and seen as aggression. With the right motives, true assertiveness will always tear down walls and build positive foundations for healthy relationships that will weather any storm.

When Push Comes to Shove—Literally

What is the role of assertiveness when it comes to domestic violence and how much abuse should a woman take? We know realistically the answer is "none," yet because of my personal experience and also through my volunteer involvement with various women's shelters, I am aware that millions of women each year are severely assaulted by their current or former mate and repeatedly return to the situation. In my own past, the times I spent in hospital emergency wards and family court confirmed that one of the leading sources of injury for women is domestic violence. Why do women passively yield to this abuse and choose to stay in these relationships? In many cases, they want to be good, faithful, devoted wives. They sincerely want to raise their children in a two-parent family. They are loyal, dedicated women who are devoted to assisting their spouses in getting help with their problems. But being committed to a relationship does not mean allowing yourself or your children to be victimized.

Nonassertive behavior is one of the reasons women tolerate physical and emotional cruelty and stay where they are being mistreated. Women who approach the situation with a passive nature want "peace at any cost" and are willing to overlook their spouse's appalling behavior. On the flip side, those who attack the problem from an aggressive stance may secretly blame themselves for igniting the violence with their own outrage, angry words, or irate actions after being provoked. With a non-assertive approach, whether passive or aggressive, we can fall into the trap of justifying the abuse and making allowances for it. Then we defend objectionable conduct and inappropriate actions, or blame ourselves while making excuses for another's malicious behavior. When we do that, we are actually encouraging continued violence.

If you or someone you know has fallen into this trap, listen for clues such as explaining away obvious warning signs. See if this sounds familiar: "You just don't understand him," or "He has a lot of pressure to deal with right now," or "If you knew what his growing up years were like, you'd realize why he acts the way he does now."

Another mistake is to make excuses based on future "potential." Here's what that sounds like: "Sure he's irritable and moody these days, but once we move into our new home, I'm sure he'll be fine," or "He doesn't have a job right now, but he's planning to start his own business and then he'll calm down," or "He's a talented musician, but he hasn't found work yet so naturally he's on edge under these conditions." Women don't see the signs because we choose not to look at these behaviors as flaws. That requires a certain level of denial. We don't deny that it's happening, instead we deny these are unfavorable attributes.

Many women who have come to me for guidance and direction have lived through this denial and have not confronted the problem. Instead, like I once did, they live in that gray area, wishing their troubled situations would improve and hoping the problem will eventually go away. They don't realize that the longer the inappropriate behavior is allowed to continue, the quicker it becomes a habit that is extremely tough to break.

Who's Pushing Your Hot Buttons?

Once you have begun to take a more assertive position, you will have to deal with some common victimizers who have the potential to keep you from maintaining your new, assertive stance. Here are some typical individuals, groups, social settings, and cultural elements that seem to make us particularly vulnerable to being victimized, and what to do when you find your hot buttons are being pushed.

Family. Your family can be an immensely rewarding part of your life or the cause of complete calamity. While the family unit is definitely to be respected as the cornerstone of our society, it can also be the source of our greatest insecurities, anxiety, frustration, irritation, and even hostility. Your non-victim stance will be most severely tested with your relatives, as they can be the least receptive to your new self-determination and independent outlook. They know you well, and many would like you to stay the way you have always been, whether or not that has been a healthy choice for you. Family members somehow tend to feel they "own" each other, and will often resort to using guilt to get others to fall into line. You may, at times, feel coerced into visiting relatives, intimidated into making phone calls, pressured into picking up after everyone else, chauffeuring people around, and generally being a martyr. When this happens, keep reminding yourself that you always have the option of doing those things out of a compassionate heart and a genuine desire to be helpful, or to say "no" when you feel pressured or if your schedule does not allow it. When you are ineffective at dealing with controlling, manipulative family members, they can pull you in so many directions that eventually they'll pull you apart. If you find you are allowing family members to put pressure on you or sway you in any way, it's up to you to take charge and determine what you will and won't tolerate. Teach your family how you want to be treated and eventually, over time, they'll respect you for your resolve.

Friends. Sometimes friends want you to stay where you are so they can feel comfortable remaining there too. In some circles, there is almost an unspoken law that no one moves forward unless everyone does. If someone in the group is not ready to progress or advance, this illogical thinking hinders the rest. Once you begin to move out of your victim stance into a more assertive position, it can cause others to recognize their own passivity. If they are not ready to move ahead at the same pace, their insecurities can be magnified in their own minds, causing them to try anything to hold you back, too. If you find yourself acting in ways that you believe are out of character for you, this may be a signal that friends are pushing your hot buttons and it is time to find some new ones.

Work. You may feel victimized by your job because of some powerful myths that are prevalent in the workplace. One absurd notion is that you must stay at your job no matter what and that you could never get another one if you were let go or chose to leave. It's no wonder we buy into this. As children, many of us were told repeatedly, *"You always start projects and never finish them."* We heard it so often when we were growing up that the mere thought of changing jobs, never mind careers, makes us feel immature and irresponsible, especially if we are the ones making the decision to leave. If you dislike yourself and your job for 50 years, the diploma or watch you receive on retirement will be no compensation.

As a young woman, I carefully worked my way through the ranks from sales representative to manager, then trainer, consultant, and eventually business owner. As I moved from job to job, well-meaning friends and associates often asked me, "What are you doing *now?*" The underlying question was, "Are you ever going to settle down?" I was even asked once, "When are you going to get a *real* job?" I guess they had a hard time adjusting to my new identity each time I changed companies or switched the products and services I offered. Had I not been so excited about the changes and sure of the fact that I was moving upward with each one, I might have let the old tapes in my mind rule, convincing me that I, too, "always start projects but never finish them!"

Coworkers can victimize you and often use criticism as their tool. Whenever you dare to step out of the crowd to attempt something new and different, you are automatically setting yourself up as a target for criticism. When you want to contribute more and go the extra mile, you may be labeled as someone who is trying to impress the boss. Giving in and backing off in these situations only opens more doors to victimization. Stand your ground and follow your heart.

Employers, supervisory personnel, and bosses can manipulate through intimidation, causing you to feel you have to give up your human rights and become mere chattel. Your job expectations can also be frustrated or deflated by the unsettling office politics that take place behind the scenes, certain company policies, or seemingly unreasonable institutional regulations. You may feel like a victim on the job because you feel pressured into compromising your values, morals, or ethical standards, or because long hours force you to be away from loved ones for extended periods. Being a workaholic or excessive loyalty to a job can cause you to forfeit family time and personal freedom. If you are feeling victimized at work, take a few moments out to ask yourself what is the cause and what you can do about working in a position that exploits you as a person.

Authority figures. You may find yourself unnerved, intimidated, or threatened by people with positions of authority or fancy titles. If you have exalted them so far above yourself that you cannot imagine them lowering themselves to notice or respect you, you will accept whatever they have to say without question. If a dentist suggests surgery, you will feel too embarrassed to seek a second opinion. If you are charged an exorbitant fee for any service, you will not feel you have the right to question the cost. When the restaurant host seats you facing the men's room, you won't feel comfortable asking for another table.

To avoid being victimized by authority figures, start to see that they are simply human beings with a job to do. As individuals, they must deal with their own insecurities, doubts, and life challenges. Their position or title does not mean they have more rights to fair treatment than you. Being overly impressed with people causes you to feel inferior and then you cannot deal with them on equal footing. I remember once being in a store and seeing a well-known artist, who happens to live in my area, shopping for groceries in the next aisle. I was awestruck and raced out to the car to tell my husband. He chuckled and told me that I obviously did not realize how many people he's overheard say the same thing when they see me in a store or restaurant! People in high positions may be performing tasks for which they have been highly trained to do but are no more important than you or me.

For years I have taught customer service workshops and seminars to professional organizations, companies, and businesses. One principle I have stressed over all others is that if anyone should be elevated in importance it is the person being served—the customer, the one paying for services rendered. Yet as a customer, you cannot expect to be regarded as important if you do not esteem yourself. If you can't see yourself as an equal, the best you can do is hope that others will treat you nicely, that you won't be overcharged, and that you won't be taken advantage of by some professional who won't discuss fees up front or does so in a condescending and belittling manner. Authority figures and those with positions and titles will respect you if you command that respect, while treating them with consideration and politeness in exchange for their professionalism.

Institutions and the people hired to serve you. If you've ever received threatening letters about an invoice that's already been paid, tried to correct an error on your phone or electric bill, or attempted to get through endless forms, voice mail options, departments, and red tape, you know what it's like to be victimized by organizations and their employees who don't seem to care one way or another. In fact, sometimes it seems as though these people were intentionally hired just to get your goat!

The first rule is to never let yourself get angry. Whenever possible, simplify your dealings with these agencies. Remind yourself that these people are not in positions of power, even though they may act the role. Their job is to enforce the organization's policies, rules, and regulations, and they normally do not have the authority to make changes on your behalf even if they wanted to. The very nature of the role they were hired to fulfill is to keep you from violating policies that cost their company time, money, or effort.

So, unless you enjoy being victimized, avoid dealing with them at all costs. Of course, always be respectful of people in those positions. Maybe you are one of them! It's what I did for a living for quite some time, and I always appreciated the customers that practiced the Golden Rule—to treat others the way you would like to be treated. But when it's time to see results and get what you feel you deserve, whether it's from a government agency, your landlord, the school your child attends, the local library, a department store, or an insurance company, avoid the front desk or clerical staff and seek out the person who is in a position to truly be of service to you.

The bottom line is that the one who victimizes you the most is... YOU! Yes, *you*. In spite of all the people, situations, and categories you can be victimized by, you are ultimately the one who decides whether you will be upset, hurt, depressed, irritated, worried, angry, fearful, or guilty about anything.

You have the right to...

- take control of your life
- make your own choices

- be what you want to be
- have your own opinion
- make your own decisions
- go against the status quo
- stand up for what you believe
- establish boundaries for what you will and will not allow
- express yourself and your opinions, beliefs, and view-points
- live by your chosen values, ethics, and moral standards
- be happy!
- say "no"

Let go of the belief that choices you made years ago are still binding. Remember the fib we looked at in chapter 2—"You made your bed, so now you must lie in it"? You do not need to be stuck in your teenage decisions anymore now that you're no longer a teen. If you aren't happy with yourself, your life, or your work, you have the wonderful option of making some changes. Whatever has happened until today is now over. Stop checking with what you've done in the past to determine what you can or cannot do in the present. Start seeing yourself as assertive, composed, self-assured, and confident. Begin acting the part and soon others will treat you accordingly.

Dear God,

Thank You for the calm, comfort, and refreshment You offer when I take one day at a time. I pray that I will always stay in the moment regardless of what I have had to overcome in the past or what I face in the future. Please help me to see that my problems are really pearls in disguise, and to know that those precious gems will be revealed when I allow the principles of Your truth and love to flow over me and saturate my life. I thank You that You never forsake me or leave me to face my difficulties alone. You were there even when I didn't know You, and now You draw closer to me as I draw closer to You. Please keep me flexible and adaptable so that I can bounce back from adversity. Help me to place the burden of my emotional complexities onto Your shoulders and be so filled with Your inner peace and joy that I spill serenity to everyone I meet. Thank You that You have given me a sound mind so that I will not be tormented by confusion but will greet each new day with clarity. I trust You for the courage I need to handle whatever the future holds. Thank You for revealing to me that I can be a peacemaker without being a doormat and that You never meant for others to walk all over me. Most of all, help me to appreciate each new day and to live my life in the moment. I offer up today into Your hands and ask You for divine direction for tomorrow.

In Jesus' name, Amen.

Part Three
Rebuild Your Future

Look not mournfully into the Past. It comes not back again. Then, wisely improve the Present. It is thine. Now go forth to meet the shadowy Future without fear.
HENRY WADSWORTH LONGFELLOW

Eye hath not seen, nor ear heard, neither have entered into the heart of man, the things which God hath prepared for them that love him.
1 CORINTHIANS 2:9 KJV

Where the Spirit of the Lord is, there is liberty.
2 CORINTHIANS 3:17 KJV

To rebuild...

Synonyms:
Start again, remake, transform, recreate, reconstruct, remodel, overhaul, refashion, alter, fine-tune, streamline, reconstruct, revamp, improve, develop, expand

Antonyms:
Tear down, demolish, destroy, deteriorate, degenerate, collapse, shut down, wipe out, dismantle, take apart

Chapter 15

Tomorrow

*So don't be anxious about tomorrow. God will take care
of your tomorrow too. Live one day at a time.*
MATTHEW 6:34 TLB

*Be strong.
It matters not how deep entrenched the wrong,
How hard the battle goes, the day how long.
Faint not, fight on! Tomorrow comes the song.*
MALTBIE D. BABCOCK

YOUR TOMORROW IS ON THE HORIZON, dear friend. It is brimming
with potential and possibilities. It overflows with opportunities and an
abundance of what is yet to come. Here you are—standing on the
threshold of a brand new beginning, looking ahead to the future. But
what holds you back from living a new tomorrow that is radically different from your past or your present? One thing, more than anything
else, robs us from taking the next step and having positive expectations
for a joyous future. That one stumbling block and biggest joy-robber is
worry. The future will come whether or not you worry about it. The

only difference is that you will have missed out on the pleasure and delight of it with all of your agonizing.

Misusing Your Imagination

Worry is born out of fear. In fact, worry could be called "the fear of what might happen." It can also be labeled "expected pain." Anytime you anticipate the worst, your imagination goes into overdrive. When you worry, your thoughts, energy, and expectations are focused on failure instead of success, poverty rather than wealth, lack instead of abundance, sickness versus health, and problems not solutions. When we choose to focus on what might go wrong, we are not trusting in God for answers. You can *"let him have all your worries and cares, for he is always thinking about you and watching everything that concerns you"* (2 Peter 5:7 TLB).

Besides, what you focus and dwell on is often what you get. Life has a strange way of giving you what you expect. As Job said, *"The thing which I greatly feared is come upon me"* (Job 3:25 KJV). Without realizing it, we can develop a "poverty mentality" and go through life expecting the worst.

One year, my grandparents gave us a wonderful gift at Christmastime—a side of beef for our freezer. Since those were lean years, and we had been suffering "malnutrition of the bank account," we sure appreciated the comfort and reassurance it brought us knowing we had a supply of tasty meals readily available. I made big pots of homemade beef and vegetable soup and kettles of beef stew with dumplings. We enjoyed many meals of meatloaf, liver with onions, and meatballs with spaghetti. But I went to the freezer one day and began to cry when I discovered all we had left were the more expensive cuts—prime rib, T-bone steaks, and sirloin roasts.

With my constant worry about the future, I had developed a "poverty mentality" which caused me to think we didn't deserve the best cuts even though we had a bountiful supply! How many times does God provide us with the finest "cuts of life" while we, with our scarcity thinking, continue to live in a "soup bone" world?

When you choose to worry, you end up living in the nerve-racking world of "what if." That's when you're always on edge and thinking, "Just suppose this or that happens—then what will I do?" In the days when I used to be a true worrywart (one of my mom's favorite expressions!), I'd be almost sick if Cliff were a little late coming home for dinner. In my mind, I'd have him dead and buried before he even had a chance to get home safe and sound. I was convinced he was lying in a ditch somewhere. So, I'd mentally live through the funeral, say my last goodbyes, and thank everyone for being there to comfort me. Then I would change out of my black dress and try to decide whether I should sell the house and move to a condo by the lake—or hire a gardener and a maintenance man so I could stay in our country home.

Soon, though, I would start to miss him terribly and long to see him just one last time. I'd promise myself that if I ever saw him alive again, I'd hug him, kiss him, and tell him every day from now until eternity how wonderful he is. Then, I'd never let him out of my sight again and care for him tenderly all the days of my life. At that moment, in the middle of my worry exercise, he'd walk in the door and I would shock myself by launching an all-out attack, shrieking, "Where have you been? How could you put me through this? I can't believe how inconsiderate you are!" and a few other choice things that I'm certain made him really glad he came home to me.

It took me years to learn that, chances are, he was probably coming back sooner or later, and that it wasn't worth putting myself—or him—through all that torture each time he wasn't home exactly when he said he'd be. Besides, even if something tragic happened, it would be beyond my control, and all my worrying wouldn't change the outcome.

A Diseased Habit

Worry is a potent emotion and a dreadful disease with the power to cripple us. It spreads through our lives, much like the infamous Blob of horror-movie fame, until it covers every part of us, draining our joy, depleting our energy, and sapping our strength. Worry has been known to cause everything from headaches and upset stomachs to conditions of dread and terror that emotionally paralyze people and keep them bound to their homes for years.

The Greek word for worry is *merimnao,* which is a combination of two words—*merizo,* meaning *to divide,* and *nous,* which means *mind.* To worry is to divide the mind. Once your mind is divided, your faith is destroyed by your fear about what might happen. It is impossible to trust that God is working everything to our good when we are in this condition.

There is no end to the things we can find to worry about. We worry over inconsequential things like what the salesclerk will think about the run in our pantyhose when we're trying on new shoes, or which outfit to wear to the job interview. We also worry about more significant things like what will our kids have to cope with when they go off to school, will we have enough money to pay the bills this month, and how will we manage to care for our aging parents plus raise teenagers at the same time. We also worry about things beyond our control—other people's attitudes, behaviors, and choices; adverse weather conditions; earthquakes; high prices; wars; and everything we hear on the news. But one of the biggest joy-robbers is worrying about tomorrow. What scares most of us is the future, and more than anything, the unknown.

In our culture today, worry and anxiety seem to be accepted as the price we must pay for running the "human race." On the one hand, we are subtly given the message that being troubled and concerned over tomorrow is the norm. After all, considering everything we must deal with, it should be expected that we lose sleep and spend our nights and days agonizing over matters beyond our control. Apprehension, dread, and fretfulness about what the future holds have become a standard way of life for many.

On the other hand, we are bombarded with stress relievers and natural remedies in the form of relaxation techniques, massage therapy, deep-breathing methods, various herbs, meditation practices, physical exercise, and diet approaches. Helpful solutions and suggestions are everywhere—magazine and newspaper articles, television programs, self-help books, and the Internet. In spite of all these beneficial strategies designed to ease the strain of worry's side effects, we can still be suddenly overcome by our worries, like a giant wave that engulfs us without warning. We can know in our heads what to do, but until we have faith and believe in our hearts that there is Someone bigger than us who loves us and is still in control, there is that space in between that provides the richest breeding ground for anxiety.

Worry is like a seed and our minds are like the lush, fertile soil. One of God's universal principles is that whatever you plant, you will also reap. When you allow the tiniest kernel of worry to fall and take root, it grows and develops until it is a habit. Then worry becomes part of your daily thought patterns and you get accustomed to it. Worry feels so oddly familiar and comfortable to us that we may not even be aware we are caught in its trap. When worry has become our everyday manner of thinking, it can also be our comfort zone. Chronic and toxic worriers gather their concerns together until they are surrounded by them, almost as though they feel unsafe without them. I am convinced that if some of us chose not to worry, the freedom we'd have would be so foreign that we wouldn't know what else to think about!

Sometimes, as women, we feel we are born into the role of worrier. It seems to be our natural calling. It's what we do and we do it well. Like a badge of honor, we wear it proudly! In our minds, we believe worry can somehow boost our image because the more we worry, the more it appears we are caring and concerned people. We might feel as though we come across as sensitive and compassionate when we worry about others. There is a difference between living in a condition of anxiety and fretfulness, and expressing true caring and compassion to others. God calls us to *"Stoop down and reach out to those who are oppressed.*

Share their burdens and so complete Christ's law" (Galatians 6:2 MSG)—but He never calls us to worry.

One woman, after hearing me speak about this topic, was sincere when she said to me, "If I don't worry about the things going on in my home and everyone in my family, who will?" She was obviously uncomfortable with the suggestion that she didn't have to worry about anything. I thought she seemed almost fearful that this would put her out of a job! As we chatted, I could see she saw worry as her calling in life, and it made her feel needed. This unfamiliar concept of not having to worry threatened to take away that sense of purpose. Instead of choosing to increase her faith and trust God with these matters, she opted to defend her self-destructive pattern of caring for her family through worry.

Imagine what your tomorrows would be like if you were free from the crippling effects of worry. What would be different if you refused to allow anxiety to kill your joy, your peace, and your faith? Worry may even be killing your health. How many times have you heard someone say they were "worried sick"? Maybe you've even said you were "worried to death" about something. The medical profession backs up this truth by quoting alarming statistics concerning the number of stress-related illnesses, some of them leading to death, and most stemming from the harmful patterns of worry.

How to Stop Worrying

Can we truly be free from the worries that cause so much destruction in our minds and bodies? The answer is yes! We do have a choice. Start by recognizing that worry is the most useless emotion you can experience. If you worry about something that might happen and it never does, your life energy is being drained right out of you for no reason. If you worry about something and it does happen, you obviously haven't changed a thing by worrying. Since those are your only two options, worry is never beneficial. Someone said worrying is like trying to go somewhere in a rocking chair. It takes a lot of energy and you don't get anywhere.

1. Say "no" to worry. Making a conscious choice not to fret is a key step in overcoming the tendency to be a worrier. That may seem simple but it's not that easy to do. Many of us have become so accustomed to carrying the burden of responsibility for our own and others' happiness, well-being, safety, and security that it is difficult to relinquish controlling thoughts, and to transfer the ultimate responsibility to the One who is really in control. *"Give your burdens to the Lord. He will carry them"* (Psalm 55:22 TLB). When troubling thoughts start to invade our minds, we need to choose to let them go. We must plainly refuse to worry and cast all our care upon our Source of security because He cares for us. Worry and trust cannot coexist. One will always win out over the other. Which one will you nurture? The prophet Isaiah writes that God

> *will keep in perfect peace all those who trust in him, whose thoughts turn often to the Lord!* (Isaiah 26:3 TLB).

2. Refuse to give fuel to your worry. Watch what you allow to permeate your mind and imagination. Filling your mind with the perversions of talk shows and gossip magazines and dwelling on the horrific things you hear or read about in the evening news only fuels anxiety and concern. While I believe in being up to date and current with some knowledge of what is happening in our world, I also believe it's a good idea to go on a strict "current-events diet." Determine how much unsettling information you really need to know and how often you want to dwell on it. We have a guideline in our home that we do not read the newspaper or listen to the news just before going to bed. When you sleep, your conscious mind shuts off, but the subconscious plays over and over what you programmed into your mind before falling asleep.

When I found out about this, I thought, *It's no wonder we sometimes wake up more exhausted than when we went to bed.* First thing in the morning is not a good idea either. Filling your mind with negative thoughts and images isn't the best way to start the day. The middle of the day isn't the greatest either. In fact, I am not sure when it's the best time to update your current events. Maybe more of us should be like my friend who says, "If it's really important and you absolutely have to know, I'm sure someone will tell you!" At the very least, you be the judge and determine how much of that information you need on a daily basis.

3. Bring things back into perspective. When we worry, we tend to get tunnel vision. That means we only see what it is upsetting us, and we block out the many blessings all around. When you find yourself worrying, take time to step back and notice the big picture. Like an artist who is working up close to her canvas and has to stop every now and then to move back in order to see the entire painting, so must we look at our life as a whole to regain our focus. Perspective is a real key in combating worry.

Even bad news can sound like good news if it is seen from a certain vantage point. Your perspective is always a choice. One powerful way to see things in proper perspective when you are tempted to worry is to ask yourself, *What will this mean to me in one year? In five years? In the light of all eternity, is it worth losing sleep, damaging relationships, and making myself ill?* Without the proper perspective, the situation can be exaggerated and blown out of proportion.

4. Use a journal to identify and write out your current worries. One woman claimed she would run out of room and there wouldn't be enough paper for her long list. If this sounds like you, begin by grouping your worries into categories including family, health, home, finances, friends, church, and community, and so on. Then break those categories down into more specific segments. When you use this journaling technique and see your worries on paper, they become tangible and concrete, which makes them easier to deal with.

5. If necessary, book a worry appointment with yourself. If you cannot seem to shake the worry habit, try setting aside a certain day and time to worry. Then when you are tempted to worry in between, you can remind yourself that there is no worrying allowed until your appointment. When the time comes, find a comfortable spot where you can sit still and be quiet. Then, you will either have a good old time of worrying or you might find that you're not in the mood after all! If you do go ahead with the exercise, allow yourself to think about all the things you were concerned over and get all your worrying done at once. Write each one out on a piece of paper and lift it up to God in faith. Then destroy your notes and *"let not your heart be troubled"* (John 14:1 KJV). If you are not in the mood to worry, promise yourself you'll put it off until your next scheduled worry appointment.

6. Talk things over with someone you trust. Women have a deep, intrinsic need to talk out what is going on inside their heads. Whether you share your concerns with a caring friend or a trained professional, simply expressing to another person what it is that disturbs you can be beneficial. There's a danger in staying isolated and becoming a passive victim. Many times when I have been going over a problem with a good listener, before I knew it, the solution became very clear. When you decide to discuss the things that worry you with someone else, it's not because you believe they have the answer. The solution is not "out there" but rather deep within you, for *"the Spirit in you is far stronger than anything in the world"* (1 John 4:4 MSG). But by brainstorming with someone else and talking things out, you'll be able to see the problem from a different angle, gain a fresh perspective, and be open to discovering a new approach.

7. Stop worrying and start praying. One woman said, "Even God would worry if He watched the evening news!" Would He really? God already knows the beginning from the end, and He tells us not to worry, but rather to pray:

> *Don't worry about anything; instead, pray about everything...If you do this, you will experience God's peace,*

which is far more wonderful than the human mind can understand (Philippians 4:6-7 NLT).

Each time you are tempted to worry, meditate instead on God and His goodness. Study His Holy Word and keep turning your thoughts back to Him and His faithfulness.

One of the greatest sources of human misery is worrying about what might happen tomorrow. I think of the women on their way to Jesus' tomb on Easter morning. They probably missed the beauty of the morning sun and the glory of the flowers along the way because they were worrying about who would roll away the stone. Then, when they got there, they discovered it had already been rolled away. All that worrying for nothing. Does that sound familiar? Make a simple decision not to worry anymore.

Chapter 16

Where, Oh Where, Has My Self-Esteem Gone?

No one can make me feel inferior without my permission.
ELEANOR ROOSEVELT

Love your neighbor as yourself.
MARK 12:31

SALLY RAN HOME FROM SCHOOL, EAGER TO tell her parents about the mark she got on the math exam. Hers was the second-highest in the class and she was excited. Because Sally had been struggling in this subject, her mom and dad were thrilled, too. Later on, when Sally's friend came over to visit, the proud parents mentioned their daughter's exciting news. Her friend thought for a moment and then replied, "I suppose that's true, since everybody else got perfect!" Well, little Sally had a choice to make that day. She could either see herself as having the worst mark in the class or the second-highest grade. Did Sally make the right choice? Sure she did! You and I have to make choices like that nearly every day.

Have you been allowing others to determine your value or letting outside circumstances rob you of your sense of worth? The truth is…you always get to decide how you will view yourself. No one else can do that unless you allow it. That's what Eleanor Roosevelt meant when she said that no one could make her feel inferior without her permission. When I speak with my seminar attendees, I am astounded by the incredible number of women who have bought into a poor image of themselves based on the comments of others—parents, siblings, friends, teachers, instructors, or coaches. Worse yet, they believe the demeaning things they've told themselves.

Letting God Determine Your Self-Esteem

God wants you to know you are His beloved daughter, and that your life—past, present, and future—is not a mistake. Be encouraged that your heavenly Father accepts you just as you are today—hangups, quirks, habits, burdens, and all. He is not disappointed in you, even if you or others are. He wants you to recognize your incredible value. God has uniquely gifted you with ability and talent, and you have tremendous worth in His sight.

Countless sincere and devout women mistakenly believe that having confidence, feeling good about themselves, and appreciating their own worth is being vain, self-centered, and egotistical. Some even believe that having low self-esteem and continually putting themselves down are symbols of true humility. Along the way, we've been fed the lie that a healthy self-esteem just isn't right for godly women.

This all changes when we realize that to esteem something simply means we appreciate its value, hold it in high regard, and look upon it with respect and admiration. If that is true, how can we go on putting down one of God's most magnificent creations of all? A healthy self-esteem doesn't say, "Notice me. Aren't I fantastic?" It does say, "Because I am God's child, I am valuable and worthy of leading a meaningful and influential life."

Recognition of your own significance and inherent abilities means you have an unconditional acceptance of yourself and belief in your God-given potential just the way you are—learning, growing, changing, and developing. You cannot begin to work on your shortcomings until you accept yourself fully despite them. Self-esteem is not about being arrogant, proud, or conceited. On the contrary, a healthy self-worth is one of the most important ways we can give honor to our Creator. It is also a vital key to attaining excellence in our marriages, family relations, friendships, church fellowship, ministry contribution, community involvement, career advancement, and business associations.

When our core desire, first and foremost, is to be pleasing to God, we can mistakenly interpret His command, *"Do not think of yourself more highly than you ought"* (Romans 12:3). We can take it as meaning, "Other people matter more than you, so don't have any faith in your own abilities or belief in yourself or your talents." We often believe that particular verse is a command to think that other people are more gifted and deserve a rich, full life even though we don't. Instead, it seems to be telling us to be honest in our estimation of our personal value and not be overinflated. Our main interest in having a high regard for ourselves is not to meet our own needs but to have a closer relationship with God and others, and to glorify Him with our lives. That's difficult to do when our self-image needs a makeover.

Most of us would have no difficulty standing in awe of nature, whether it's the majesty of a mighty waterfall, the remarkable pattern on a butterfly's wings, the splendor of a rainbow, or the brilliant colors of autumn leaves. Yet what do we think of ourselves, the most amazing creation of all? Sometimes, not much. We need to tune in and listen to the things we silently say about ourselves. We can be most unkind when we are referring to God's magnificent work of art. I wonder what He thinks when we tear ourselves apart any time we fail, make a mistake, have a setback, or look in the mirror.

If there is a secret to leaving your past behind and building a future with confidence, it's to realize that you are an extraordinary human being. You don't have to strive to be a worthy person. You already are because you are made in God's image. You are a competent, bright, and talented woman. There is no one else exactly like you, and there never will be. You are a limited edition, one-of-a-kind, and only you can accomplish what you were designed to do.

This does not imply that your value comes from what you do. You are a human *being*, not a human *doing*. Yet God has uniquely gifted you to contribute your abilities with your own special flair, to go out and make a difference in this world, whether you are involved in a career, working as a stay-at-home mom, devoted to full-time ministry, operating your own business, caring for foster children in your home, cleaning up after incontinent elderly patients, helping illiterate adults to read, teaching emotionally disturbed children, nursing AIDS patients, or offering support to others in countless capacities. You were designed to carry out a worthy mission.

The one thing that can keep you from fulfilling your calling is believing you don't have personal worth. The biggest hindrance to accomplishing your destiny is that deep down inside you do not feel you deserve a satisfying and rewarding life, one of vibrant health and energy, a loving spouse, meaningful relationships, a nice home, comfort and security, a fulfilling purpose, or a rewarding job. With low self-esteem, you won't feel worthy of flourishing and living in prosperity. But Jesus said, *"My purpose is to give life in all its fullness"* (John 10:10 TLB). He came to give us an abundant life—bountiful, overflowing, and more than adequate!

Understanding Low Self-Esteem

Why is it that some very capable and talented women find the doors of personal acceptance, relationship success, and career opportunities continually closed to them, while others with apparently equal or even less potential seem to have unlimited opportunities for success in every area of their lives? It just doesn't seem fair. Of course, we know that God's timing is perfect and He is always working in us what needs to be completed to prepare us for what He has in store. Knowing this can bring peace and the assurance we need to wait on the Lord for His blessings. But, there can be another reason for the struggle—a woman's self-perception. With a poor self-image, doubts about our value and what we are worthy of achieving will seep into everything we do. Others who sense our insecurity may be uncomfortable and unsure how to deal with it, and start avoiding us. This in turn will affect how we relate to our spouse, family members, and coworkers. Then because we expect to be rejected, it's exactly what will happen.

Unfortunately, your self-esteem is often based on the image you have of yourself rather than what God's Word says about you. Your self-image is a picture you carry in your mind's eye that reflects what you believe you are capable of, worthy of, and deserving to receive in this life. Without a proper understanding of what God has to say about who you are, the way you view yourself can negatively influence everything else—how well you deal with stress, make decisions, handle change, manage relationships, and care for yourself and others.

Many women who work at having a healthy, balanced view of themselves still find it extremely difficult. Running away from their own poor self-concept, some throw themselves into their work and service to others in an attempt to conquer it. They might think they have forgotten self in favor of giving of their time and talents, and concentrating on the needs of others; however, this often results in futile efforts, feelings of emptiness, and eventually total exhaustion.

Here's a little test you can try. If someone looks at everything you're able to accomplish and says, "I don't know how you do it all," then you need to ask yourself not only *how* you do it but *why* you do it. It may be that you find it too difficult to say no, or you may find it necessary to fill your life with "esteem-building" activities when your sense of personal worth is lagging. Sometimes by taking on too much we are actually inviting abuse. In a sense, we are sending the message, "I'll be the doormat. Go ahead. Walk all over me and take advantage of my need to serve…that's all I am worth."

Our inner longing for healthy self-esteem can send us down countless dead-end pathways—searching for acclaim in frenzied volunteer work or seeking attention with the best casseroles, highly elaborate desserts, and the most elegant dinner parties. We long for approval with our beautifully decorated homes and meticulously landscaped yards, or look for compliments with the latest fashion find we picked up at a sale. We'll even try manipulating our children toward perfection in their own lives to boost our sense of worth and prove our value to outsiders.

Add to that the subtle whisper of the world, prompting, "Try this... then you'll feel good about yourself," or "Buy that and the lonely ache in your heart will be quenched." When we hear that voice calling, we must recognize that none of these endeavors will fill the gaping hole at the center of our hearts. Instead, with all our striving, the hole only gets bigger. Our poor self-image, which is the opposite of pride and just as harmful, tears us apart and opens the door to other deadly sins: anger, envy, jealousy, lust, greed, and gluttony. We are unhappy because, rather than giving God center stage in our lives, we have substituted something else. It's only when we come back to Him that we are fulfilled and our need for approval, applause, admiration, and appreciation drops away.

As a speaker, I had to come to the realization that my worth and value are not determined by my audiences' evaluations, comments, applause, and ratings, or whether they laughed at my jokes or gave me standing ovations. I am valuable because God says so. The psalmist David wrote,

> *How precious it is, Lord, to realize that you are thinking about me constantly! I can't even count how many times a day your thoughts turn towards me. And when I waken in the morning, you are still thinking of me!* (Psalm 139:17-18 TLB).

The Problem with Having a Lopsided Self-Concept

When we miss the truth about God's perfect love for us, we have an unbalanced self-image and one of two things can take place. Either we feel unsure of our God-given talents, gifts, and abilities, and end up underachieving when it comes to carrying out God's will in our lives, or in our search for true significance, we attempt to overachieve and work to the point of exhaustion with activities and tasks that do not have lasting or eternal value. We keep trying to please others and God, but always feel as though we are falling short.

God is a loving Father who wants you to love yourself. When Jesus taught, *"Love your neighbor as yourself"* (Mark 12:31), the word used for love is the Greek *agape,* which is an active term. It refers to a love that protects, nourishes, cherishes, and wants the best for another. *Agape* love of self means unconditional acceptance and always seeking the very best for ourselves and others.

Loving and caring for ourselves is such an innate part of our nature that we even see it practiced by some mentally and emotionally unbalanced people who participate in self-destructive behaviors. To them, this is an attempt to protect themselves from feelings that are even more painful, those feelings associated with certain traumatic incidents or prolonged life situations they have experienced. Abuse victims often have a tendency to suffer from eating disorders such as anorexia, bulimia, or obesity, as well as some serious addictions. Subconsciously, they are saying to those who have abused them, *You may have battered my body, you might have abused me sexually, verbally, or emotionally, but you can't control what I eat. So I will either eat or drink myself into oblivion, or starve myself to death.* Their eating disorder or other addiction is simply a reaction, a subconscious attempt to control something in their lives, even if it is just their weight or their habits.

If you have an eating disorder, an addiction, or any other symptoms of unusual behavior, you must recognize they most often come from the emotional scars of some form of abuse. The first step in freeing yourself from these scars in your life is to open up and look at your life with honest eyes, ready to see the truth and face the memories so you can allow God to help you deal with the pain little by little.

How Is Our Self-Esteem Formed?

The way you regard yourself today as an adult is a choice and not dependent on somebody else's opinion. In fact, what others think of you is really none of your business. It's what God thinks of you that matters. But over the years, many factors have played a role in determining how you see yourself. Let's take a look at some of the most common ones.

1. What others told you. Many of us grew up thinking that we were unacceptable and not valued in our parents' eyes. In school, if we were teased, bullied, or had difficulties with certain subjects, our feelings of unworthiness multiplied. If we grew up believing we were the awkward child, the unattractive one, the student with a low IQ, or the sibling with no talent, as adults we continue to believe those lies. Being labeled in certain ways by a family member or a peer takes its toll and carries over into our adult life. Labels like "clumsy," "chubby," "four-eyes," "loser," "slob," or "stupid" imprint themselves on our mind and emotions and come back to haunt us even when we are grown adults achieving our own levels of success. Then, when things suddenly don't go as we'd like, we tell ourselves, *Perhaps my mother was right after all, and I'm never going to amount to anything,* or *Because I'm not very good-looking, maybe my husband will leave me for another woman.* We need to go back and ask, "Who was it that said I had no talent or that I was ugly or fat or would never find a man who would love me?"

Perhaps this way of thinking may explain the "impostor syndrome" that holds so many women back. Even though they have achieved a certain degree of success and are fulfilling their life's mission by making valuable contributions to their families and this world, they never get to experience the victory because they feel like impostors. They think to themselves, *I must have been in the right place at the right time when I was given this opportunity or promoted to this level. Someone thinks I have what it takes...and I hope they never find out that I don't!* Feeling like a phony robs you of the joy of your accomplishments.

During your childhood years, your self-esteem was formed almost entirely by your family. You depended on them to affirm your worth and abilities. You were told what to do and what not to do, and may have been bombarded with negative messages or constantly reminded of your mistakes, failures, and shortcomings. Because your faults were emphasized, they became magnified in your mind, and now you wear them like labels. See if you heard some of these messages growing up:

> *"You're just like your father, and look what a failure he is."*
> *"With grades like that, you'll never amount to anything."*
> *"You're such a slob. Just look at your room."*
> *"Why can't you play quietly like your sister?"*
> *"You're so gabby. Do you have to talk so much?"*
> *"You only think about yourself."*
> *"Being born into this family means you are doomed to a life of poverty."*
> *"Just be satisfied with what you have."*
> *"You don't have the brains to go to college."*
> *"How could you believe such gibberish? No one else does."*

Whenever we can tie together our feelings from the past—both positive and negative—with where we are today, it allows us to better understand why we view ourselves and our world as we do.

2. What you told yourself. Often, we don't even realize we are carrying on a conversation with ourselves all day long, but on a subconscious level, that's just what we are doing. Try listening to the words you use when you speak to yourself. I have heard some people say some pretty nasty things to describe themselves. For example, "I'm not the brightest crayon in the package," or "Guess I'm one sandwich short of a picnic." While it's good to be able to see the humorous side of yourself once in a while and not take yourself too seriously, reinforcing these things on a regular basis will have a definite impact, and not the kind you want.

Here are some of the other ways we program ourselves with negative self-talk. Do any of these statements sound familiar?

> *"What a dummy I am!"*
> *"How could I be such a klutz?"*
> *"I'm not very creative."*

"Why even try?"
"I have no talent."
"I'm a born loser."
"I am so stupid."
"I always make a fool of myself."

Rather than spending a lot of time trying to erase these self-limiting beliefs and programs, what we can do instead is reprogram new beliefs over the old ones. Think of your mind as a computer. God has given us the most fantastic bio-computer on the face of this earth! It follows instructions and you're in charge of what you tell yourself. Start programming in the instructions that will produce the results you want to see happen in your life.

If you have been abused—mentally, emotionally, sexually, or physically—your self-talk may be even more critical, judgmental, and damaging. You must know that you are an innocent victim and stop the judgmental, personal put-downs. You may be thinking, *Oh, but Sue— you don't know what I have gone through or what I have done.* You may have told yourself, *I deserved the abuse I received.* No matter what you've done, whether you said or did something you believe led to the abuse, you still did not deserve to be abused. You were a victim. Abuse is a hostile action and violation against you. It can be one of the biggest contributors to your negative self-talk.

3. Messages you receive through stereotypical images, our culture, and the media. Through our culture and the media, we are bombarded with messages that try to convince us that all women act in certain ways—they are lousy drivers, poor at math, love to shop, and always gossip. We are also fed messages that all women should be alike when it comes to our physical image. When I interviewed women while writing this book, I found that one thing affects a woman's self-esteem more than anything else, and that is the beauty illusion.

When it comes to our physical image, I have good and bad news. The bad news is that there is nothing we can do that will truly make us more eternally beautiful. The good news is that we are already amazingly beautiful because God created us that way. Beauty cannot be given to us by anyone. There is no shopping mall or makeover program in the world that has what it takes to improve on our genuine beauty.

Instead, this exquisite loveliness is a radiance that shines from deep within us as we grow in our relationship with a loving God. You've probably known women you may not describe as physically beautiful, but who so powerfully exude genuine love, compassion, kindness, empathy, and joy that the result is the image of a beautiful woman. We've also known women who are next to physical perfection to the outward eye but have no light shining from within. Until they invite Christ into their lives, they will go on relying on all the outer beauty tricks of the trade.

When I was newly in love with the Lord, I was working in a cosmetic salon. I remember customers wanting to purchase the exact shades of makeup I was wearing because they said it made my skin glow and my eyes shimmer and sparkle. But when I gave them samples to try, they were almost always disappointed because the products didn't have the same affect. It took a while before I caught on and realized that what they were noticing on my face was the inner glory of God. I still find it amazing that His wondrous love can shine through and show up on the outside! The Bible says,

> *If you are filled with light within, with no dark corners, then your face will be radiant too, as though a floodlight is beamed upon you* (Luke 11:36 TLB).

When we are overflowing with God's love, the glory of His image gets imprinted upon us and the resulting radiance is visible to the world!

Our authentic feminine beauty is not the result of clothing or cosmetics or hair products, although we have been convinced by advertisers that it is, so we spend billions of dollars each year on these products. Besides, we are programmed through the media's subliminal messages that we could not possibly be truly desirable to our husbands or content as women unless we are able to arrive at the current standards of physical beauty. It isn't until we become aware of our true inner-spiritual glory that we will be set free from fretting over a wrinkle here or a blemish there. When we do, a gray hair or two, or a few extra pounds won't seem like such a big deal.

What to Do When Your Self-Image Needs a Makeover

1. Focus on your positives, not the negatives. If I were to ask you to make a list of your positive traits and inner qualities, you may have trouble coming up with a few. However, if you were to start jotting down your faults on a blank sheet of paper, and if you're like most women, you'd probably run out of room. We are all too familiar with our flaws, imperfections, weaknesses, and shortcomings but don't spend a lot of time thinking about our strengths, virtues, and assets. Choose to make a list of positive attributes and read it now and then. If you're stuck, ask a good friend to help out. Here's the secret: God thinks you are a treasure, and the more you see yourself through His eyes, the less you will need the approval of others!

Change doesn't come overnight when long-held thinking patterns have to be broken, but by the power of God you can be free to hear God's truth about your positive qualities.

2. Quit pointing out your flaws. You'll be amazed that when you stop drawing attention to the qualities you dislike, others won't notice them either. On the other hand, if you keep telling me about a feature you're not happy with, guess what I'll see more than anything? Most people are not as aware of your defects as you are. They are not looking at your teeth, but your smile. They don't notice your fingernails as much as they feel the warmth of your handshake. To take your mind off your own inadequacies, concentrate on making others feel more at ease.

At a very large conference where I was nervous about being the first speaker of the day, I had spent a lot of extra time in prayer for my audience and the message I would deliver. A woman arrived at the last minute and was visibly perturbed. She had been stuck in traffic, and when she finally made it, there was no place to park nearby so she had to walk 15 minutes in the freezing rain. By the time she got to my "Stress Survival" presentation, she was stressed to the max. I intuitively took her hands in mine to warm them, and I literally felt her calm down. That encouraged me as I went on stage to deliver the opening keynote. Afterward, she told me that when I touched her hands, she miraculously felt all tension drain from her body. She was able to enjoy my session and the rest of the conference. Sometimes we may never know the effect we can have on others once we quit concentrating on our own limitations.

3. Lighten up! One of the biggest self-esteem lessons I've had to learn is to quit taking myself so seriously. At a different speaking engagement, the woman who hired me was glancing in my direction when I overheard her say, "Can't you just shoot her before she starts?" I was startled and nearly fell off my high heels before I realized she was talking to some photographers from a national newspaper. Apparently they wanted to sit in the front row to take my picture during the entire presentation and she wasn't crazy about the idea. At my very next engagement, the audio team was having problems with the sound equipment. I went to the back of the room—as if I could make a difference—and as I was returning to the platform, I heard one of the technicians holler, "We found the problem. There's a screw loose in the speaker." I'd like to think he was referring to the sound system.

I'm finding that in this business and in life, you can't take yourself too seriously. We all have to have a good laugh at ourselves now and then. Besides, if you haven't laughed at yourself lately, someone else probably has. A woman I hired to help promote my course "Maximize Your Time & Energy" had to learn this, too. She sent out hundreds of flyers before she noticed a typo. Instead of saying, "7 Ways to Tackle Your 'To-Do' List," it read "Do-Do" list. I think it was worse because it came right after the line about clearing away paper clutter: "How to shrink your piles without using Preparation H."

I could be really embarrassed about each one of these incidents, but I'm learning that angels fly because they take themselves lightly. Have you ever had an embarrassing moment? How about one that wasn't funny at the time but now you can laugh about it when you tell your friends? It usually requires a bit of time between the humiliating experience and when it eventually becomes funny. Why not shorten the gap and start laughing right away? We normally say, "I was so embarrassed I could have died." We put embarrassment and death on the same level! When we take ourselves too seriously, we lose our ability to acknowledge our human frailty. Laughing at yourself is a way of saying, "I'm not okay and you're not okay, but that's okay." As believers we can always add, "God loves me anyway."

The Power of Your Self-Concept

Low self-esteem and a negative self-image can be the biggest reasons you become a victim in life. The way you see yourself determines how well you manage your relationships, respond to other people, deal with stress, make decisions, and handle changes. What you believe to be true about yourself becomes your reality and the basis of your reactions to situations. While no one can pretend the past didn't happen, it's possible to pray that all the negative effects are removed. You are not destined to live with them forever.

Ask God to break the bonds of self-loathing and pray you will be molded into His image. With a healthy self-esteem, you'll recognize your true worth and act accordingly. God wants you to know how valuable you are. Jesus asks,

> Are not five sparrows sold for two pennies? Yet, not one of them is forgotten by God. Indeed, the very hairs of your head are all numbered. Don't be afraid; you are worth more than many sparrows (Luke 12:6-7).

Discover your true worth just as you are. Remember, God isn't finished with you yet.

Chapter 17

God Is Talking—
Are You Listening?

*Enlightenment is the moment of truth,
the sudden emergence of new insight in an act of intuition.*
ARTHUR KOESTLER

*If any of you lacks wisdom, he should ask God who gives
generously to all without finding fault, and it will be given to him.*
JAMES 1:5

HAVE YOU EVER FELT THAT THE CREATOR of the universe was trying to get your attention? Sometimes I refer to these times as "aha" moments. They come as red flashing lights alerting us to something significant we need to be aware of or as signals warning us to change direction. We can choose to heed them or ignore them, but these insights are genuine and always trying to keep us from harm. How comforting it is to know you can trust God when He says, *"I will instruct you and teach you in the way you should go; I will counsel you and watch over you"* (Psalm 32:8).

Over the years, I've discovered when these insights come, the best thing I can do is pay attention. For example, at my seminars and book signings, I can't begin to tell you the number of women I've met and talked with who told me they had the distinct gut feeling they shouldn't marry a certain person, but went ahead anyway because calling it off seemed to be more difficult than going ahead. Besides, walking away at that point would be a humiliation to them and their family. Some convinced themselves that it was probably only pre-wedding jitters and tried to ignore it. When my dad whispered to me on my first wedding day that it wasn't too late to change my mind, he knew I was making a mistake. Because of that inner nudging, I knew it too, although I wasn't sure if it was simply the wrong timing or the wrong person. The "red light" came as a warning, advising me to rethink my actions, but I chose to ignore it.

Then again, years later, as I sat in family court, heavenly wisdom spoke to me once again, and this time I listened. Through continuous promptings, I began to consider making changes in my situation. There were subtle clues and unremitting nudges to take practical steps, such as apply for my own personal credit cards, open savings and checking accounts, make duplicates of car keys, house keys, and identification papers, and start to stockpile household items I would eventually need in order to set up housekeeping in a new home. I started to talk with my former husband about the possibility of a trial separation in order to get some help and sort out our problems. My heart's desire was always to restore the relationship, and I knew I had to trust God for that, too.

Someone to Listen To

Although I may not be completely capable of running my own life, I can trust the One who is. To be honest with you, most of us are not very good at managing our lives, but we can read the owner's manual— His holy Word—and listen for His voice. When left to our own devices, we can make decisions that are not always the best, do things we later regret, and say things we wish we could take back. Before making a move, it's always best for us to ask for divine counsel, heavenly wisdom, and God's directives. Then,

> *When you walk, they will guide you; when you sleep they will watch over you; when you awake they will speak to you* (Proverbs 6:22).

If you've had the experience of waking up in the morning with a miraculous solution to a problem or a brilliant idea, you know the benefit of listening to your heart. You've probably found it helpful to keep a pen and paper handy to capture those insights. Well, that same experience can continue all day long when you develop the habit of asking for divine guidance, expecting to hear from God and listening to His voice.

Although I teach this and believe it, I still have days when I revert to ignoring that small, still voice and doing things my way. I am almost embarrassed to tell you this story, but I am convinced God has a sense of humor and you can go ahead and laugh, too. Besides, it makes a good point.

When I was speaking at a national women's event held in the Bahamas, I was the only speaker to address a group of business and professional women for the entire conference, with a number of topics I speak on. The organizers who hired me were also excited because their conference was the first to be held in a luxurious hotel after it had been totally refurbished. What a posh place it was—so of course I dressed the part, including three-inch stiletto heels to match my cherry-red suit. One thing I do when I wear high heels, especially if I am speaking for the whole day, is slip them off right after my introductory remarks and discreetly slide into a pair of comfy flat shoes I've hidden under the podium ahead of time. Then when it's time to break for lunch, and again at the end of the day, I put my stylish shoes back on. (I know, it is so vain—but those red pumps look so stunning with my suit!)

Well, this particular day, as I went to change my shoes for lunch,

God said, *Leave your flat shoes on.* Have you ever argued with God? I said, "Lord, I love those heels. They match my outfit and I paid a lot of money for them. I *really* want to wear them." Again, I heard God say, *Don't change your shoes.* I continued to whine, "But Father, those high heels are so striking, and besides, I can't think of one logical reason not to change." There's a major key. God's voice should always win out over logic.

Well, I quickly convinced myself I hadn't really heard anything, and decided to wear the heels to lunch. As I was making my way out of the ballroom where we'd had our morning session into the dining room, there was a small step just outside the door. It was carpeted in a beautiful gold plaid to match the rest of the rug, creating the visual illusion that there was no step. Without warning, the toe of my shoe went forward onto the floor while my heel caught the edge of the step, and down I went. I had been chatting with two women—one on either side of me—and this left them staring at each other, wondering where the speaker went. As I lay on the floor, I thought the same thing everyone does when they trip: *I wonder if anyone saw me?* Well, 500 women saw me! After someone helped me up, the manager was called and also a nurse who packed ice around my swollen knee while I tried to eat my lunch. That afternoon, I delivered the rest of my presentation perched on a stool on the stage. My message that day was titled, "With Wings, There Are No Barriers," and I jokingly asked my audience if anyone noticed me trying to *fly* to the dining room. I went on to confess the argument I'd had with God and we all had a good laugh, especially because the point I had been making before the lunch break was about the importance of listening to our still small voice within!

Unfortunately, that's not the end of the story. As I got ready to leave at the end of the day, I packed my notes, slides, flat shoes, and props into my briefcase and prepared to head off to a resort where I was staying for a few days. As I made my way to the elevator, I thought I heard God say, *Go back and check the podium.* Again I argued, "But Lord, I've remembered to pack everything. Really, I have." Just then, a lady came running toward me holding a pair of reading glasses—and of course, they were mine. Am I a slow learner, or what? I am so grateful our God is patient.

God's Voice in Creative Problem-Solving

Vera's boss called to say that the CEO of their company would be coming to her location for a routine inspection and he wanted her help in getting the place in ship-shape order. His biggest concern was the storage room where they stashed everything that didn't have a home of its own. Vera knew what a mess it was and that it would take a miracle to make a difference in the short time before the men arrived. So she said a silent prayer, believing God would provide a solution.

A few minutes later, as the CEO and her boss made their way down the corridor toward the storeroom, they noticed the door was shut. When they got up to it, they saw a small sign that read, "WOMEN." Now that's what I call creative problem-solving. As Albert Einstein put it, "When the solution is simple, know that God is answering." Sometimes I wonder if we work much harder than we really have to!

The Power of Calling Out for Help

Answers are there, solutions are within reach, and protection is available. Help is closer than you could ever imagine. The most astonishing reality I am aware of is that we have a divine guardian continuously looking after us, healing us, comforting us, and teaching us. It is the Spirit of God who is always ready to care for us, hold us, and protect us in warm, tender, invisible hands. What will bring His help when we need it? The answer is simple: asking. According to Scripture, *"You have not because you ask not"* (James 4:2 NKJV). When you need heavenly guidance, call out believing you will be heard.

I am convinced there are times when we are divinely led into circumstances that appear to have no solution—until we cry out for help.

One thing that builds our faith is to be in the midst of a problem where, if God doesn't answer, there is no way out. Those are the times when God says to us,

> *Call unto me, and I will answer thee, and show you great and mighty things, which you do not know* (Jeremiah 33:3 KJV).

Your heart's cry may be for help in a moment of serious danger, provision in a time of deep need, or clear direction in a period of confusion, turmoil, and indecision. It might be a call for freedom from emotional baggage that has weighed you down long enough, or for the desperate needs of someone close to you. In any case, God is waiting for you to call on Him to provide a solution.

Even when you forget to ask or don't know how to pray or what to request, there's a small, still voice that is always speaking deep in your heart. It's the incredible intuitive part of you that goes beyond logical intelligence, sensible reasoning, and analytical thinking. It's the perceptive part that remains unrestricted by your doubts, inhibitions, fears, and limited thinking. It is always providing direction and guidance, solutions to seemingly unsolvable problems, and answers where there seem to be none. Because what God wants more than anything is to have a personal relationship with you, He is always speaking to you in the form of hunches, impulses, and urges. I call them "holy nudgings" or "divine promptings." It's when you *just know* you should do something in a particular way or head in a certain direction. One true value of this inner knowing is that it allows us to gain perception, understanding, and compassion concerning our past and then use it to make insightful decisions about the future.

Learning to Trust Your Feminine Intuition

Over the years, after having thousands of women share with me their personal stories of surviving devastating circumstances and overcoming horrific situations through incredible insights they have received, I have come to confirm and support the validity of a woman's intuition. While some women can look back and recognize that they've become victims by not heeding their inner voice, many others told of how they were able to avoid being victimized by trusting their intuition.

It's time that women recognize we've been blessed with this gift, whether we call it intuition, a gut reaction, or our sixth sense. Intuition is actually a kind of inner wisdom, a discerning sense our Creator has endowed us with, so we can maneuver safely through the twists and turns of life on this earth. It's our inner knowing, the part of us that serves as an internal guidance system, allowing us to perceive outside the range of our usual five senses.

Intuition is one of the most powerful and trustworthy sources of authentic knowledge and probably most underused resources available to us. It enables us to tune into potential problems in a most remarkable and unique way. We are actually able to make "feeling" judgments based on this miraculous inner knowing.

Sometimes women say we get an idea "out of the blue," or we have a notion to change direction that appears to come suddenly from nowhere. Ideas flick through our mind that at first seem quite illogical, impractical, and unrelated to any of our past experiences. Subtle insights come into our senses, minds, and bodies that have no relationship to fact or rational reasoning. Usually the men in our life don't understand it, or they take it lightly and tend to refer to it as "feminine radar." They see it as emotional, unreasonable, or at the very best, inexplicable. When I use intuition to explain to my hubby a choice I've made or some concern I can't seem to let go of, he is likely to roll his eyes and write it off. He much prefers logic and reasoning. He wants the tried, true, and tested—something that can be backed up and supported by facts, figures, and data. For the most part, men have a hard time believing we could be correct in our analysis of a situation or estimation of a person without a shred of logical evidence. They want us to prove our opinions and feelings with spreadsheets, grids, flow charts, bar graphs, and laser pointers.

Lana and Joe have operated their own business for a number of years. Occasionally Joe would proceed with a business deal that Lana didn't feel right about because he had statistics and other data to back up his decision while she could only offer her suspicions. One time, a particular job candidate was applying for the position of general manager, and although this man had the education, background, experience, and qualifications Joe was looking for, Lana had a creepy feeling. "I wouldn't trust him," she told Joe immediately. When he questioned her about this impulsive evaluation, she said, "I can't explain it, but I just don't feel right about hiring him." Based on his extensive personal analysis, Joe disregarded her comment and hired him anyway. Sadly, within a few months, this man had embezzled funds from the company, stolen thousands of dollars worth of equipment, and left the country. These days, although Joe still doesn't comprehend it, experience has proven Lana right so often that, when she has misgivings, he now pays attention.

Women get intuitive feelings about people and events. Once we are tuned in, we instinctively know when to avoid a situation for our own safety. Deanna was training to be a fitness counselor at a well-known center and one of the recommended courses was a class that introduced a particular type of stretching exercise. She thought it would be interesting to see what it was all about and talked her teenage sister, Evelyn, into signing up with her to attend a few sessions. As the group was practicing the new technique, Deanna noticed the male instructor staring inappropriately at some of the younger participants in the class, including Evelyn. The girls stayed until the end of the class, but later on, the more Deanna thought about the situation, the more uneasy she felt. She shared her fears with her sister who accepted Deanna's misgivings and they both decided not to return to the class. Some time later, they found out that the instructor had been let go from his position for immoral misconduct. Who knows what might have happened, but by quitting the course, they eliminated any possibility of wrongdoing.

Decision-Making Beyond Logic

Just as Eve was deceived into thinking she would become wise by eating the fruit, so am I often misled into wrong choices because they appear to be good. Logically they make sense, but if I allow analytical thinking and reasoning to override my deepest, innermost impulses, I am usually proven wrong. I am learning to trust these God-given intuitive gut feelings more and more.

Paying attention to my intuition was a hard lesson for me to learn both personally and professionally. In my personal life, I chose to disregard that inner wariness, cautioning me before I walked down the aisle as a teenage bride. The result was that I lived for many years as a battered wife before gaining the strength to move away from a life destined for domestic violence. Although I am grateful for the person I have become as a result of the trials and tragedies I endured, I have also discovered how crucial it is to respect this inner voice of wisdom.

In my business and ministry, I have discovered the importance of listening to that inner guidance, too. Something happened a number of years ago in my speaking profession that left me wailing, "If only I had trusted my instincts." A woman I will call Jill came to our area and introduced herself to me as an international promoter of speakers and authors. She told me she had been following my career path, she was impressed with the passion I had for the work I was doing, and wanted to contribute to my mission to help women. Because she told me she had experience working with other professional speakers internationally and knew that I wanted to make my business grow into a worldwide organization, I was excited about what we could accomplish together. When she described her vision of taking my programs to various cities across the continent, it was so much like my own vision that this seemed like a good partnership. It seemed too good to be true. (My father always told me that if something *seems* too good to be true, it usually is!)

Jill and I had many meetings where we spent time getting to know each other and discussing a strategic plan of action for our dream of bringing women together so they could be encouraged and inspired to transform their lives. Meeting by meeting, she was winning me over with her expertise and background, the professional and media contacts she had within her network, and her impressive client list. The whole thing made sense logically, even though something didn't feel quite right. All the while I had a nagging feeling deep inside me, warning me not to go ahead with this venture. It was like a red light flashing, a signal alerting me to be cautious. Because I wanted so much to see this dream materialize, I chose to ignore my gut instincts. I also wondered if it was fear of the unknown holding me back.

Not wanting to be governed by fear, I gave her the go-ahead. The plan was to book several hotel conference rooms across the country and hire a graphic image consultant to start designing promotional materials. One evening Jill called to say she would need cash up front for down payments on the hotels and deposits on advertising materials. She asked me to write her a check for the funds she would need which amounted to thousands of dollars. Foolishly, I went ahead—and the instant I handed her the check, I had such a sick feeling that I knew I had done the wrong thing.

Well, the bottom line is, she took my money and left! By the time I tracked her down again, she was beautifully tanned from being on an island vacation (something I could not afford to do at the time). Jill told me our events had to be cancelled because of low registration and we had lost the down payments she had supposedly made. I found out later this was not true; she had done the same thing to several other career women in our area. At least a dozen business people wanted to start a costly and time-consuming class action suit against her. I chose not to get involved with that, but here's what I did do.

When I was through beating myself up with my invisible baseball bat and calling myself a dummy and lots of other things I won't mention here, I picked myself up off the floor and asked myself, *What did I learn?* and *What would I do differently next time?* Instead of berating myself continually over the next few years for being such an idiot or wailing about the fact that I had lost all that money, I had to tell myself that it's over and done, and I cannot go back to change it. What a waste of time and energy it would be to dwell on something that is now out of my control. It's in the past and I can't fix it. If I could I would, but I can't.

On the plus side, I have learned to trust my instincts. Everything in my life began to improve once I discovered the truth that I can make choices based not on what seems to make sense or what others think best, but on God's voice and the gift of inner wisdom. The next time I am in a similar situation, I will ask God for direction and listen to my hunches and gut feelings rather than trusting only logic or going with an all-consuming desire to fulfill my personal dreams and plans. I've learned to pray and ask for supernatural guidance in all life and business decisions.

Next time I will not only take the matter to God in prayer, but will talk over the situation with a prayer partner, a trusted friend, or a trained professional. The Bible says,

> *Where no counsel is, people fall: but in the multitude of counselors, there is safety* (Proverbs 11:14 KJV).

Next time I'll do my homework and find out more about the person I'm dealing with by doing background checks, asking for referrals, and following up to confirm my findings. There will always be times when people will try to take advantage of us and situations that won't go as we planned. But in the future, we can be equipped and prepared as to how we will respond.

You Always Know What's Best for You

Another time we run into trouble is when we are tempted to look outside ourselves when we need a solution, as though the answer is "out there" somewhere. We tend to believe that someone else will be able to guide and direct us better than we could do ourselves, whether it's a family member, close friend, business coach, personal trainer, health professional, marriage counselor, personal therapist, or financial advisor. While it may be a good idea to seek the help of professionals on occasion to gather information, gain a fresh perspective, benefit from their expertise, or devise an action plan, the final decisions must be ours.

Here's a news flash for you. You can always know better than anyone else what is right for you. When it comes to making significant life choices and major decisions, develop the habit of asking God in prayer, and then listening and trusting the insights you receive.

Sometimes when God talks we are tempted to chalk it up to coincidence. It might seem like a fluke or a twist of fate, but there are no coincidences. We can receive clear direction from the Holy Spirit through a number of sources—a book we just "happen" to pick up and open to a certain page, a TV show or radio program we tune into "by chance" at exactly the right spot, a nugget of wisdom within a sermon or seminar, or a perceptive suggestion from an insightful friend. Divine guidance may emerge as a whim to attempt something new or go in an entirely different direction with a project. Intuition is an internal guidance system that serves as our own inner compass, and is one of the most underused resources available to us. God's nudgings are trustworthy sources of wisdom because He always has our best interest at heart. This is actually the language through which God can miraculously get our attention and speak to us.

However they come to you, train your heart to listen to these insights. Tune into God's voice by adjusting your spiritual antenna. As author Julia Cameron encouraged us, "Become willing to see the hand of God and accept it as a friend's offer to help you with what you are doing."

Hearing from God in the Midst of Danger

Unfortunately, there is no checklist outlining what to do when you find yourself in a dangerous or potentially hazardous situation, but divine insights can guide you. Because each woman's circumstances are unique, there are no cookie-cutter approaches. For example, some experts say if you are being attacked to always resist, while others tell you never to fight back. When you find yourself in an abusive relationship, some would say to leave immediately, while others may recommend, for your own safety, to plan ahead and be cautious about how and when you walk out. While some would recommend separation and perhaps even divorce, others would suggest to never give up on anybody because miracles happen every day.

None of these strategies is right for every situation, but there is one approach that is: Listen for the voice of God. You are unique and so is your situation. He will guide you through your special circumstances in a way that's just right for you. No one can tell you what is best for you in any heartbreaking or dangerous situation, but you can always know better than anyone what's right for you. No matter what your need, and regardless of your current situation, you can listen closely, *"and thine ears shall hear a word behind thee, saying, This is the way, walk ye in it, when ye turn to the right hand and when ye turn to the left"* (Isaiah 30:21 KJV).

Heavenly wisdom and the gifts of awareness and discernment are available to you. Take them seriously. Not only will they warn you of impending danger, but they let you enjoy the serendipitous events that take you by surprise and fill your life with joy.

To hear the voice of God, you must take a leap of faith. Trust your intuition. Listen to your conscience. Go within and seek the wisdom and guidance God has planted deep within you. Ask for insights, expect to receive them, and believe they are true. Then, remember to act on them. When it comes time to make changes and decisions about your future, listen to your heart…the right way is built in.

Chapter 18

Be Still, My Heart

Prayer begins by talking to God, but it ends in listening to Him.
BISHOP FULTON J. SHEEN

In quietness and confidence is your strength.
ISAIAH 30:15 TLB

IMAGINE THAT I'VE ASKED YOU TO MEET me for coffee because I need to talk with a caring friend about some things that are troubling me. Then as soon as I finish pouring out my heart, I get up, say "thanks," and leave before you have a chance to respond. That's the way it is sometimes when we pray. Too often we hastily present our troubles and concerns to Him, say "Amen," and then go on about our day, never taking the time to listen to what He has to say. Then we wonder, *Where is God when I need Him?*

God is always speaking directly to us. He does it in many ways— through His Word, our daily experiences, other people, nature, our circumstances, our conscience, our thoughts, and our gut feelings. But His voice is often drowned out in the noise and confusion all around us. Even during our quiet times of prayer, we tend to do all the talking. "Listening prayer" is one way to clearly hear His voice.

If you feel you've never heard from God, it could be that you haven't actually taken the time to listen. That's not surprising. Women today are so busy. We spend our lives running on the treadmill of life and we begin to feel that any time spent in quiet reflection or fervent contemplation is "wasted time" because we could be accomplishing so much more through activity. In a world that encourages women to multitask to the nth degree, it's understandable that we find it hard to sit still and quietly listen for God's voice of divine wisdom. I have been known to run through the house foaming at the mouth because I've thought of five things that needed to be done right in the middle of brushing my teeth.

Our culture seems to promote "busyness" as an acceptable lifestyle. An article I read recently suggested I double up on chores by cleaning the grout with an old toothbrush while I'm in the shower waiting for my hair conditioner to work. It went on to say I could maximize my time by investing in a waterproof cassette player to listen to motivational tapes while I shower. One night when I couldn't sleep, I watched a TV infomercial for an electric hair styling brush that twirled on its own (I'm not kidding!), and this would be good because, after all, who has time anymore to brush her hair 100 strokes like our moms suggested. Now, I'm thinking if we no longer have time for personal grooming, this might be an indication that we need to re-examine our priorities. With our hectic lives, it is becoming increasingly difficult to *find* quiet time, so maybe we need to *make* time.

Creating Stillness

Just as children can benefit from having an occasional "time out," you and I need to have some special periods of refreshing. Retreating every now and then is one way we can create the stillness we need in order to hear God's answers we so desperately long for. Leaving the past behind to move on to a wholesome and productive future requires that you make some pretty significant decisions and major life changes, and for these you'll need powerful insights to guide you. God longs to speak to you and have you hear Him. He tells us, *"those who search for me shall surely find me"* (Proverbs 8:17 TLB).

To get started, take a moment to find a spot where you will be free from distractions. Sit quietly and choose to consciously empty your mind of the day's concerns and the other hullabaloo that goes on inside your head. Next, take a journal and write out your thoughts and concerns, letting God know you are sincerely and openly looking into your past to come up with the reasons you feel and react as you do now. Then, begin to calmly listen. Your goal is to free your mind so God can talk to you and reveal whatever obstacles are holding you back from fulfilling your purpose. With pen and paper handy, you'll be amazed at the way God speaks to you. Begin to record your thoughts, jotting them down as He reveals them.

Have you heard this revised version of a well-known phrase: "Don't just do something—sit there"? Normally, instead of sitting quietly, silencing our minds, and listening to our heart when we have a problem to solve, a decision to make, or a project to complete, we think in terms of taking action and doing more. In today's culture, it is easy to become obsessed with busyness and productivity. We think finding an answer requires extra effort and more work when simply being still can be much more fruitful in the end. Jesus knew the benefit of getting away from the hustle and bustle of everyday life to sit quietly in the presence of the Father. He is calling us to do the same:

> *Are you tired? Worn out? Burned out on religion? Come to me. Get away with me and you'll recover your life. I'll show you how to take a real rest. Walk with me and work with me—watch how I do it. Learn the unforced rhythms of grace. I won't lay anything heavy or ill-fitting on you. Keep*

company with me and you'll learn to live freely and lightly (Matthew 11:29 MSG).

Continuous activity seems to come naturally to women, whereas spending a few moments in quiet stillness feels somehow strangely unfamiliar. Unless we make the effort, very few of us have even five or ten minutes of total, complete quiet time during an average day. We wake up to the alarm clock, listen to the kids' squabbling while we shower, or the radio blaring as we dress. We hear traffic noises, conversations, pagers, beepers, phones ringing all day, and the television once we get home again at night. But how often have you moaned, "I just need a little peace and quiet?" That just might be the Holy Spirit letting you know He can't get through to you unless you have hushed the clamor that goes on around you and inside your head. You need to get into the habit of finding nuggets of silence and solitude throughout your day. Turn off the radio when you are driving. Get out into nature alone during your lunch break. Get up a few minutes ahead of everyone else or stay up a little later at the end of the day. The key is to get away from it all, even temporarily. A few minutes may be all you need, so don't put it off waiting for "leftover" time.

Finding Creativity

If you've ever wracked your brain trying to remember someone's name or the title of a book or movie, you know that the more you focus on it, the more it eludes you. It's not until you finally get away from routines and let it all go that it comes to you. It's when you are not striving and focusing on the issue that your mind is free to hear the answer. The same is true for any problem or need you have. When you are most stressed out and need divine guidance, retreat to your cocoon. Take a nature break, have a nap, go for a stroll, or enjoy a drive in the country alone and you'll be surprised at how quickly God will speak to you. That's when solutions begin to emerge.

When I am writing and need to be inspired, I can count on certain nurturing routines to prime the pump and get ideas flowing. For example, any water experience ignites new ideas so swiftly that I have to keep a journal and pen, or a hand-held tape recorder with me. Some of my most creative ideas have come to me while soaking in a warm bubble bath, standing in a steamy shower, hearing waves slap against the shore while lying on a beach, or listening to rain on the roof of my screened sun porch.

Getting entirely away from familiar surroundings also inspires me. I have done more innovative writing in hotel rooms because I am in a new environment. There I've been still and quiet long enough to ask for inspiration and had the silence and solitude I needed to listen for answers. Whether I am taking a leisurely drive in the country or cruising down the highway with the convertible top down, being alone in my car has the same effect. Listening to gospel, classical, or inspiring instrumental music, looking through old photograph albums filled with pictures of favorite people and happy times, flipping through a gardening magazine, doing a crossword or jigsaw puzzle, or relaxing in a rocking chair near a blazing fire wrapped in my favorite quilt handmade by my mom are other ways I have found to kindle new thoughts. Experiment and find out what works for you.

Missing Out on Nurture

Time out to nurture ourselves is such a crucial ingredient when we want to pay attention to our intuition, listen to our conscience, or hear insightful messages, yet so many of us feel guilty about investing the time, effort, or money required. However, it's when we take the time to do those things that we stay in touch with our inner knowing. They allow us to listen to the very voice of God, gently making every effort to get our attention and offer guidance and new direction.

Beth is a woman who is missing out on God's best for her life because she's never developed the habit of nurturing herself. I met this 39-year-old wife and mother of two teenage sons when she attended one of my seminars. She was tall, slim, noticeably fit, and looked stunning in a fashionably coordinated pantsuit with a paisley scarf and classic pearl jewelry. She could pass for being much younger than she really is, except maybe for the tiny lines around her mouth and eyes—laugh lines she jokingly says aren't funny anymore. The truth is she feels there isn't anything about her life that is funny these days. Right now she is experiencing an agonizing struggle between following her heart or doing what she knows intuitively is right. Beth is considering leaving her marriage of 19 years to start a relationship with a young man she's only known for a few months. This vibrant 24-year-old fellow has captivated her with his electrifying personality and the thrilling suggestion that she ride off with him into the sunset on the back of his motorcycle to start a new life together.

Until now, Beth has been relatively content with her life. "Maybe I haven't been ecstatic with the way things have been, but I've never had any major cause to be dissatisfied either. It's just that I see how drab and dreary my life and marriage have become now that I've had a chance to get to know Ed. He makes me feel so alive."

How does a responsible, seemingly mature, and sensible woman find herself in a situation like this? While Beth's case may be a bit unusual in that she has fallen for someone so much younger, it is fairly typical in that many women who devote their entire lives to nurturing others often feel they have missed out on the best life has to offer. They wake up one morning and think, *Life is passing me by.* Beth expressed that she was so tired of being the one everybody leans on, the rock of the family, and the one who holds everything and everybody together. She had gradually taken on the role of the martyr of the family, and it left her feeling worn out and empty to say the least.

As a wife and mom, Beth had been so busy taking care of everyone else and looking after others' needs that she had never really invested the time out to nurture her own needs or even to find out what they are. She had always been the strong, dependable one, and fully committed to setting a good example and being what everyone else wanted her to be. She had not given a lot of thought to what she really wanted out of life.

Over the years, I've met a number of women who have found themselves in Beth's position, although not all of them were being tempted by an extramarital involvement. As I've tried to encourage and guide women through these difficult times, I have noticed that most of them felt tied down to their situations or held back by their responsibilities, and they longed for something more from life.

Stephanie said she met Allen when she was 18 years old and after 26 years of marriage, along with devoting her life to raising four children, and recently working at a job she finds tedious and mind-numbing, she says she feels trapped and hopeless. She admits that Allen is attractive and charming, a good provider, a wonderful father, and a passionate lover, and she doesn't want to sacrifice any of that just so she can "find herself." But that doesn't make up for the fact that playing the role of the "martyr" for so many years has taken its toll on Stephanie.

Marie was one who did leave her husband, Stan, simply because he wasn't fulfilling her emotional needs, and there was nothing anyone could say to change her mind. Now after being married and divorced two more times, she says she's come to realize that she had been looking to Stan and her other partners to fulfill in her what only God could do for her. She now sees that Stan was a pretty great guy after all and now realizes she may never find anyone else like him. Unfortunately for Marie, Stan's second wife Judy also realizes how special he is and she's not about to let him get away.

Healthy Self-Care

What is it about all these women that caused them to want to escape? Is there a common thread? As I travel and speak at women's events, I am seeing an increasing number of women who are dissatisfied and the one common denominator is they have all neglected to develop the habit of looking after their own needs. More and more women tell me they are stressed out, worn out, burnt out, and exhausted. Most of them say they feel overwhelmed, overextended, overtired, and underappreciated. They don't even think of taking time out for personal pursuits or pampering activities, especially if they cost something, because they would feel too guilty. If you are waiting for someone to come along and offer you time out and money to nurture yourself, forget it. It's probably not going to happen. Only you can take on the responsibility of being sure you are nurtured.

Somehow, as women, we have been fed the message that it is wrong to practice healthy self-care. While we can always find time, money, and energy to nurture someone else, we somehow feel selfish and self-centered if we do the same for ourselves. How many times have you bought a gift for someone else and then grumbled that you don't even have one of *those* for yourself! We are often conditioned to look after everyone else at the expense of our own health and well-being. We have taken on the position of nurturers of the entire world, but when we neglect ourselves in the process, we pay the price. While we are caring for the rest of the universe, we are often sacrificing our own enjoyment of life, and in the end we stand to lose our health, our inner peace, and even our most cherished personal relationships. Eventually every aspect of our life is affected and those we love suffer needlessly.

While we never want to relinquish our vital role as nurturers, we must always check our motives. It's important to give of ourselves, our gifts, and our talents for the right reasons. Then we can derive our pleasure and joy from making a contribution and having the opportunity to make another's life a little brighter in some way. The wrong reasons are when we need to be needed, want to earn bonus points for being so selfless, try to win approval or affirmation from someone else, or hope to look a bit better than the rest because we are so willing to give beyond the call of duty.

A lot of the time we are acting on a subconscious level and not even aware we have these motives. Sometimes, pride causes us to overextend ourselves and it becomes important that we stand out from the crowd. One woman confided to me that for many years she had placed unnecessary pressure on herself when she always had to be the best at everything—the best hostess, cook, baker, seamstress, housekeeper, and decorator. When she tackled any project, from wallpapering and painting her home to designing and sewing her own fashions, she went to extremes to be sure they were unique and perfect in every way. It wasn't until she came to the realization that she was trying to prove her worth and value through these things that she could finally let herself off the hook, relax, and let someone else be the best at some things.

Knowing when to say "no," even to ourselves, is crucial. Naturally we never want to stop contributing and giving to others. It's our inherent nature to be nurturers. But it is so critical that we replenish what we are giving away. Many women keep giving and giving until they are attempting to function "on empty." One thing I have found is that you cannot give away what you don't own. It's time to start practicing what I call, "healthy selfishness." Simply put, it means that one of the nicest things you can do for your family and other people you love and care about is to take time to nurture you. If you are going around totally exhausted, chances are you're not going to be much good to anyone, and you won't be very much fun to be with. So, get rid of the guilt. Not only will others appreciate that you have nurtured yourself and come back refreshed, renewed, recharged, and rejuvenated, but you will be equipped and ready to make the changes that will move you into a victorious future. Get off the treadmill of activity and into the classroom of silence. There's so much to learn there. It's the only way you're going to hear from God.

Chapter 19

Unlocking the Hidden Dream

God can do anything, you know—far more than you could ever imagine or guess or request in your wildest dreams!
EPHESIANS 3:20 MSG

The future belongs to those who believe in the beauty of their dreams.
ELEANOR ROOSEVELT

IF YOU WERE EVER CALLED A DAYDREAMER as a child, it probably wasn't a compliment. Daydreaming was often not encouraged when we were children, and it isn't promoted in our adult world either. We tend to think of a dreamer as someone with her head in the clouds and her eyes closed to the reality of restrictions like limited resources, changing relationships, job insecurity, and world chaos. At one time, we all had vivid imaginations and were oblivious to limitations. We started out with dazzling dreams and noble goals, and our inner knowing assured us we could soar to heights untold on wings of freedom. Then some-where along the way, we lost the dream. In all of life's harsh experiences, sorrows, losses, and disappointments, our wings became crushed and broken. We've traded our lofty dreams for what could be measured or documented or experienced with the five senses, often putting our-selves—and God—in a box. Maybe we need a fresh dream to learn how to fly all over again. "Logic will get you from A to B," said Albert Einstein, but "imagination will take you everywhere!"

None of us can live passionately without a vision for our future. Thomas Jefferson said, "I like the dreams for the future more than the history of the past." When we don't have a dream, we seem to grapple hopelessly with yesterday, struggle pointlessly with today, and wander aimlessly into tomorrow.

My childhood dream was to marry Elvis. I knew without a doubt that someday I would be Mrs. Presley. Then, when I heard he'd married a gorgeous young woman named Priscilla, I was devastated. I figured if he'd met me first, I would have had a chance. My next ambition was to find a loving husband and become a full-time homemaker and mommy. Like many young girls at that time, I envisioned living with my little family in a quaint Victorian cottage with gingerbread trim, complete with rose gardens and a picket fence.

In my dream, I'd hang clothes on the line from a wicker laundry basket, simmer big kettles of home-cooked soup on the back burner, and cool fresh baked apple pies on the window sill with lace curtains fluttering in the breeze. My mornings would be spent leisurely tending my garden where I'd grow plump tomatoes and luscious raspberries, and in the afternoons I'd stroll through the park with my beautiful babies in an English pram. At night, my husband and I would snuggle together by the fireside to read to each other and talk over our day. As the children grew, they'd play happily with each other wearing little

Laura Ashley dresses and Ralph Lauren outfits that never got dirty. Did I know how to dream or what?

Although I know now my dream may not have been very realistic, any genuine hopes of having a cozy and contented home were shattered when my married life turned into one of financial hardship, relationship tension, and ongoing arguments that escalated into domestic violence and continued for many years. I am not sure about your dreams or what's happened to them, but it's easy to see why so many of us gave up on having a glorious vision for a happy and meaningful future.

Healthy Use of the Imagination

One day that all changed for me. In my darkest hour, someone asked me these two questions that got me dreaming all over again and thinking in new directions:

1. If you could do, be, or have anything in this world and money, time, or background had no bearing, what great things could you imagine for your future?

2. If you could envision a happy, joy-filled, and significant life for yourself, what would you dare to dream?

Until then, I hadn't thought that merely pondering a better way could actually play a role in creating a happier future, but those questions set in motion what would eventually lead to a personal metamorphosis for me. My previous dreams had been such big disappointments, and I had stopped giving much thought to the "what ifs" in life. It didn't seem worthwhile to even dream about a brighter future, because I had little hope it would make a difference. Besides, I didn't know I was worthy of having a chance at a better life. I believed I had made choices that locked me into my situation and no amount of contemplating a brighter future would alter that. I have since learned that every change in direction starts with a single idea, an inspiration, a vision. Just as a fashion designer has an image of her creation before she even begins, and an architect first has a vision of a future cathedral, so we must have a dream.

If you could design the rest of your life, how would it be different from what you've experienced so far? To start anew, give yourself permission to ponder a different existence. Consider the many aspects of your life that would be part of a better future, including your family relationships, the friends you'd associate with, the church you'd attend and your involvement there, the job you would have, the way you'd furnish your home, the hobbies, entertainment, and other interests that would fill your spare time, and the vacations you'd take. This is just a starting place. Your dreams can change and evolve because they're not written in stone. It's possible, and even preferable, to make mid-course adjustments as you go along.

Here's the most important part. God can dream a much bigger dream for your life than you could ever dream for yourself. So before you even begin, preface your dreaming with a prayer. Ask God to grant you wisdom and inspiration, to open your eyes to a greater vision of your life and Him. Like me, you may hesitate to dream, wondering, *Who am I to say what's best for me? What if I dream something that isn't part of God's plan for me?* Pray that God would clearly show you the dreams He's written on your heart and ask the Holy Spirit to reveal new insights about your future. God wants you to pursue your dreams while you rejoice in Him. The psalmist said,

> *Delight yourself in the LORD and he will give you the desires of your heart* (Psalm 37:4).

Jesus taught us to "pray believing." Can you remember playing make-believe as a child? You actually lived out an image in your mind and believed it to be real. You didn't hope it was true when you played nurse or teacher or movie star, you just knew it was. Well today, in the same way, a dream is a mental image that can support your desires. We all think in pictures anyway. If you don't think you do, ask yourself if you've ever worried about something or relived an embarrassing moment! Likewise, when you're captivated by an intriguing novel, in your mind's eye you can envision the plot, scenery, and characters as you read. When you anticipate sitting down to enjoy your favorite dessert or plan a surprise party for someone, you can "see" it all in your imagination. In fact, it would be difficult to even think without using some form of mental imaging. The best part is, it doesn't cost a thing. Go ahead and dream—it's free and available to everyone.

Dreaming Up Goals and Plans

After considering the two future-altering questions I shared with you, I soon realized that in order to conquer the past, get my present life on track, and move confidently into a triumphant future, I needed to set some wholesome goals for myself—mental, physical, emotional, and spiritual. The significance of having a goal is that you will never leave where you are until you decide where you'd rather be. It's as simple as that. Start thinking about what you'd rather see happening when it comes to your health, spirituality, personal needs, spare time, fitness, energy levels, relationships, career, finances, and peace of mind. Changes in those areas are targets you can aim for.

When I first sensed God beckoning me to dream about things seemingly unrelated to my background, education, family situation, or present job, they may have seemed far-fetched to others. But some of my particular dreams—developing a word game, presenting seminars on a cruise ship in Hawaii, writing inspiring books for women, learning to play tennis, designing and installing a new kitchen in our home, and more—are now realities and bring so much joy into my life.

The next step I took was to put those dreams in writing. Once goals are written down they become more tangible, meaningful, and feasible. It's been my experience that most people who are successful in seeing their dreams come to pass do much of their thinking on paper. Not only did I write my dreams on index cards so I could post them and see them regularly, I backed them up with pictures. Using images cut from brochures, catalogs, and magazines, I created a "dream collage" that helped to keep the dreams alive. Today, I actually have a dream binder with dividers in it and sections for various dreams including marriage and relationship goals, travel ideas, business objectives, home decorating and landscaping concepts, and personal health and wellness targets. It makes goal planning tangible and so much more fun.

When you provide a target for your thoughts, you will find you automatically move toward it. For example, whether you spend your day thinking about all the TV shows you're going to watch when you get home, or focus on some good inspirational books you'd like to read, either way it becomes your target and determines what you will accomplish. If you're focusing on devoting an hour to praying and studying God's Word, you will miraculously find the time; or if you concentrate on how tired you're feeling, you'll be compelled to lie down on the couch and take a nap instead. When you can envision in your mind's eye the development of something you desire, it can become your reality. This is why it is so important to set a careful watch over our thoughts and desires. Like my grandmother used to tell me, "Be careful what you wish for, you just might get it!"

Having a dream for your future is critical when it comes to nurturing your life back into balance as you recover from a hurtful past. However, it doesn't necessarily mean you'll know all the specifics about what's going to happen along the way. It's more about gaining a sense of direction and restoring the hope that you do have a future and a purpose and it is full of promise. Any vision for your future that is without hope or one that is filled with thoughts and images of failure is not of God. He only wants the best for you.

How do you start to have a different vision for your future? Begin in prayer by asking God to reveal His will for you. When we bring the presence of the Lord into our thinking and planning, it will block out negative and discouraging thoughts brought by the enemy. God can restore a vision where it has been lost and give you the hope to dream again. Then, decide to abandon all your excuses. It's easy to come up with reasons for not having a dream. But with God, you are never too old or young, too single or divorced, too black or white, too male or female, too short or tall, too fat, skinny, or broke to have a dream! Envisioning a great future is something that's available to everyone. Whether you are a mother, student, day-care worker, teacher, sales representative, nurse, real-estate agent, or own your own business, be sure God has a future with a mission in mind for you to fulfill.

Next, be sure to dream big without any restrictions. God's plans for you are grander than anything you could imagine for yourself, so remove all the mental and emotional limitations and boundaries, real or imagined, that may be hanging on from your past. Let go of all reservations and past programming that would cause you to fear the unknown. Stop checking into your past to see what you are capable of today. Be aware of discouraging thoughts and silence the inner skeptic.

For instance, when I began writing my first book, my inner critic chided, *Me, a writer? I haven't had the proper training or education. What could I possibly have to write about that would be of true value to a reader?* That's when God assured me He was the one who had something worthwhile to say and I would be an instrument. By pinpointing your qualms and uncertainties, you'll be better equipped to discern whether your dreams are truly from God, yourself, or the enemy whose main purpose is to distract you from God's ultimate purpose.

No More Limits

We need to quit defining our limits. Allow God to determine what you can or cannot do. There have been many times that I've disagreed with God about my capabilities. I am living proof that arguing only wastes time and blocks blessings. When I was building my business as a conference and retreat speaker, I felt comfortable presenting keynote addresses before large audiences to open or close corporate events. But when God opened a new door for me to do a series of customer service workshops for smaller groups of managers and staff across the country for an international automobile corporation, I thought, *No way! I can't do workshops. I'm a keynote speaker, not a workshop leader. Besides, I don't know a thing about the auto industry!*

Finally, I stepped out in faith and accepted the contract, and I discovered I truly enjoyed this new aspect of my profession. Not only that, I found I had a knack for leading workshops I never knew I had. The next five years turned out to be one of the highlights of my career, not to mention being extremely profitable. It was a valuable learning experience that went on to open many more doors. God loves to take our weaknesses and seeming impossibilities, and work through them. Truly, *"with God all things are possible"* (Matthew 19:26), and His *"power is made perfect in weakness"* (2 Corinthians 12:9). Dream big about things that couldn't possibly happen by your own strength and ingenuity, but only by the power and grace of God. We can never out-dream Him!

If you're still not sure about God's will concerning your dreams, here's a prayer that never fails. Ask the Lord to "block it or bless it." Go ahead with your plans trusting that if it's His will for you, He will make the way smooth and open doors. And if not, believe He will close doors while taking away the opportunity and the desire.

Knowing a dream is God's will for you doesn't guarantee you won't feel scared. It's okay to be afraid. In fact, if your dream doesn't scare you a little bit, it's probably not big enough! When you allow yourself to have a dream, you can soon move into a realm where miracles are not just some strange and occasional phenomenon but a natural daily occurrence. When God gives you the dream, He'll also equip you. Remember,

> The One who called you is completely dependable. If he said it, he'll do it! (1 Thessalonians 5:24 MSG).

If you're afraid to pursue a dream, start with the first step and then let yourself go. When a baby eagle is pushed from its nest, it flutters and thrashes about with apprehension at first until it catches a current of air called a thermal. With amazement, it discovers this invisible sea of support is capable of holding it up and then flying happens with ease and comfort. You, too, will find the support you never even knew existed will suddenly be available for you.

Three Powerful P's of Successful Goal-Setting

The power of purpose. A purposeful goal is one that has a reason, a motive, or a specific intent. It's been said that when a woman is given enough reasons, she can go out and accomplish almost anything. Knowing the "why" behind your dream gives vitality and significance to your goals and plans. Even the most routine tasks take on new meaning when they are backed by purpose.

For instance, when you make the bed in the morning because you want it to be fresh and comfortable at bedtime for yourself or someone you love, it stops being just one more item on your to-do list and isn't such a boring chore anymore. When you sing in a choir or play guitar in the church band with the intent of inspiring others to have a closer relationship with God, it becomes an act of love and not merely another commitment you've made in your already overloaded schedule. It's purpose that inspires us to do whatever it takes, for as long as it takes. There's power in having a specific and steadfast incentive behind your dream. It will give you the stamina to continue when you think you can't go another step.

Having purposeful goals lets you envision the end result before it is accomplished and gives fresh meaning to your life. Something miraculous begins to happen when you have a definite motive for pursuing a God-given dream. You may have an unshakable desire to begin a certain type of work, or start a ministry that until now you have felt excluded from or held back by barriers, real or imagined. Maybe you long to get moving in a certain area and believe God is calling you to do it, but you feel stuck. Seeing the purpose in your goal is one way to get unstuck.

You need something bigger than yourself to live for. If you haven't discovered it yet, you must long for it and search for it. Keep searching until the Holy Spirit reveals it to you. Ask, seek, knock, and keep knocking until the door is opened. You are God's instrument in this world and when you've discovered your purpose, there's a tremendous peace that comes from knowing you are at the center of His will.

The power of passion. Has your dream become a burning desire? Are you so fervent about something you enjoy doing that you'd do it for free? It's when your dream becomes a magnificent passion and you are filled with flaming enthusiasm that you will take action and see it through regardless of the obstacles. For a long time I would say, "I want to write a book so much that I feel there's one inside me trying to get out!" I was filled with passion, and sure enough, I've had the privilege of writing several books.

I have also been saying I'd like to learn to play the flute and take up woodworking as a hobby, but I haven't done either of these yet. Do you know why? I'm tempted to tell you that I'm a busy woman and don't have time for flute lessons or I can't afford all those expensive woodworking tools. I know the truth is I simply don't want to do those things bad enough. When I desire them as much as I wanted to write books, I believe they will happen. Miraculously, I will find the resources I need. Our hectic schedules or lack of finances are perceived limitations, and they sure come in handy as excuses for not pursuing our dreams. When we have genuine zeal and fervor, we'll pray with the intensity that shows God we believe He will answer. Our focus will be on God and we'll concentrate on the intention of our prayer, not on the obstacles.

Years ago, when I was selling products door-to-door, I had been so inspired by the sales trainers I sat under that I was able to begin making the powerful choices that dramatically changed the direction of my life. I soon became passionate about wanting to become a motivational speaker so I, too, could go out and challenge and inspire others who felt held back like I did. I believe God planted this desire in my spirit.

I wrote out my goal to be the sales trainer for the organization I worked for. Well, that was quite a stretch because there was no such position, but I was so passionate that I didn't let that minor restriction stop me. Someone suggested that I fill in all the details of my dream and appeal to all five senses. In my mind, I saw myself wearing a red business suit, carrying a leather briefcase, getting on an airplane, flying across the country, and being on stage inspiring large audiences. That was all quite a stretch, too, because I had never worn a suit, owned a briefcase, or flown anywhere. To top it off, I had a fear of public speaking! To make the dream more believable, I went to the dress shop and tried on all the red suits and modeled them in the three-way mirror. I put them back on the rack because I couldn't afford a suit, but told the sales clerk I'd be back. Then I went to the leather store to try out the briefcases and model them too, and told the clerk there the same thing. Then I envisioned myself on stage at the podium, in front of huge audiences, and imagined them becoming excited and challenged by my messages.

I held onto that whole image and then worked hard on my existing sales career. After my group's sales escalated phenomenally, I was given the opportunity to travel across the country, speaking at all the company conventions, and eventually offered the position of company sales trainer! Of course, I said, "I knew you'd be calling, and I know where to get a suit and a briefcase!" If your dream was to suddenly appear, do you know where the suit and the briefcase are, or whatever those represent in your dream?

Sadly, there are very few people with great desires. Wishful thinking is more common. Some of us need to replace our wishbones with backbones, plus a whole lot of passion. When intense fervor is missing, our dreams lack power. The amazing thing is when we truly want something, if we want it as much as we want air to breathe, yearn for it as we might crave our favorite food after a long fast, and when it lines up with the Word of God and His plans for us, we will somehow find a way to see it through to fruition.

The power of persistence. Are you facing some difficulties and challenges as you attempt to move forward and achieve your dream? If so, that's normal and it's to be expected. There is not an achievement worth remembering that isn't marked in some way with the scars of annoying setbacks, the blemishes of disappointment, and the wounds of frustration. It takes true commitment and tenacious perseverance to see a dream through to fulfillment.

Yet this kind of dedication and determination has become a rare quality. Helen Keller believed that "we can do anything we want as long as we stick to it long enough." It's too bad that genuine "stick-to-it-iveness" is a trait we are seeing less and less often in our society. I am not suggesting that persistence means accepting situations that are harming you or blindly agreeing to stay in relationships that are potentially life-threatening. But when it comes to the day-to-day challenges and difficulties that could cripple your dreams, decide that you are going to persist and go ahead regardless of the obstacles, and then refuse to look back.

Steps to Following Your Heart

Listen to your heart by setting aside some time to be alone in a quiet place—maybe a scenic spot you enjoy by a lake or in a nearby park. Nature has a way of helping us "think big" as we notice the grandeur of God's creation around us. Even a quiet corner in a café or local library can provide a reflective atmosphere for contemplation. Bring a journal, pen, and perhaps some related books to browse through. They'll stimulate your creativity.

Then, pick up your pen and start to list your dreams. As in any brainstorming session, there are no "bad ideas" at this stage. You can edit them later. For now, get out of your box. Try coloring outside the lines. Let yourself go and write down even the wild and crazy ideas: starting a business, becoming a foreign correspondent or a missionary journalist, learning to speak Japanese, parasailing, deep-sea diving, or hang gliding. The first time I made my list, I felt a surge of exhilaration, excitement, and positive expectancy inside me.

In my travels, I have met many women who have done this exercise and ended up listening to their hearts to follow their dreams. Jennifer had such an amazing flair for decorating that her friends often referred to her as the "Martha Stewart" of the neighborhood. She would offer her services to them for free just because she enjoyed decorating so much. Their encouragement, along with much prayer, led Jennifer to start her own interior design business. Now she is able to earn her living doing what she is naturally gifted to do.

Becky has a knack for gourmet cuisine and entertaining, and with the support of family and some good friends, she started her own successful catering service. Sharon used to enjoy treating her family and friends to pampering indulgences—massages, facials, pedicures, and manicures—just for fun. At their prompting, she eventually decided to follow her heart, studied to become a registered massage therapist, and now operates a beautiful spa in a charming older home where she also lives. She is able to make her talents available to so many more women in need of some special pampering and build a business at the same time.

What can you think of doing that would allow you to use your innate gifts, talents, and unique strengths? What can you become so involved in that you lose all track of time? Which activities give you a sense of being fully alive? The answers to these questions can help you to determine and fashion your dreams.

When you regularly set and achieve goals, you can leave behind past hurts and disappointments, while living in the moment and anticipating an exciting future ahead. You'll become a more interesting person with new ideas, concepts, and information to discuss. You'll have a brighter and more hopeful outlook, and will not be as focused on what's wrong, including past disappointments or current struggles. What can you imagine doing with the rest of your life? George Eliot told us "It's never too late to be what you might have been!" It all starts with a dream.

Where there is life, there is hope.
Where there is hope, there are dreams.
Where there are dreams, there are goals.

Chapter 20

Building Foundations Day by Day

You know these things—now do them! That is the path of blessing.
JOHN 13:17 TLB

Getting an idea should be like sitting down on a pin.
It should make you jump up and do something!
E.L. SIMPSON

IT'S WONDERFUL TO HAVE A DREAM WHEN it allows God to expand your horizons while using you to fulfill His purpose in your life. Nevertheless, having a dream for your future is only the beginning. We need to follow through with our dreams by developing specific strategies that are attainable and measurable that will also give us direction and keep us on track. An effective, productive life doesn't just happen. It requires a plan and some action steps. Sadly, most of us spend more time watching television, making out a shopping list, reading a novel, preparing for a vacation, or organizing a party than we do planning our lives. Why is that? One reason is that planning takes time and can seem like a lot of work, even though in the end it can free up time.

If you want to leave your past behind and move forward, you can't live "by the seat of your pants." You must devise a plan and put it into action. We seem to accept this when it comes to handling money, managing our careers, and operating our homes. But we often fail to devise a plan for things far more important—getting to know God, becoming more Christlike, traveling our spiritual journey, overcoming past limitations, conquering former hurts and regrets, rebuilding relationships, and maintaining our physical, emotional, and spiritual health.

Imagine what life would be like without goals and plans. We need to set specific targets regularly if we hope to accomplish certain tasks and activities. Think about these points:

- Without a plan, you may not pray, meditate, or read your Bible consistently.

- If you don't plan, you won't attend church regularly or get involved in a ministry.

- If you don't decide ahead of time, you won't go for a walk or exercise every day.

- If you don't have a plan, you won't eat healthy foods, drink eight glasses of water a day, or take your vitamins.

- Without planning ahead, you won't volunteer your services or make a contribution in your church or community.

- If you don't save your money, you will never be able to buy a home or take a vacation.

- If you don't put money away early, you won't be able to afford your child's education.

- Unless you plan your route for a trip, you'll probably get lost.

- If you don't decide ahead what you are going to say at a meeting or in a speech, you will ramble on incoherently.

- If you don't set up a realistic budget, you will not have the money to pay your bills.

I know that I have to plan if I want to put supper on the table by a certain time or get the laundry folded and put away. It takes planning to enjoy a weekly date with my husband, spend time with my family, take time out for personal pampering, stay in touch with friends, open my home to entertain guests, take a vacation, record my thoughts in a journal, and read a book every couple of months. Planning is so crucial to every aspect of our lives.

The best way to begin building your future is to make plans for restoring balance into your life—body, soul, and spirit. Most of us are out of balance much of the time in one or more of those areas. When one area is out of whack, they're all out of whack! Picture a three-legged stool, and imagine what would happen if one of its legs was suddenly taken away. Obviously, the stool would topple over. That's basically what happens to us when we neglect either body, soul, or spirit. As you begin to make changes in your life, leave the past behind, and move out into the unknown to build a new future without all the baggage, balance will be a key component. Here are some guidelines and action steps to help you regain your balance—physically, emotionally, and spiritually.

Plan Balance for Your Body

1. Get moving! I know you hear about exercise all the time, but the truth is you need to be in good physical condition to take your life to a new level. Exercise not only helps you to experience vibrant health, energy, and vitality, but is also a powerful coping strategy when you are working toward healing your emotions and restoring happiness. A vigorous workout will release endorphins and other chemicals into your body that will help you to feel more positive and hopeful.

If you're out of the habit, start slowly and build. Find something you can do each day that gets you moving. Whether it's putting on some big band music and dancing alone in your living room, going for a stroll around the block, walking or jogging on a treadmill, doing jumping jacks, or going to a gym, the key is to move more. Whatever you do, choose an activity that is easily accessible for you and something you really enjoy so you'll be more apt to do it regularly. The good news is the more out of shape you are, the quicker you'll see results.

2. Pay attention to your eating habits. A number of years ago, because of my personal illness, I decided to study nutrition and its effects on our bodies. What I discovered was that wholesome nutrition plays a critical role in the health of our immune system, our moods, energy levels, and ability to think clearly, and also influences how well we cope with stress and change. Your body is an energy system and functions with efficient food fuel.

A good starting place for vibrant energy and vitality is to eat food in a form that's as close to its natural state as possible. You won't find sugar-coated cereal with green marshmallows growing in a garden, or diet cola and coffee flowing in a stream. The fields are not full of instant rice and fast-cooking oats, which should tell us a lot about the way we are fueling our bodies. When I see what goes into some women's shopping carts, and the growing numbers of families that regularly eat at fast-food restaurants, it makes me sad. God created your body to be self-cleansing and self-renewing, but only if you provide the nourishment it requires.

For starters, eat lots of foods that are rich in water, which makes them natural cleansers for your body. Those high-water content foods include almost all fruits and vegetables, preferably fresh and raw, or their fresh-squeezed juices. In addition, try replacing tea, coffee, and soft drinks with juice and water. If you still crave the bubbly carbonation in soft drinks, have a mixture of fruit juice with club soda or mineral water with a wedge of lime. The message is simple: Eat well, live well.

3. *Take time to rest*. Retreat periodically throughout the day from the hectic pace of raising a family, going to work, maintaining a household, and nurturing everyone else, especially while you're attempting to make major life changes. I think the psalmist put into words the longing of our hearts when he said, *"Oh, that I had wings of a dove! I would fly away and be at rest"* (Psalm 55:6). Whether it's a mid-day snooze, time out to put your feet up and read a magazine with a freshly-brewed cup of tea, or a few minutes to work on a favorite hobby or craft, you'll come back to your regular activities with increased energy and a fresh perspective. Interestingly, as an added benefit, you will sleep better at night if you go to bed rested. I know that seems contradictory, but many sleepless nights are caused by falling into bed totally exhausted. Periods of non-action and times to do nothing during your day contribute to the healing process. Jesus regularly encouraged His disciples to set aside periods of quiet time away from the crowds.

Plan Balance for Your Soul

Aside from bringing your physical body into balance through a regular fitness routine, healthy diet habits, and periodic rest throughout the day, you can nurture your soul into balance as well. Your soul includes your thoughts and feelings, so try being a good, wise friend to yourself and imagine what you'd suggest to someone you care about who is going through a major transition. Then practice those suggestions yourself. Here are some simple delights, innocent indulgences, and pampering pleasures you can practice.

1. *Create an oasis of stability and order*. You can do this through the patterns you incorporate into your day-to-day living. You need to have some routines that are predictable and dependable, to give you a sense of rootedness and certainty. They will counteract the effects of all the changes you are making while relinquishing your past. Your dependable oasis may be a particular place you visit, a certain ritual you practice, a special person you can depend on, a loving pet you can snuggle with, or an enjoyable hobby that brings you pleasure.

2. Develop a personal support system. Whether it's a parent, spouse, sibling, grandparent, counselor, friend, or coworker, look for someone who is always there for you, who provides dependable strength and support, and encourages you in your dreams and plans, even though they may be continually evolving. In this journey, there is no such thing as a solo flight. The devil's plan is for you to feel lonely and isolated, especially during times of change, uncertainty, or pressure. Instead of giving in, take a journal and a good pen, find a comfortable spot, and begin to list every possible source of support in your life. When I was going through my own transition, I was blessed to have the support of people who were good sounding boards, understanding listeners, empathic confidants, perceptive advisors, and thoughtful supporters. You can look close to home for your encouragement, or explore the avenues of therapeutic support including your church, pastoral staff, professional counselors, trained therapists, or doctors.

3. Make your home the most comforting sanctuary you can imagine. Surround yourself with symbols of comfort, warmth, and contentment. I always do my best writing when I first set the stage with a scented candle, a steamy pot of herbal tea with my very best china mug, and a little soft instrumental music in the background. Once I'm dressed in some especially comfy clothing, I set up my laptop in the kitchen in front of the picture window where I can enjoy the colors of nature and see birds visiting the feeders or having a bath.

Think about what makes you feel at peace, whether it's specific colors or certain textures you find calming, artwork that makes you feel tranquil, a flower arrangement that brings cheer, scents that are soothing, or the relaxing influence of a crackling fire or candles flickering nearby. Make your own safe haven, a comforting place to start each morning and a refuge you can relax in at the end of each day. Have your favorite comfy armchair ready with a footstool, some cozy comforters, fluffy pillows, stacks of good books or magazines, special music that brings solace, a bathrobe to snuggle in, and other symbols of peace and tranquility.

4. Get outdoors and allow nature to nurture you. Immersing yourself in the restorative, healing, and inspirational powers of the great outdoors is a wonderful balancer for your soul. When you take even a few minutes to step outside, you will reap benefits untold. The sights, scents, textures, and sounds of nature are not only for our physical pleasure but also provide healing for our hearts. Seek out a few special places that soothe you—a nearby park, a spot by the lake, a garden in your own backyard, a sun porch or veranda—and go there when your mind yearns to be at peace. Stand on a hill and let the wind blow through your hair. Lie on the grass and pick out shapes in the clouds. Notice the simple beauty of a sunset, a night sky filled with shimmering stars, or the brilliant colors of an autumn leaf. Appreciating nature is far from being New Age hocus-pocus. To be touched and stirred by the majesty of God's creation is a beautiful and sincere form of worship and praise to Him. You will soon face old challenges with a fresh, new perspective.

5. Arrange for some pampering. Invest in your emotional well-being with a facial, manicure, pedicure, or other spa treatment. Massages are especially beneficial. When you get a bump or a bruise, it's natural to try to rub away the hurt. The same is true for the emotional strain and mental anguish that come with the stress of overcoming past obstacles that hamper your dreams. Not only does a massage provide an overhaul for the entire body, relieving muscle tension, discharging toxins, and releasing endorphins, but it will amazingly lift a sagging spirit, too.

A relaxing aromatherapy massage is one of my favorite pampering treats that, over the years, has helped me to get through many stressful events. One reason massage is so valuable as you begin to let go of the past is that muscle tends to hold memory. I did not know this and it took me by surprise the first time I had a massage after going through a devastating separation and divorce. I cried from the beginning to the end and the tears just kept flowing even after I left. When I couldn't stop crying, the massage therapist very gently encouraged me to allow myself the freedom to experience this type of release, assuring me it is a cleansing process, emotionally as well as physically.

If budget is a concern, try trading massages with your spouse or a good friend, or give yourself a facial, scalp, shoulder, hand, or foot massage. Purchase some scented massage oil, set aside some time to relax, and enjoy.

6. *Enjoy stimulating waters and peaceful tub soaks.* Water has a rejuvenating effect on all living things with its miraculous healing and soothing properties. Yet so often, we jump in and out of our morning shower so burdened with the cares of yesterday, worries of today, and fears of tomorrow that we never get to fully enjoy the benefits. First thing in the day, revel in the warm water of a shower as it cascades over your body. There is energy in moving water, and as it pounds and bounces off your skin, it wakes up the whole body.

On days when I am having a hard time getting up, I sometimes pamper myself by luxuriating in a candlelight bubble bath. While it may seem self-indulgent, it hardly costs a thing and doesn't take much time, yet the rewards are priceless. A bedtime bath in a tub full of sparkling warm water that's been sweetened with soothing oils and calming scents is a comforting way to unwind at the end of a stress-filled day. Lying back on an inflatable pillow, with a cup of herbal tea, listening to your favorite music, you can soak away a lot of your cares—mental, emotional, and physical.

7. *Recapture your ability to play.* We can get so grown-up and serious when we are dealing with past issues, present trials, and future uncertainties. It's easy to lose our childlike sense of awe and wonder and we soon forget how to play just for the fun of it. Having grandchildren has restored my ability to make playing a regular part of my life again. Now I need no excuses for building sand castles, making snow angels, and jumping in piles of scrumptious-smelling autumn leaves.

When my dear friend Beth was attempting to overcome some horrendous trials and sorrows from her past, I encouraged her to "come out and play" with me. While her struggles were monumental and I was aware that this would not be a cure-all, I recognized she needed to have some fun and laughter as she went through her healing process. After her husband left her to live with someone he had been involved with for quite some time, Beth discovered he had somehow legally arranged their business partnership so that she ended up with nothing but the debt. Her four children, not fully understanding the situation, chose to live with their father which broke Beth's heart. Shortly afterward, she started a business of her own but was forced to declare bankruptcy.

Now she was attempting to start a new business and was in a deep pit of despair and hopelessness when I called her and invited her to go for lunch. Although there was not much I could do to alleviate her past and current problems, I felt God was giving me the opportunity to bring some joy into her life, even if it was temporary. When we got to the restaurant, I told her I wanted to buy us both lunch if she would do one thing for me—go to the park across the street and use the playground equipment. She thought I was out of my mind. Here we were, two women dressed in business attire and carrying briefcases. But she agreed, and off we went. We hoisted up our skirts to climb onto the teeter-totters. We flew through the air on the swings and hung our heads upside down to study the clouds. We climbed the steps to zoom down the slide! We laughed and played most of the afternoon away and neither of us cared whether or not we had lunch. I received the nicest note afterward from Beth and she said our day at the playground was the most fun she could ever remember having. Hidden in every woman is a child who wants to play again. Go alone or go with a friend. Splash in some puddles and make a few mud pies. You won't be sorry.

8. *Invest in your friendships.* We are relational beings. For most women, that is what life is all about. Having female friends takes the pressure off of the men in our lives. We seem to know intuitively that we need richer, deeper relationships with other women. We yearn for the stability and reliability provided by strong and lasting "forever" friendships. Time with friends becomes even more meaningful as we go through trials, troubles, and transitions. A genuine friend knows all about you and loves you anyway. She knows your secrets and keeps them. She coaches you through tough times and isn't judgmental.

Regardless of what you are going through, friendship is a two-way street. Be sure your friendships are balanced by honing your communication skills and learning to listen deeply. Otherwise, one is bound to feel taken advantage of or imposed upon. Friends can be our best supporters in times of loneliness and our greatest encouragers in times of change.

By planning balance for your soul, you are creating an environment for healing and building up personal strength and inner resolve. Use the above suggestions to work out a series of coping strategies that will come to your rescue when you are attempting to restore joy and happiness while releasing a healthy future.

Plan Balance for Your Spirit

If your goal is to know your heavenly Father in a new and more intimate way, you'll want to find ways to work balance into your spiritual life, too. The best way to know Him is to hear from Him. Hearing from God involves spending time reading from His Word, praying, listening for His voice, and then meditating on what you've read or heard. Meditation means contemplating and pondering a thought God has planted in your heart or a particular verse of Scripture. It's an active process, not passive. Listening is also active and something we choose to do. God will not do for you what you can do for yourself. You must do what you can and then trust God to do what you cannot. Here are some ideas for lingering in God's presence while you listen for His voice:

- Make an appointment with yourself each day to spend time in prayer. Mark it on your calendar in advance if necessary and take it as seriously as you would any other engagement.

- By scheduling it the same time every day, it will be easier to keep as a routine. Decide ahead of time that you won't let interruptions keep you from this most important part of your day.

- Prepare a quiet spot where you can be alone. Make it a comfortable place you'll look forward to returning to, whether it's a cozy spot near the fireplace, your special rocking chair, a porch swing, or a sunny corner of the room.

- Keep your Bible along with a few favorite devotional books, a good journal, and a nice pen in a wicker basket. Choose one with a handle if you're like me and appreciate the variety of moving from spot to spot.

- Physically unwind by consciously relaxing each muscle in your body. Start at your face and neck and end with your toes.

- You might want to brew a pot of coffee or steep some tea, listen to soft worship music, and light a scented candle to unwind and prepare your spirit.

- Empty your mind of schedules, relationship challenges, worries, and problems. Meditate on a scripture you've just read or a favorite one you've memorized.

- Pray a prayer of thanksgiving and worship to the Lord and open your mind to what He has to say as you rest in His presence and love.

- Keep a prayer journal to record prayer needs for yourself and others. Also record the answers to your prayers and keep a gratitude journal to count your blessings.

Following the steps and ideas in this chapter will help bring balance into your life—physically, emotionally, and spiritually. They will keep you calm, comfort you, and remind you of God's goodness and availability in the midst of the storm. Balance is the foundation that refreshes you and gives you renewed energy and strength. As Isaiah tells us,

> Those who hope in the LORD will renew their strength. They will soar on wings like eagles; they will run and not grow weary, they will walk and not be faint (40:31).

By taking time out to practice balance in your life and by lingering in God's presence, you can receive His peace and direction to build new foundations day by day.

Chapter 21

Set Free—at Last!

Christ has set us free to live a free life. So take your stand!
Never again let anyone put a harness of slavery on you.
GALATIANS 5:1 MSG

Look up, dear, look up to the heavens.
There is more in life than this. There is much more.
GEORGE BERNARD SHAW

THROUGHOUT OUR JOURNEY TOGETHER over the course of these chapters, we've found that it all comes down to this: We long to be free. We want to soar with eagles to magnificent heights, free-fall through the air, and float away on the clouds. We yearn to be back in the Garden where we can experience pure and total abandon, dancing, skinny-dipping, rolling down grassy hillsides, jumping and singing and shouting! What could possibly be better than absolute and complete freedom?

All of us can think of something we'd like to be set free from. For some, it's hurtful memories, past regrets, or bitter resentment. For others it's sorrowful remorse, frightful insecurities, or deep-rooted grudges. Imagine what it would be like to be free from worrying about your appearance or weight, your marriage or singleness, your children or parents, financial burdens or health problems, workplace disputes or world affairs, illness or death, or whatever the future holds. Be assured, dear reader, the One who created you and me, and the entire universe, *wants* you to be free. Not only that, He *can* set you free by the same power that raised Christ from the dead because He's the same yesterday, today, and forever.

There is hope for you or someone you know who struggles with an imperfect or painful past. What happened yesterday does not have to follow you around anymore, continuing to hold you back or cripple your dreams. Every single thing that's happened to you until now, good and bad, has brought great opportunities for emotional and spiritual growth. I trust you've discovered that through the concepts and principles presented here. I pray they've helped you to gain clarity about relinquishing your past, renewing your present, and rebuilding a brand-new future for yourself.

My Journey into Freedom

While I am thankful for my past, heartaches and all, I am the most grateful for the one way we can truly end our old life and begin again. It goes beyond turning over a new leaf, making New Year's resolutions, or any mental gymnastics and positive thinking techniques. The Bible says,

> *If anyone is in Christ, he is a new creation; the old has gone, the new has come* (2 Corinthians 5:17).

One day I experienced that transforming power—a true metamorphosis—and became a brand-new creation. My life could not have been so totally renewed except for the beautiful mystery I will share with you now.

What if someone could tell you the secret to being free once and for all? That's exactly what I was searching for at a very devastating time in my life when I happened upon this quote by St. Augustine:

> O God, Thou hast created us for Thyself and we are not satisfied until our souls rest in Thee.

You and I were created with a soul that yearns for something beyond ourselves, one that longs for communion with God. When I read that quote, it produced an inner stirring that caused me to believe something remarkable was about to be birthed into my life.

It was springtime in 1975. I started keeping a journal to record my thoughts, feelings, hopes, and dreams, something I'd never done before. My first entry started with a line a friend had written inside a greeting card:

> God has written the promise of resurrection not in books alone, but in every leaf in springtime.

In almost every entry after that, I expressed that I sensed a prompting deep down inside me, letting me know that my springtime was about to happen and something new would soon take place. With incredible anticipation, inexplicable joy, and a peace *"which is far more wonderful than the human mind can understand"* (Philippians 4:7 TLB), I began to look forward to whatever changes were in store for me, not knowing where or when they would happen. It was a most peculiar experience for me to have such amazing peace in the midst of the storms that continued to rage in my former marriage and home.

At the same time, my health seemed to be on an uncontrollable downward spiral. I was losing weight and my strength was quickly fading away. Feeling so extremely exhausted all the time made it especially difficult to continue caring for the children while working part-time and looking after our home. My doctors were baffled as to what was going on in my body. I spent many hours and often entire days having tests, blood work, and X-rays, with little satisfaction and virtually no answers.

Not surprisingly, my poor health stirred in me a desire to know more about this life and the hereafter. I suddenly had many questions about where we came from, our purpose on earth, and what lies ahead of us when we die. I started to read everything I could get my hands on. I asked a lot of questions and went on an all-out quest for answers. Most of all, I wanted to know the truth. I was convinced there must be *one truth,* not many truths based on popular theories, assorted philosophies, various religions, and individual personal beliefs. I could not comprehend how many things could be considered "the truth" simply because someone had decided on it.

Although I had attended a traditional church as a girl growing up and received wonderful teaching from the Bible, I had never developed a personal relationship with God. More recently, the path I had chosen over the few years leading up to my illness had taken me in a totally different direction. It included exploring astrology, studying transcendental meditation, visiting fortunetellers, reading daily horoscopes, and attending the church services of many different denominations.

Yet nothing gave me the inner peace or concrete answers I was searching for. Instead, they left me feeling empty. I was more agitated, confused, and desperate for answers than ever. I have since come to understand the danger in following some of these practices. One of the attractions in pursuing these rituals is to find out what the future holds. But God doesn't want us to know the future, only to know Him. He wants us to trust Him to guide us into the future one day at a time.

Also at that time I was beginning to make very poor choices in my personal life. When I speak to women's groups, I have a session I call "Looking for Love in All the Wrong Places!"—and they get the idea without my spelling it out. I have a hunch you may have even looked in a few wrong places yourself.

But let me tell you about the worst piece of advice I ever got. It came directly from a therapist my doctor had referred me to in the hope I would gain the confidence and strength I needed to make positive changes. He also hoped I would get off the tranquilizers I was taking and then make better choices for my children and me. After I sat sobbing in this therapist's office for the better part of an hour, he advised me that, if I couldn't muster the courage to leave my marriage, and if I was going to continue tolerating the abuse while merely wishing it would go away, the next best thing I could do was to treat myself by having an affair.

I could not believe what I was hearing. Now, when I think back, I believe that his offensive suggestion annoyed me so much it was one of the irritants that finally provoked me into making better choices on my own. It was the kick in the pants I needed, and also the beginning of the end of a sad chapter in my life.

Two Key Events

Shortly after that, two key events happened that were life-changing. First, my little girls began attending Sunday school by riding on a bus that picked up neighborhood children every week. The church workers on our route visited us every Saturday to be sure we knew who they were and what the children would be experiencing the next morning. I had never met such peaceful and caring people. They were so genuine, sincere, and full of joy that I felt intriguingly comfortable having my girls go with them.

Although I had stopped attending services anywhere, and this denomination was new to me, I was excited that my children would learn the old familiar Bible stories, hymns, and verses that had made such an impact on me during my growing-up years at church with my family. Besides, having the girls occupied every Sunday morning meant I could go back to bed and get a bit more sleep! What made it even better was that they loved going and even counted off the number of "sleeps" on the calendar until they could go back. One night while I was tucking my children in bed, they asked, "Mommy, are you in the army of the Lord?" I remember thinking, *Oh, dear, my kids are in the army of the Lord and I don't even know what that is!* I decided it was time to find out.

I made up my mind I would go with them one Sunday. I had been invited often but kept putting off going because I was modeling professionally at that time and convinced all the makeup, jewelry, and bright colors I wore would not be acceptable in such a church. The day I finally attended, I worked hard at modifying my image. My face was scrubbed clean, my nails were free of polish, and I styled my hair as straight and plain as possible. The black dress I chose to wear had a very high neck and a hem that went down to my ankles. I carried a great big borrowed Bible and with one last glance in the mirror, was satisfied that I looked appropriately "religious." Then off I went.

Was I surprised when I got inside! There in the pews were some of the most beautiful women and handsome men, dressed quite attractively—not at all dowdy or drab as I had expected. In fact, I will never forget one man wearing yellow plaid pants. (Of course, it was the 70s, but imagine that—yellow pants in church.) I was blown away and at the same time embarrassed by how I looked. Obviously, I was sadly mistaken about how one should appear in an evangelical church.

I had also been mistaken about why a person would go to such a church. My impression had been that only people who led dull, boring lives would want to spend their valuable time sitting in a pew. But that church was anything but boring, and the warmth and love I felt that day made me want to bring our beds and belongings, and move right in. Eventually, that was the church I attended regularly for nearly 20 years.

The second event happened one afternoon while I was sitting in the waiting room in family court for yet another session involving domestic violence. I looked around at the other women there. Like me, they had made an attempt at concealing swollen lips, bruises, and black eyes. Aside from my modeling jobs, I also sold makeup in a cosmetic boutique, so I had the expertise and the products needed to artfully disguise most of my injuries. Yet, for the most part, we looked like clones, lost and forlorn, dejected and despondent, with a familiar sadness coming from deep within our dark, empty souls. Then, for the first time something hit me like a bolt of lightning: I did not belong here, nor did any of these women. This was not the life we were created to live. There was a better way—for me and for them. Why had I not seen it before?

Crying Out to God

One of us had to step out and make the first move, and I was ready. My prayer that day was, "God, show me the path I am to take, and then I can come back and lead the way for others." I recognized that I needed divine guidance and power to make the right choices and to let me know what changes I should be making.

Soon after that, I was introduced to an exercise program involving Yoga and began taking classes at a local fitness center. It wasn't long before I realized the class went beyond focusing on exercise and that it would delve into things of a supernatural, spiritual nature. My first reaction was that maybe this was the divine power I had been seeking over the past few months. However, something did not feel right. Then, just days before the class in which we were to practice a candle-gazing and meditation exercise, my health took a drastic turn for the worse. After fainting at work, I ended up in the hospital and was never able to return to the classes.

Although I did not recognize it at the time, I see clearly now how God had a different plan for me. I now know that as much as there is a God who loves us and wants the very best for us, there is an enemy at work in the world attempting to destroy us. This illness turned out to be a blessing in disguise, as I believe I was actually being protected from the dangers of this treacherous practice. There are many sincere and committed Christian women I meet and talk with who are still following some of these rituals and not aware of the dangers. I believe God is faithful and when we genuinely turn to Him and seek His truths, He will not let us continue going down the wrong path.

My illness advanced quickly. I had never been so sick in all my life. My throat was lined with blisters, and I was coughing up blood and bleeding profusely through my nose, kidney, and bowel. I had a fever that would not budge no matter what the doctors and nurses did for me. Glands in my neck were so swollen and bulging they could be seen from across the room. Eventually, my head, neck, and shoulders all seemed to blend into one body part. At one point, my own doctor walked right past me and did not recognize me. There was tremendous swelling in several of my internal organs including the spleen, kidney, and pancreas. My skin became so sensitive that the slightest pressure from even the flimsiest clothing was nearly unbearable. It became too painful to even brush my hair and teeth because my scalp was so tender and my gums would bleed. Every muscle in my entire body ached, and I was becoming more fragile each passing day. A torrent of tears would stream down my cheeks regularly and without warning.

Eventually, my doctor called in other professionals to help determine what was happening and what to do about it. They tested me for leukemia and several other life-threatening diseases, but they were stumped. Finally, I was released from the hospital when it was determined nothing more could be done. Family members were taking care of my children, and my mother came to my home every day to bring food, clean nightgowns, and fresh bed linens. My former husband seemed most at ease when I was in a weakened condition, and he was glad to care for me as well. Thankfully, the usual battles and struggles did not exist while I was sick. Although it was not a cure for the relationship, my illness oddly alleviated some problems for the time being.

Then, one day something happened that altered my life in a way no other event ever had. It was a moment in time that transformed me forever. What do you do when you have five doctors and they practically give you a death sentence by sending you home from the hospital with no hope of surviving? You might do what I did and call out to God!

As I lay there in my sickbed, I knew I still did not have the answers I had so sincerely sought. But if this was the end of life on earth for me,

I needed to know the truth more than I needed anything else. I cried out to God for answers about heaven and hell, and about life after death—and that is when I felt divinely directed by a still small voice within to go to the Bible. I remembered that I had a little white Bible with a zipper my parents had given me for my tenth birthday. I found it packed away in a box in the basement with other childhood mementos. (This is the Bible I take with me when I share my testimony at retreats, in churches, and on Christian TV. As you can imagine, it is now the most precious and cherished tangible possession I own.)

When I took that Bible back to bed with me and opened it at random, a verse jumped out: *"Ye shall know the truth, and the truth shall make you free"* (John 8:32 KJV). Ah, there it was at long last—exactly what I had been searching for! When I tried to read more, the words weren't making much sense to me, so I asked God to help me understand. Soon I flipped the pages over and the Holy Spirit helped me to understand when Jesus said, *"I am the way, and the truth, and the life. No one comes to the Father except through me"* (John 14:6).

I kept turning pages and reading verses that assured me, *"By grace are ye saved through faith; and that not of yourselves: it is the gift of God: Not of works, lest any man should boast"* (Ephesians 2:8-9 KJV), and *"God so loved the world, that he gave his only begotten Son, that whosoever believeth in him should not perish, but have everlasting life"* (John 3:16 KJV). What I discovered there in my sickbed was that God holds my future. He holds your future, too. Through Christ's death and resurrection, He has made a way for us to know Him. We need only to accept what Jesus has done for us. That day, I did just that when I confessed to God that I recognized I needed a Savior, asked Jesus to forgive my sins, and invited Him to come and live in my heart. That was the moment I was given the gift of new life.

Later that day as I read my Bible, I came to this verse: *"I will not die but live, and proclaim what the Lord has done"* (Psalm 118:17). Was God letting me know He wanted to heal my body, too? I quietly prayed and believed it was possible. A few weeks later, after I experienced what my doctor referred to as a "miraculous recovery," I promised the Lord I would tell this story for the rest of my life whenever I was given the opportunity. I was completely healed and went back to work a few weeks later. How thankful I am to be able to proclaim to you here on these pages what He has done in my life—and beyond that, what He can do in yours.

Wanting the Best Answer

Sadly, there wasn't a "happily ever after" ending to my marriage. Rather, things eventually got worse until I knew we could not live this way any longer. It wasn't good for any of us. One night at bedtime, I told God I would stay on my knees praying until He answered. It was the beginning of August, and my request was that this way of living would be over for us by the end of the month. I knew I would accept any answer from my heavenly Father. Up until then, I had been "putting in my order," looking for specific answers. Now, I was desperate and simply prayed, "Thy will be done." I wanted the best answer for the children, my husband, and me. I just didn't know what that would be.

By sunrise the next morning, I knew that I had heard from heaven— although I still didn't know what the answer was, only that I could trust God to work it out because *we know that all that happens to us is working for our good if we love God and are fitting into his plans* (Romans 8:28 TLB). I got up from my knees and said a prayer of thanksgiving, even though I was not sure what was to come.

A few weeks later, there was another episode of violence. Afterward, my former husband said he wanted me to take the girls and leave because he could not handle the pressure any more. He recognized his problem and, rather than seek help, he wanted it to be over by the end of the month. Even on the day I left with the children, I was convinced it would merely be a temporary situation until he got the help he needed and came to know God the way the girls and I had. Little did I know we were headed for divorce and a very different future all together.

Although I do not travel the world promoting separation and divorce, I believe there may be times when it becomes necessary, especially if there is abuse and a partner rejects all suggestions for receiving help for his problem. In spite of this, some women like me continue to stay in the marriage for the sake of the children, enduring inexcusable abuse themselves and causing the children to suffer emotional damage beyond measure. I thank the Lord every day that my children know and love God, and are experiencing their own remarkable healings from the past.

There are so many hurting and frustrated women who continue to feel trapped in devastating situations. They may be living with a cruel, vindictive, or spiteful person, whether it's a spouse, child, or parent. Maybe they go to work every day for a mean and insensitive boss. Perhaps they must tolerate family members or coworkers who seem bent on destroying any remnant of self-esteem they have left. In any case, these are women who are wounded in their spirits and some in their bodies, too. Who knows what has gone on in their past? Sometimes even they don't know the whole story themselves.

When I meet them in person or read the letters they write to me, there's one question they ask me more than anything else: "Should I leave my hurtful situation?" While that was God's path for me, it's something I cannot answer for others. There isn't one solution for all. There's no pat formula or magic wand to wave. The best answer I can offer is to pray and trust almighty God. In fact, pray your heart out. Be diligent and never give up. Call out to God with all your being and keep praying until you get an answer. God hears the cry of your heart. He wants to show you a new and better path. He alone can do this because He's the only one who knows every detail of your unique situation and what the future holds.

No one else could possibly advise you as accurately as your heavenly Father, who knows you intimately and cares deeply about every aspect of your life. He also knows the other party or parties involved and their futures. In some instances, it would be best to leave a hurtful situation immediately, especially if there is anything inappropriate happening or it is potentially dangerous to you, your family, or the lives of others. In other cases, when there is hope for restoration, leaving would be a mistake. Our loving God, who knows the beginning to the end, knows what the future holds and whether you should escape the pain or ride out the storm. He can tell you what you should do in your unparalleled situation. He cares and wants to guide you. Put all your faith and trust in Him and then watch what He will do for you.

In my case, it became clear that moving on was part of God's plan for us, although life as a single mom wasn't easy. It did, however, give the children and me the opportunity to observe God working and doing miracles regularly in our home, our family, and our finances. At times, the loneliness and grief seemed absolutely overwhelming, but it was a means of drawing me into a deeper relationship with God than I had ever known before. Each time I realized my helplessness without Him, He would draw me closer. I was driven to my knees and developed complete dependence on my heavenly Father as my Protector and Provider.

I spent hours in intense prayer and studying the Word. One day, I remember falling to the floor sobbing after the reality struck me that I might never enjoy a loving relationship with a husband. There, alone in my kitchen and weeping uncontrollably, I heard a voice that clearly and gently said, *Be still and know that I am God.* Suddenly, I felt as if a hand, a strong and loving hand, were placed on my back, although I didn't feel it as much outwardly as inwardly. Instantly, my body stopped shaking and the sobbing subsided. Although today I regularly hear from God in many ways—deep in my spirit, through His Word, and through the words of others—I must say I have never felt His touch or heard His voice in such a tangible way since.

Our Only Solution

After that episode, my prayer became, "Lord, please just get me through this day." Then it was "Just this next hour, Father." And eventually, "God, please get me through the next minute." I found the only way I could do that was to keep a Bible open in every room. I hugged a Bible while I slept; I placed one on the countertop while I did dishes or ironed. I had Scripture verses written out on index cards and posted everywhere throughout our tiny apartment. I had learned I could not survive even a few minutes without God's Word. It provided the reassurance, comfort, and safety I longed for.

Eventually, God in His mercy did bring me a life partner. Cliff and I met at a Christian dinner meeting and have been married more than 25 years now. My girls were thrilled to have this big, fun-loving guy in our lives. When he and I went away on our honeymoon, they stayed with family members, and together they got out their art supplies to make a huge greeting card to welcome us home. We still laugh about what they wrote on the inside—and I have asked the girls permission to share it with you. Apparently, they searched the Bible looking for the ideal scripture to complete their card, and for some reason they chose the verse, *"Father, forgive them for they know not what they are doing!"* (Luke 23:24). We're still not quite sure why they chose that verse, but over the years, in spite of our love for each other, there have been days when we wondered if maybe they knew what they were talking about!

I love to share the story of how God brought me out of my devastating circumstances because I know there is hope for you and your future, too. Sometimes the painful past we've experienced seems bigger than we are. Try as we may on our own strength, we can't seem to overcome the obstacles that cripple our dreams. Feelings of fear, failure, heartache, and disappointment keep looming over us and frightful memories come back to haunt us. We can't seem to get beyond the point of anguish, torment, sorrow, and misery that comes in waves to overtake us.

This is when the only solution is to put ourselves completely into God's hands. If you have been looking for love in all the wrong places, this is where you'll find what you've been searching for all your life. Are you ready to take that step, my precious friend? If you haven't done it before, why not turn to Jesus and ask Him to come into your life right now. Be assured that the One who healed the sick and raised the dead can come and touch you where you are this very minute. He is the same yesterday, today, and forever. He loves you. Accept His love. Trust Him with your life.

Dear God,

Even though I am ready to leave my hurtful past behind, tomorrow can be a scary place. I thank You for the promise of Your hand of protection on me, and those who are close to me, as I go through this incredible transition. Keep me from worrying, I pray, for I understand that worry is a sin. Thank You for being with me wherever I go and for the angels who keep watch over me to keep me safe as I face the unknown. I ask You to fill me with Your comfort whenever I feel alone or abandoned.

Lord, remind me that You are always thinking of me and want to bless me, and in Your eyes, I have incredible worth and value. Help me to recognize the unique qualities You have placed in me and to be able to appreciate them. I ask You to free me from the self-consciousness and self-focus that can imprison my soul. I accept the new life that You have chosen me for, and I listen to hear Your voice in a fresh, new way.

I am so grateful I don't have to make decisions alone. Help me to heed the godly wisdom and advice You provide for me through so many sources, whether it's Your Word, a caring friend, a good book, a radio program, a sermon, or the small, still voice in my heart. Your words are music to my ears. Show me new ways to quiet my mind so I can meditate on Your Word.

Thank You for the dream You have planted in my heart. You have given me a new vision for my future. Help me, Lord, to persevere in prayer for that vision even when the answers don't appear to be coming. I trust You to bring good from my time of waiting. Grant me faith, and help that faith to grow. Even so, remind me that the size of my faith doesn't limit the greatness of Your actions. Even in my most passionate pleadings, I pray that my spirit would come into agreement with Your will. Help me to see clearly the plans that You have for me and show me how to build strong foundations day by day.

Thank You, Father, for providing spiritual, physical, and emotional nourishment to bring balance to my life when I'm feeling frightened and overextended. Lord, thank You most of all that I can come boldly into Your presence and for the righteousness I have because of the cross. Make me a new person, Father. Give me a fresh perspective, an optimistic outlook, and a renewed relationship with You through Jesus Christ.

In the name of Your precious Son, Amen.

Afterword

FOR NEARLY 20 YEARS, I HAVE HAD THE privilege of listening to hundreds of women share the stories of their lives. As they have graciously invited me into the most intimate parts of their past and present, I have laughed and cried with them as they've tried to overcome stumbling blocks and prepare for their futures. Through it all, I have held steadfast to the belief that freedom is possible for all. I trust by now you have recognized that my faith in the reality of freedom is not because people have within them the power to change or heal themselves. It is because of the hope of Jesus Christ in us. After all, *"It is for freedom that Christ has set us free"* (Galatians 5:1). This power to free us transcends the natural world in a way that is nearly impossible to explain unless we have witnessed or experienced it.

Your path to freedom will not necessarily be like mine. The way is unique for each of us, but there are enough common threads to which we can all relate. One commonality is our need for God. He tells us that it's truth that sets us free. The truth is that freedom is found in accepting His love, walking in faith, and being obedient to His Word.

Any problem you face can be overcome by the power of God in you. There is nothing that is hopeless or cause for despair. You can walk in confidence even though so much of life seems like a struggle. My intent in sharing all of this with you is to help you move beyond your past where you've been stuck to a place where you will be living a victorious life, overcoming the fears and obstacles that hamper your dreams. You see, you can be free from your past—at last!

More from Sue Augustine

Stress-Proof Your Life with...
5-Minute Retreats for Women

Do you long for the pure and simple things in life?

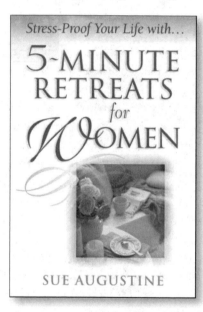

Have endless responsibilities taken the fun out of your days? Are you experiencing more stress and anxiety, and less peace and joy? Has it been a while since you felt truly rested?

Drawing from her professional expertise and sharing from her own experience, Sue Augustine helps you find new meaning in the ordinary experiences of everyday life. Each of these short chapters will help you recapture the joy of such simple pleasures as welcoming the wind in your hair, going barefoot, and escaping in a good book.

Take a break. Enjoy the kind of life God has designed for you. Revive your spirit and refresh your soul with *5-Minute Retreats for Women.*

More Harvest House Books to Nourish Your Spirit and Feed Your Soul

Seven Secrets to Timeless Beauty

Discover and Maximize Your Personal Style

by Norma Day

Norma Day helps you discover the special beauty inside you, and how that inner radiance can be reflected on the outside. The practical tips and ageless advice she's gathered during her remarkable career of walking the fashion runways and directing a top modeling agency reveal secrets to such things as…

- *makeup basics:* the ways to get maximum impact with minimum time
- *personal style:* the characteristics of a woman who knows who she is
- *elegance:* the bodily poise that comes from a heart filled with love

Seven Secrets to Timeless Beauty shows you how to enhance what is beautiful about you—inside and out—and encourages you to be all you were meant to be.

When You Need a Miracle

Experiencing the Power of the God of the Impossible

by Lloyd John Ogilvie

Are your greatest needs—with family, work, relationships—going unmet? Are you limiting your life to only what is possible in your own strength and talents? From his longtime pastoral experience, Dr. Ogilvie points the way to the God who can meet your *every* need because He is Lord of the *im*possible—the One who can bring about miracles of healing, reconciliation, and growth!

When Pleasing Others Is Hurting You
Finding God's Patterns for Healthy Relationships
by David Hawkins

You want to do the right thing—take care of your family, be a good employee, "be there" for your friends. And you're good at it. Everyone knows they can depend on you—so they do.

But are you really doing what's best for them? And what about you? Are you growing? Are you happy and relaxed? Are you excited about your gifts and your calling, or do you sometimes think...*I don't even know what I want anymore.*

In this engaging and provocative book, psychologist David Hawkins will show you why you feel driven to always do more. You'll see how you can actually lose vital parts of your personality and shortchange God's work in your life. And you'll be inspired to rediscover the person God created you to be.

Becoming Who God Intended
A New Picture for Your Past • A Healthy Way of Managing Your Emotions • A Fresh Perspective on Relationships
by David Eckman

Whether you realize it or not, your imagination is filled with *pictures* of reality. The Bible indicates these pictures reveal your true "heart beliefs"—the beliefs that actually shape your everyday feelings and reactions to family, friends, and others, to life's circumstances, and to God.

David Eckman compassionately shows you how to allow God's Spirit to build new, *biblical* pictures in your heart and imagination. As you do this, you will be able to accept God's acceptance of you in Christ, break free of negative emotions and habitual sin...and finally experience the life God the Father has always intended for you.